PROPERTY

PROPERTY

Hypotheticals, Self-Assessment Rubrics,
and Tools for Success

Jill M. Fraley

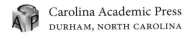

Carolina Academic Press
DURHAM, NORTH CAROLINA

LIBRARY OF CONGRESS CATALOGING-IN-PUBLICATION DATA

Names: Fraley, Jill M., author.
Title: Property : hypotheticals, self-assessment rubrics, and tools for
    success / by Jill M. Fraley.
Description: Durham : Carolina Academic Press, 2021.
Identifiers: LCCN 2021006957 | ISBN 9781531018177 (paperback) |
    ISBN 9781531018184 (ebook)
Subjects: LCSH: Property--Examinations, questions, etc. |
    Students--Self-rating of.
Classification: LCC K720 .F73 2021 | DDC 346.04076--dc23
LC record available at https://lccn.loc.gov/2021006957

Carolina Academic Press
700 Kent Street
Durham, North Carolina 27701
Telephone (919) 489-7486
Fax (919) 493-5668
www.cap-press.com

Printed in the United States of America

For my students, past, present, and future.

And for Halie, always.

Contents

About the Author

Jill M. Fraley is a Professor of Law at Washington and Lee University School of Law, where she has been teaching for 10 years. She practiced as a litigator, before first teaching in 2004. She was the Tutor in Law at Yale Law School for two years before moving to Washington and Lee University School of Law. Professor Fraley holds a B.A. from Yale University, a J.D. from Duke University School of Law, and an LL.M. and J.S.D. from Yale Law School.

Professor Fraley is a native of Appalachia, specifically a farm in eastern Kentucky, and is passionate about issues of equality, access to education, poverty, homelessness, environmental protection, and just property laws. She is a professional photographer and passionate about the work of NGOs. She spends as much time as she can outdoors, in the mountains, traveling, gardening, quilting, and writing.

Introduction

Hard work in law school does not necessarily translate to good grades. It is frustrating, but true. One of the main reasons is that law school deviates from the method you have used to learn your whole life: practice, evaluation, feedback, repeat. Then you get to law school and there is a single exam at the end of the semester or maybe also a midterm but without grades or individual feedback. Students feel anxious, depressed, frustrated, and as though the system is random or unfair.

Worse, that single exam is probably a hypothetical, which is different from the kinds of exams you have taken all your life. Answering a hypothetical requires you to apply rules in a robust and thorough manner. It is not as easy as it sounds, and law school classes rarely provide an explicit methodology for writing an application. Legal writing courses often teach analysis, but the best strategies for writing a brief are not exactly the same strategies for getting the most points on an exam. I test this out regularly by asking second semester 1Ls to tell me how to go about applying a rule — without using the word "apply." They can never do it. They do not have a methodology; they just think they know how to apply a rule intuitively. Exam results suggest otherwise.

Checking your own work on a hypothetical meant to be ambiguous is also not easy. Think about it this way: You know that you understand how to multiply, because if you multiply three by two, you get six. The calculator agrees. What did your agreement with the calculator tell you? Not just that you got the right answer, but that you know how to multiply. In other words, we normally check our understanding of processes by checking the accuracy of our conclusions. Hypotheticals are usually balanced, or nearly so, meaning that there is no one correct conclusion. You can't use the answer to check your process.

It is also difficult to practice hypotheticals. You are likely to have trouble finding samples of hypotheticals, particularly samples paired with some type of scoring device or sample answer. Oddly enough, even when students have samples, they sometimes focus entirely on study rather than practice. This is not a good plan. Answering a hypothetical is a skill, not knowledge. You would not give a piano concert after trying to play once or reading a book about playing. You would give the concert after regular practice, correction, and progress reports from a teacher. Except law school does not usually provide practice, detailed corrections, or progress reports.

After the first semester, students are often still in the dark. Exams are often not returned to students or have limited comments. In many courses, if you want your exam back, you must ask the professor to "review it" with you, which feels like challenging your grade even when it is not and is approached with similar levels of apprehension and dread by both parties. If students score well enough to avoid crying on the bedroom floor, they rarely request such meetings, even though some feedback might help take them up a grade the next time around. When a student does take this opportunity, exam reviews often fail for lack of genuine feedback. Students often receive a simple numerical total and a series of checkmarks across pages of their answer with no indicators of what was missing.

I do not like this situation. I do not like that students can work hard but fail to do well in law school. I do not like that grades seem random because students do not understand what they did well or poorly. What I want is a world where hard work actually works, where you get the grade that you deserve. I've done that in my own classroom, and this book is my plan for world domination, so to speak.

The purpose of this book is to give you back some control. This book works as a review for property law, a workbook as you learn property law, a course in academic success, or a review for the bar on common law real property.

You can learn how to write a robust application of the rules. More importantly, you can practice this skill. Then you can grade yourself accurately and see how your score compares to other law students. You can diagnose problems with your answers, learn strategies to fix those problems, and keep practicing to improve your scores.

The Secret of This Book: Rubrics

The real secret of this book is the scoring rubrics. You can find hypothetical prompts or fact patterns in a variety of places. You could write them as a study group. But they're not useful. You need a scoring rubric to make those hypotheticals actually useful. Why? Because you need specific, individualized, and detailed feedback on your performance to improve. A scoring rubric provides that.

You might think a sample answer would work just as well. It does not. During my first year of teaching, two of my students were very close friends. They were close enough to each other to have shared their grades and their answers to a practice hypothetical I had given as a midterm. One had an "A-" grade and the other a "B-" grade. Here is why they came to see me together: Neither one of them could tell the difference between the two answers. The one who had the higher grade said, "I did well. You would think I would know! But I do not understand why my answer was right, so I do not know if I can do it again or not." That was when I decided that I had to share scoring rubrics with my class, even though I had given a sample answer.

A sample answer is someone else's work. It is not detailed feedback on your work. It is the feedback that matters, along with continued practice to improve.

The rubrics in this book allow you to grade yourself and to provide yourself with that detailed and individualized feedback. Write in this book. Do the work of practice, grading, and more practice. Get a study partner or small group. Then it is easier because you can grade for each other using the rubrics.

This system works. Students in the bottom 10 percent of the class have used these materials to be in the top 10 percent the next semester. Your job is to put in the work of practicing. This book makes it as convenient and exam-realistic as possible.

Why Would I Give Away Secrets?

You already know the first answer to that question: I want the world where your hard work matters, and you get the grade that fits with that work. I want a fair system where study and practice count. I want you to have a system of techniques for writing an application, so you do not wing it.

There is another answer to the question, though. As someone who came into the academy as an outsider, I am very conscious of how failures in transparency create an unequal playing field for students. I did not come from a professional family. I came from a small farming community in the Appalachian Mountains.

But I was lucky enough to get an excellent education. I have a bachelor's degree from Yale University, a J.D. from Duke Law School, followed by an LL.M. and J.S.D. at Yale Law School. These multiple law degrees put me on rather unusual ground. Most professors hold only a J.D. A growing number hold a Ph.D. in another field such as history, philosophy, or sociology. Only the tiniest percentage holds multiple degrees earned within the legal academy. What that means, in terms of this book, is that I have spent more than twice as long as most professors navigating legal education *as a student.*

Going from Appalachia to Yale in 1995 was like moving to another country at 18 without your parents, without any friends, and without knowing there could be culture shock without leaving your own country.

Insider knowledge presents itself more readily in upper-class families, where a student is able to consult family members and friends who have been to law school. Students from blue-collar or impoverished families just do not have the same opportunities. Success in law school is unevenly available to those with more social capital and those who come from professional families, creating unintentional, but nonetheless significant, barriers for others.

Additionally, failures in transparency likely generate much of the stress and distress that law school is known to create for students — stresses that are already known to fall disproportionately, in terms of gender, and likely across other differences such as race and socioeconomic status. And that bothers me. America long ago fell short of the ideal of a classless society — and I do not want law school, my intellectual home, to perpetuate social stratifications. Put another way, the secrets are already available to those who have or forge the right relationships. I am making them available widely.

How the Rest of This Book Works

Part 1 of this book is a primer on hypotheticals. Read it first. It tells you how to go about answering a hypothetical, with a particular focus on the techniques you need to write a thorough application of the rules. Most importantly, the primer teaches you how to answer a hypothetical in the way that should get you the most points.

Part 2 contains the practice chapters. Each begins with a brief discussion of rules on a particular topic. Without a clear set of rules, it is impossible to issue spot or to develop a robust and structured application. Thus, each chapter begins with a brief set of relevant rules. (Note, you may learn different or additional ones in class.) Next, each chapter organizes those rules into a short outline. The outline provides a structure that you can use (and memorize if it fits the rules taught in your class) so that you can organize an application into a nested IRAC structure.

Then the chapter presents a sample hypothetical question. The question will require the rules given to you at the beginning of the chapter (and no others). As you get to later chapters with multiple issues, the hypothetical may draw on rules from earlier chapters as well. Once you have learned the rules, do the hypothetical. The earlier chapters, which present property rules, tell you the issue for each hypothetical, so there is no issue spotting. This is intentional to allow you to focus on the depth and breadth of your application. Later chapters require issue spotting, and Part 3 has some issue spotting practice.

It is best to do the hypothetical immediately after reading it. Reading it first gives the brain an opportunity to do background thinking in a way that is unrealistic to exam situations.

When you complete the hypothetical, use the rubric to score yourself. (There are directions in the primer, and they are simple.) Finally, you can compare your answer to the sample answer. This allows you to see how well you followed the model structure and to also see how an ideal answer addressed problems that you might have skipped. Throughout the book the samples grow in complexity to those that are closer and closer to exam length hypotheticals. Timing yourself is ideal, even if you do not set a limit, but rather just monitor your time to make sure that you are improving.

Finally, Part 3 of this book focuses on diagnosing errors and giving you strategies to fix your errors. You can refer to that chapter repeatedly as you do the practice hypotheticals.

PART ONE **THE PRIMER**

ONE

The Hypothetical, or Welcome to Comparative Grading

Meet the Hypothetical

The vast majority of law school exams contain three to four questions in a format called the hypothetical. Hypotheticals resemble college exams in that they require essay answers but introduce an entirely new type of question. The hypothetical question is not really a question. It is a story, sometimes called a fact pattern. True to their name, hypotheticals propose an imaginary factual scenario, generally complicated (if not convoluted) and raising a number of different legal issues or potential causes of action. The question mimics a (definitely crazy) client walking into your office and pouring out a story in a stream-of-consciousness narrative. Your job, as it will be in your career, is to sort out possible legal options arising from that factual situation and then to analyze those options. In an odd way, this means you are the one who has to find the questions. You must figure out what legal issues are worth discussion.

Why There Are No Right Answers

Hypothetical questions rarely have a correct answer. Most issues have facts that sit right on the line in terms of who should win. Take, for example, the question of whether mudflats are wetlands. Are mudflats more like *wetlands* such as marshes or more like *land* for purposes of federal environmental regulation? Your professor does not know, and that is precisely why she would use this as an exam question. Professors choose facts that make the conclusion iffy. Why? Because it places all of the emphasis on your ability to argue, as well as to see the merits of the two sides.

The problem is that this grates against your last 20 or so years of schooling, where for the vast majority of the time, the emphasis fell on locating or recalling the right answer. You must actively fight this impulse.

Hypotheticals and Comparative Grading

Most American law schools have a system called *mandatory means* that govern grading. It means that professors do not have full control over grades, as they usually do at undergraduate institutions, along with most other educational institutions.

Mandatory means require the professor to submit grades that average to a particular number. Information about the required mean is generally found in the student handbook or on the registrar's website, and it is sometimes different depending on the type of course (1L or 2/3L, exam or paper) or the number of students enrolled.

Additionally, the mandatory mean varies from institution to institution. The mean could be 2.6 (a B-), 3.1 (just over a B), or 3.3 (a B+). The mandatory mean comes from a regulation set by the faculty as a whole, the law school administration, or the university. The origins of mandatory means lie in trying to prevent grade inflation, which frustrated potential employers of graduates.

What do mandatory means change for a professor? If a professor is teaching undergraduates and there is no required mean and the professor has 10 outstanding students in a seminar, she can record 10 A grades. That cannot happen in a mandatory mean system. The mandatory mean almost guarantees that in any given class there are very few A grades. For example, in a small section class of 17–24 students, the professor can likely assign only three to four A grades. The mandatory mean limits a professor's ability to assign very high grades without also giving very low grades. It has to balance out to get to a mean such as 3.3. So, a professor can assign several A grades, but only if she is also willing to assign several C+ grades. At many law schools, grades lower than a C+ are rare, but that also requires that A grades are rare.

Mandatory means also make law school grading comparative. Consider this example: there are 17 students in the class. Precisely 15 of those students write very good, but not excellent, exams. Out of the 100 points possible on the exam, all of them scored between 83 and 86. The professor assigns those exams a grade of B+. The remaining two students score 94 and 99. Only the student who has a 99 can receive an A, simply because the mathematics of two A grades would go above a 3.3 mean. It gets worse. The student who has a 94 can't even have an A- grade. She will receive a B+ just like everyone else, even though she scored a 94 and the others scored between 83 and 86.

Assigning the student scoring 94 a B+ creates a mean of 3.341176, which falls just under the maximum of 3.35 (assuming a discretionary margin of +/- 0.05). If the professor assigned two A grades, the course mean would violate the rule by being too high (3.38). She cannot even assign an A- grade to the student who has a 94, because that would make the mean 3.36.

If the professor wanted to assign an A- to the exam scoring 94, she must make one of the other grades lower. But, in this example, all of the other scores are within three points of each other, so it does not really make sense to give them different grades. In addition, it might be that there are four exams all scoring 83, so there would be no way to choose which exam to give a B rather than a B+. The professor may not be pleased with the 94-scoring student receiving a B+, but neither can she randomly choose an exam scored at 83 to drop. Neither outcome seems fair.

This grade assigning problem illustrates why professors prefer hard, long exams. It is unfortunate but true. Long, difficult exams are more likely to produce a wide spread of scores. It makes the task of assigning grades much easier when the scores are distributed over a wide range.

What if the 17 student scores are more widely spread? It would be possible for the professor to assign three A grades and three A- grades, but only if she also assigned three B grades and three B- grades. She would also need to have five exams in the middle as B+ grades. This seems reasonable.

But if the incoming students had a mean college GPA of 3.7, more than half of them may be receiving the worst grades of their lives. It is naturally very distressing for students coming from college grading systems, which are often (but not always) more generous.

A student could be disappointed with an A- grade and not realize that she also has the highest grade in the class. (And if the distribution of the scores had been different, the professor would have loved for her to have had an A.) Not realizing how the mandatory mean works can give students both entirely unrealistic expectations and more distress than necessary over their grades. Even the student who graduates from law school with the highest GPA almost certainly does not have a 4.0.

This is why the class rank (which did not necessarily matter so much at college) suddenly becomes so important in law school. The class rank is a better indicator of how you are performing compared to your classmates than your GPA is. Class ranks allow employers to evaluate students against their peers at their own school and other schools, without looking at the GPA. This is particularly helpful when different schools have different mandatory means. Many legal employers require class rank to be included on a resume for precisely this reason.

What Does Comparative Grading Mean for You?

In college, if you were confident in your knowledge of the subject matter and your abilities with that type of exam, you could relax about the outcome. With comparative grading, the question is not how much you know or how well you can write. The question is whether you can do it better than the majority of your classmates. In real life, that translates to the fact that you are never really done preparing for an exam, because you are always trying to outrun your classmates, so to speak.

And you probably have no idea how well your classmates are doing. If you do not have graded exercises before the final exam, using a mandatory mean, there is almost no way to know. Discussions in class sometimes represent a student's abilities, but often they do not.

Comparative grading also means that the distribution of points given in a syllabus is somewhat misleading. For example: A syllabus might say that the final grade comes from two quizzes (25% each), a midterm (25%) and the final exam (25%). If there are 100 points total, then each task counts for 25 points. That is all true. But if you are thinking of the percentages as a measure of relative importance, those percentages lie. Why? Because in a comparative grading system, the importance of a task is determined by the distribution of scores. In mathematical terms, the most important task — or the one that determines the final grades — is the one where there is the most range.

Say five students (Rose, Lily, Basil, Verbena, and Ginger) take the two quizzes, midterm, and final exam, but there is almost no distribution of the scores except on the first quiz. That first quiz will determine the grades in a comparative grading system.

The weirdest thing about this system is that the professor does not control it. It depends on the range of scores, so it depends on student performance. The best that a professor can do to change this is to make some items worth so few points that there cannot be much of a range or to score things so "lightly" or "gently" that there is no range.

Range and the Relative Importance of Graded Course Components: Example of a Quiz Determining Final Grades							
	Rose	Lily	Basil	Verbena	Ginger	Mean	Range
Quiz 1	5	10	15	20	25	15	20
Quiz 2	15	15	15	15	15	15	0
Midterm	15	15	15	15	15	15	0
Final	14	15	14	16	16	15	2
Total points	49	55	59	66	71	60	
Final grade	B-	B	B+	A-	A		
GPA	2.67	3.0	3.33	3.67	4.0	3.334	

While the range is also important in non-comparative grading systems, the importance is amplified in comparative systems, because the professor does not have the power to just determine a competence threshold for each grade. For example, in the class above, if the professor determines that 55 points demonstrates excellent knowledge of the subject matter, then there would be four A grades and probably one A- grade.

Estimating Your Own Performance

Comparative grading and hypothetical-style exams combine to make it nearly impossible to estimate your own performance when you finish an exam.

First, hypotheticals require the student to find the questions. The student finds the questions by spotting the relevant legal issues. Imagine you read a hypothetical and see four issues: nuisance, trespass, gifts causa mortis, and inter-vivos gifts. Most of your classmates see all of those issues, but also see an issue of adverse possession. You leave the exam thinking you had plenty of time and covered those four issues wonderfully. You did. You are not wrong about that. But you did not see the adverse possession issue and will have no points for that issue, while your classmates will score higher because they did see the issue and respond to it.

This is different from a typical college exam. If you have a test with 30 multiple-choice questions, you leave the exam knowing how many you did not have time to finish. If you finish the exam knowing you had to completely guess at 10 questions, you also have a good sense of how you did. With a hypothetical, you may not know that you did not finish or that you listed six important rules, but there were 10 important rules.

Second, you do not know how your classmates did. You do not know how many issues they spotted or how many rules they remembered. Even more importantly, you do not know how well your classmates developed a robust analysis of the facts.

This Book and Knowing How You Are Doing

The purpose of this book is to give you back some control. You can learn how to write a robust analysis. More importantly, you can practice these skills. Then you can grade yourself accurately and see how your score compares to those of other law students. You can diagnose problems with your answers, learn strategies to fix those problems, and keep practicing. By practicing, you regain control and make your hard work matter.

TWO

Recipe for Hypothetical Answers

This chapter covers the basics of responding to a hypothetical, while the next chapter goes into more detail about the all-important application section, which contains the reasoning and arguments.

Reading the Hypothetical

A single hypothetical story — often called a prompt or fact pattern — is generally a page to a page and a half in length. It is single spaced and dense with facts. Simply reading the question eats up precious minutes of exam time. Yet exam success requires reading the question slowly and carefully.

To tackle a hypothetical, begin by searching out all of the causes of action or questions about causes of action that you can find. Ask yourself:

- What claims could be made in court?
- Do you see any defenses?
- What facts will make it difficult for you to apply the rules? (Note these carefully — these might be called the "sticky" facts.)

All of these questions likely point to issues that you should address within your answer. Make a list of these issues in the margins. The process of locating these issues is called issue spotting and it often makes up a significant portion of your exam score.

Issue Spotting

Issue spotting refers to the process of locating the facts within a hypothetical that produce a legal question. Law professors (and bar exams) tend to test your ability to issue spot precisely because legal practice centers on this skill. Excellent issue-spotting skills pave the way for excellent exam answers.

At the beginning, achieving perfect issue spotting may seem unreasonably difficult. Unfortunately, that is naturally the case. Because issue spotting requires looking at a set of facts and picking out which of those facts give rise to a legal question (and naming that question precisely), it just does not work without some knowledge of the law. The law tells you which facts are relevant and which are not. Searching for sympathetic or problematic facts helps, but does not always work because the law provides remedies for some issues and not for others. If students struggle with issue spotting, it is often because the student does not know the rules or understand the rules thoroughly. Success requires both memorization and thinking.

Take an example:

Short Hypothetical: Caroline's Bad Day

Attorney John Smith can hear Caroline whining to his secretary from outside the door. "But I've got to see somebody today!" With a sigh, he opens the door and invites her to sit down.

"What seems to be the trouble?" John situates himself behind his desk and nudges the box of tissues closer to Caroline.

Reaching for a Kleenex, she explains, "I heard a phone beeping around 3:00 a.m., and after rummaging on the bedside table, flipped it open while half awake. Turns out it wasn't my phone, but my fiancé's. The message said, 'I'm so glad you spent the night last night. Can't wait to see you again. Miss your touch already. xoxo.' The contact name was String Bean, which is a nickname for his buddy Rodney from work. I looked at their text history and it was a string of the same, going back months!"

"He is your fiancé?" John asks when she pauses to sob.

"Yes. Well, no. He was until this morning, but not anymore. I kicked his shin good to wake him up. The little $#@$#* said, 'What are you doing with my phone?' I threw it at him and asked how long he'd been sleeping with his buddy. Stupid idiot yelled that he is not sleeping with Rodney. He just put Sandy Turbington's name in as String Bean so I'd never get suspicious if I saw it on there. Stupid idiot!! I told him to get out and he said that was fine by him, since he took care of the rent and all the bills anyway, even though both our names are on all that stuff. He said I did not even care if he was happy."

Between her sobs John interjects, "Both your names are on the lease?"

"Yes. Now Patrick says he wants all his stuff back. He says he wants the ring and the above-ground pool he set up for my son in the back yard. He is even threatening to rip up the new sidewalk that he put down to the back deck and to take out the tool shed he built back there. When he left, he took the television he'd given my son for Christmas and the car we bought together last June. And even worse, that %$#$%@#% Sandy found out that I know and now she is just rubbing my nose in it, texting me with all these lewd pictures of them together. And my heart is just completely broken. I thought Patrick and I would be together forever!!"

Analyzing Caroline's Bad Day

By learning the potential causes of action (reasons one is allowed to bring a suit in court) and remedies, a future attorney also learns what the law does and does not address. As you have learned since childhood, plenty of things unfold unfairly in life. The law provides remedies for only a few of those, and only in very specific circumstances. In this example, Caroline suffers a broken heart, which the law will not recognize as an injury.

You might even say that Caroline's primary injury at the moment is a broken heart. The fact that the law will not provide her a remedy (even though her fiancé might well be a $%#@#$^& by objective evidence), does not mean there aren't legal issues raised by Caroline's story. In fact, there are many, falling across multiple areas of law.

If this were a criminal law exam, you would want to ask:

- Did Caroline commit battery when she kicked her fiancé?
- Did Caroline commit assault and battery by hitting her fiancé with his phone?
- Is it theft for her fiancé to have taken her son's television? Or the car?
- Would it be theft for her fiancé to take the pool and shed?
- Would it be destruction of property to rip up the sidewalk (given that he obviously can't just relocate it to his new house)?
- Can her fiancé enter the property to get his things without committing trespass?

If this were a torts exam, you would want to ask:

- Did her fiancé or Sandy intentionally inflict emotional distress on Caroline by having an affair?
- Was there an alienation of affection?
- Did Caroline personally injure her fiancé when she kicked him or threw the phone at him?
- Did Sandy intentionally inflict emotional distress by texting the photos to Caroline?

If this were a property exam, it would present a completely different set of issues.

- Who rightfully owns an engagement ring after a split? Does that change based on fault or who asked for the split?
- What are the rights and obligations under the lease? Does Caroline continue to be liable for the full rent after her fiancé's departure? Does she have a right to end the lease?
- Can her fiancé collect Caroline's half of the back rent?
- Is the car jointly owned?
- Was the television a gift?
- Are the above-ground pool, tool shed, and sidewalk fixtures or not? Are they removable or must they remain with the lessor of the property? Does the lease speak to improvements or fixtures to the property? If they are removable, was the pool a gift to her son?

This short hypothetical does not provide enough facts to answer many of these questions, but it does provide enough to spot the issues and answer some of the questions. (Exam questions will tend to be much more detailed, offering enough facts to argue the application of the law.) The important thing to notice here is how easy it is to wrap many issues into a small space and how common it is for issues to overlap different areas of law.

Unless, you are taking the bar, where subject divisions do not matter, write your exam answers for only one class at a time. Remember to think in terms of causes of action and to segregate those into the different areas: property, contracts, criminal law, etc. Your professor for property is not allocating points for a criminal law or torts issue. In fact, she may not have even noticed it within the hypothetical due to her focus on her own area. Do not waste time on criminal issues during your property exam.

At the same time, remember that some facts give rise to both property and tort claims, or to both criminal and tort claims. Also, some causes of action sit at the dividing line of subject areas. For example, nuisance is often thought of as both a tort and a property cause of action. Trespass can be a matter of property law or of criminal law. In those cases, make sure to tackle the issue fully.

Your task is to search out those facts that give rise to a cause of action, elaborate on the relevant rule, apply that rule while ideally arguing both sides, and reach a conclusion on the issue. Seek out the relevant parts — as the attorney tries to do when he repeatedly redirects the conversation with Caroline in an attempt to gain information about the specifically legally relevant portions of her story.

While it seems both straightforward and understandable to say that the law simply does not cover all of the unfairness in life, students often struggle substantially with this idea. Many choose law school because of a well-developed sense of ethics and fairness or because of a specific desire to remedy unfair situations. Simply put, law students tend to hate to hear Caroline cry and hate to say that while there are some things the law can do for her, such as protect her assets, it can't punish her fiancé for simply being a *%$@$#^.

To succeed as well as persevere without losing a sense of hope, students must accept that a complex legal system already exists and they as beginners must learn this system and how to apply it rigorously, without bending rules purely for sympathy. Only then will they be ready to challenge — and be respected for challenging — the system's assumptions and inadequacies. There are plenty of problems within our system, but in law school (or at least in your first year), do not waste your time and energy pushing against the system. Learn, understand, and then challenge.

Structuring Your Answer for the Most Points

Once you have located the issues, there is a long-standing and quite useful formula for organizing and drafting the essay: IRAC, or Issue, Rule, Application, and Conclusion. This formula repeats for each of the issues located within the hypothetical. Here is a quick summary (with more detail to follow later in this chapter and in others):

First, tell the reader the legal question that you are answering. That is, state the issue.

Second, for the rules section, state the major or central guiding rule or test that applies to that issue. For example, in property a bailment requires a transfer of personalty with mutual assent. A trespass requires an entry onto the real property owned by another. There are, of course, many other smaller, clarifying rules. But these are the key rules for each issue. After stating the key rule, add any important information about weighing problematic cases — i.e., burdens of proof, shifts in burdens, or weight of particular parts of a rule or test. Save the more detailed rules for now because they are best incorporated in the application.

Third, apply the rules. The application is where most of the points reside in a hypothetical. It is also the easiest place to go wrong in your answer. The application needs strong organization. Otherwise, it is likely to become a repetitive muddle that gains few points. That is why it gets an entire chapter to itself next.

Finally, the conclusion gives an outcome. Tell the reader who wins and the most important reason why.

Why CRAC Supports Lower Scores

Some professors and guidebooks suggest using CRAC as an organizational-analytical tool rather than IRAC. This approach both begins and ends with the conclusion. The first line of an exam answer then might be, "Jane has a claim against Mr. Chandler for nuisance."

Over the years, I have tested how students performed on exams using IRAC versus CRAC. Students who write in CRAC inevitably write one side of the argument more effectively than the other.

It is, perhaps, subconscious — if you already have what you think is the right answer on an exam, why develop both sides of the argument equally? Students who write in the IRAC format are more balanced in their work and get more points simply because they create a more robust analysis of the issue, considering all of the arguments on both sides.

Remember that most points are within the application or analysis. Approach the application with an open mind. It can even help to begin with an iffy statement about how things will turn out. This helps students to write a more thorough and balanced analysis. To earn the most points, begin with the issue as an open question and make your way to the conclusion incrementally, using the facts and your knowledge of the law.

What if your professor loves CRAC and asks you to use it? Consider writing your answer using IRAC first, and then go back to the beginning and change the I to a persuasive C. Then add one or two extra sentences to that side of the argument in the application. With this strategy, the conclusion-first mindset will not impact the robustness of your analysis.

The Rules Section Generally

The purpose of the rules section of IRAC is to set forth the primary rules that will answer the legal question posed in the issue statement. Focus on the key rules here. It is often appropriate to introduce small, clarifying rules within the application itself.

You do not need to include rules that are clearly not useful in light of the facts in the hypothetical. For example, if the prompt says that the plaintiff filed suit immediately, there is no reason to discuss the three-year statute of limitations. Yes, it is a rule. Yes, it is a rule for this cause of action. It is just not relevant given these facts. The trick with the rules section is to be thorough, but not irrelevant.

Understanding the Common Types of Legal Rules

To be sure that you both understand how the rule works and are thorough in stating the relevant rules, it can help to be aware of the types of rules students typically encounter in law school classes. Professors rarely talk about the different types of rules, particularly in terms of their structures, so this is likely something you must add for yourself. But it can be very useful.

There are two ways you can use types to describe rules: you can organize rules by the type of structure they have or by when each rule is utilized during a lawsuit. Both can be useful, particularly for 1Ls. It can help you begin to see the patterns so that every case you read does not feel quite so new and foreign. Understanding both the structure and the legal function of a rule helps you plan and execute a better analysis.

Structures of Rules

As you read, brief, and outline the cases, you should begin to recognize that there are similar patterns in the structures of many of the rules you encounter. Courts rely on a series of standard types of tests (rules) for deciding the outcome in particular types of cases. To analyze and synthesize cases most efficiently, you should be familiar with the different types of tests and, as you read, note the type of test that the court is creating with each legal rule. This will double-check your outline's organizational structure and also give structure to your argument when you apply the rule in an essay.

Here are a few basic types of tests that appear frequently:

1. All elements required (a.k.a. an and-type test)

This type of test provides a number of elements (requirements), all of which must be met. The adverse possession definition fits here.

Example:

Adverse possession requires: (1) visible, (2) continuous, (3) exclusive, AND (4) hostile possession, (5) proven for the statutory minimum length of time.

This type of test is essentially a list with all elements required. Note that this test is an all-or-nothing approach. The court does not care if you have beautiful proof of elements one through four — if you cannot provide evidence of element number five, you cannot pass the test for having adverse possession.

2. Alternative elements

This type of test lists a number of elements in the alternative. Proof of any one element in the list is sufficient to meet the test. Trespass works as an example here.

Example:

A trespass has occurred when someone physically enters another's land, directs her personal property onto the land, or allows the entry of other tangible materials.

One word makes the difference here: *or.* Any *one* of the listed actions suffices. John might walk onto his neighbor's lawn (physically enter another's land), drive his car onto his neighbor's lawn (direct his personalty onto another's land), or allow dust from his home repair project to settle on his neighbor's lawn (allow the entry of other tangible materials onto another's land). Any one of these actions meets the rule's requirement.

3. All elements (with some alternatives)

Occasionally you will encounter a merger of these two types — a list requiring almost all of the elements to be present with an option presented. Consider "mutual mistake" in adverse possession law. Some jurisdictions allow mutual mistake to substitute for the hostility requirement.

Example:

Adverse possession requires: (1) visible, (2) continuous, (3) exclusive, AND (4) hostile possession OR mutual mistake, (5) proven for the statutory minimum length of time.

This works like an all elements test except that the fourth element can be proven two different ways.

4. Balancing test or factors test

Balancing tests diverge nearly completely from the first three types. A balancing test also lists elements, but does not require any particular arrangement of the proof of the elements. A case might be successful with wonderful proof of three out of five elements, or sloppy proof of five out of five elements. While wonderful proof of one element alone is much less likely to be successful, it is not impossible. Essentially, the balancing test provides courts with a list of relevant factors to consider, but usually no real direction in terms of how to weigh those factors with respect to each other.

Example:

When determining whether the action of one landowner is a nuisance to her neighbor, courts balance the utility of the action to the one landowner (or society as a whole) against the detriments suffered by the neighbor.

What that means is that if the one landowner is digging large pits on his property, and his neighbor's home ends up covered in dust that drifts over from the digging, the court might decide the dust is a nuisance if the pits are dug randomly and for no apparent reason, but not if the pits are being dug to farm organic mushrooms. Similarly, dust from your personal home renovation project might not be viewed as sympathetically under a balancing test as a like amount of dust generated by a power plant that serves thousands in a nearby city.)

5. Definitional test

Remember that the test for trespass in number 2, above, included a requirement that materials entering another's land are tangible. Naturally, some cases provide a definition for "tangible." This is also a type of rule or test because you know that something entering another's land must be able to be defined as tangible in order for there to be a trespass. (This turns out to be tricky when it comes to things like dust and smells, which in some states are covered by both trespass and nuisance and in other states only by nuisance.)

But be careful, because courts often present much more complicated tests in ways that make them seem definitional. For example, the court could say: "Texas law defines adverse possession as an actual and visible appropriation of real property, commenced and continued under a claim of right that is inconsistent with and is hostile to the claim of another person." This sounds like a definition of adverse possession, but it is, in fact, a list of required elements.

Others can be even sneakier. Think about driving under the influence ("DUI"). A court might define DUI as the operation of a motor vehicle while under the influence. Again, that sounds like a definition, but actually contains multiple required elements. For DUI, there must be operation of a motor vehicle, so it is very likely that you can sleep in your back seat while drunk without violating the law. You need a definition of "operating." (In many jurisdictions, by the way, simply inserting the keys counts, even if you do not start the engine.) You also need a definition of "motor vehicle." Do tractors, bicycles, and skateboards count? In many jurisdictions, you will need to turn to statutes passed by the legislature rather than court decisions to find definitions for these terms (e.g., a blood-alcohol concentration of 0.01 may, by statute, constitute "under the influence").

To the best of your ability, take any definitional rule and break it down into subparts to create a test of required elements. A DUI requires (1) operation, (2) of a motor vehicle, and (3) while under the influence. If it cannot be broken into pieces, then it is a simple clarification or definition of a single term or element.

6. Exceptions

Some rules complement others by explaining when the primary rule does not apply.

Example:

Damages are required except where the claimant can establish the doctrine of anticipatory nuisance.

Legal Functions of Rules

It is also useful to understand when rules are used in the lifespan of a lawsuit, and that means organizing them by their function.

1. Procedural rules

Procedural rules govern the who/when/how of creating and pursuing a legal claim. They are all about details.

Example: The statute of limitations for trespass in Vermont is three years.

Example: Claims must be brought by the Attorney General unless the private plaintiff is able to show a special injury.

2. Basic tests (a.k.a. prima facie case rules)

These are the key rules for any cause of action. They are the heart of the argument.

Example: Trespass requires an entry onto the real property of another person.

Example: To establish a nuisance, the plaintiff must prove an unreasonable interference with the use and enjoyment of land, causing a substantial harm.

3. Defense rules

These rules explain what is and is not a defense to a cause of action. They also provide the details of what is needed to prove or establish the defense.

Example: Compliance with the Clean Water Act is not a defense to a nuisance action brought by a private individual.

Example: Compliance with best management practices is an affirmative defense to nuisance actions where the complaint is based on agricultural activities.

4. Remedies rules

Remedies rules tell you about what the plaintiff can and cannot be awarded by the court in the event that the claim is proven.

Example: Damages are a matter of right when the defendant proves all elements of the claim.

Example: Injunctions are equitable remedies that are within the discretion of the court.

Example: Punitive damages are not available except where the plaintiff acted with malice.

Example: In determining whether to grant an injunction, the court considers the social value of the defendant's business.

Thinking in terms of legal functions helps you to group rules in an order that is logical for your reader, because legal readers naturally think in terms of the order of tasks as a lawsuit evolves from the filing of the complaint to the dismissal.

Initially, procedural rules are very important. Later, it is all about the key tests. Then the defense argues. Finally, you must think about remedies. This is what you might call the natural progression of a lawsuit.

Writing Your Conclusion

The conclusion tends to receive the fewest points — and this makes sense given that many or most hypotheticals are meant to have credible arguments on both sides of the issue. It is generally not advisable to worry about coming to the "right" conclusion because *there very likely is not one.* Exam questions are chosen for their ability to nestle right between existing legal rules, giving them no certain outcome in court. These are precisely the questions that are most likely to end up in court because both parties refuse to settle the claim. You need a conclusion, but often it is okay to just pick one.

Occasionally, professors write exams that favor one side or the other and expect students to apply the rule, make a robust argument, and then pick the correct conclusion. Here, the conclusion will be worth more points, but the application generally still holds the largest number of points. There is no reason to write elaborate conclusions. Write good arguments. The next chapter tells you how.

THREE

Applications, or
Where the Most Points Live

When it comes to successfully earning points, IRAC looks a lot more like:

In this way, the IRAC model is a little misleading in that it appears path-driven to the final answer. Scoring well is not usually about the C. It is about the A.

The issue is important, although often less because of the points available for simply recognizing the issue and more because if you do not spot the issue, then you will not get the points for the rule and application associated with that issue.

There is a real irony about the application being where most of the points live on a scoring rubric: students constantly read bad examples of applications. Law textbooks contain edited cases and, to fit everything in, a 50-page Supreme Court decision is often reduced to four or five pages. That means what is left is often fact- and rule-dense and only includes portions of the court's extensive application of the rules. As a result, students more often read bad examples of how to do an analysis, because what students are actually reading is a partial analysis.

What Does It Mean to Apply a Rule?

How do you go about creating a persuasive and thorough application of the rules? The first step is to actually make sure that you apply all of the rules to all of the evidence. What does it really mean, though, to apply the rule? It may seem intuitive — and a very basic application of a rule to facts often is. But lawyers aren't paid high dollar amounts for very basic applications. And simple applications do not fare well in final exam scores. That means there should be a specific strategy for crafting a thorough and robust application of the rule to the facts.

Applying a rule to the facts means noting the facts in evidence that are relevant and explaining to your reader what makes those facts relevant, important, meaningful, and interesting in the context of the rule.

The basic step of analysis is determining which facts support each side. But what often happens with student exams is that this critical step occurs entirely in the student's mind and not on the paper. That means what the student writes is really just a list of facts on each side. This is a type of analysis, but not a very sophisticated one. This method is also rather fatal for success as an attorney because it assumes that the judge intuitively sees your logic and interprets the facts in the same way that you do. Likely, this is far from the truth.

The key then is to make sure that when a fact supports one side or the other, the essay should explain why the fact supports that side, rather than simply making a general assertion that the facts do support that side.

Example:

A property rule requires annexation (interpreted as attachment). Hypothetical facts state that the item in question weighs 500 pounds. The answer could say, "The item weighs 500 pounds, and this supports the item being attached." This answer assumes that in this context the reader regards 500 pounds as a lot and as difficult to move. But that might or might not be true in a variety of business circumstances. If the business is elephant transportation, that weight is minimal. If the business is mail delivery, that weight would be considered very heavy.

The better plan is to explain why the reader should regard the fact as supporting one side or the other. Ideally, the "why" given here should connect directly to the legal rule being applied.

Example:

A better answer to the above question then would be: "Five hundred pounds is difficult or impossible for an individual to move without specialized equipment, which suggests that the item is attached." And this answer improves by connecting the reasoning to the rule: "A weight of 500 pounds effectively makes the item attached because it is difficult if not impossible for one individual to move the item without specialized equipment."

The best responses to hypotheticals will not only organize the facts by how they support each side (and occasionally both sides), but also articulate the reasoning behind that organization of the two sides. Additionally, the best responses will also explain why the fact is important, meaningful, or relevant within the context of the rule.

Connect facts back to a part of the rule. The facts lack meaning or are unpersuasive without the context of the rule. (This is why the R is always first — IRAC.) The facts are most persuasive when you explain why you believe the fact is useful in terms of the rule without assuming the reader sees that relationship.

Example:

Rule	*Abnormally dangerous activities are nuisances.*
Fact	*Neighbor's blacksmithing creates sparks that cross the boundary.*
Application	*Sparks from a neighboring property create a risk of fire, which is a danger to public safety and therefore abnormally dangerous.*

Notice the structure of the application statements: fact, explanation, rule. This is the first and basic method of creating an application.

How to Structure an Application for Thoroughness

Students use a variety of inventive structures to create arguments for both sides. Here are some common models:

Model 1	Model 2	Model 3	Model 4
Divided stream of consciousness	Organized rules, muddled elements	Organizing elements, dividing arguments and rules	Organizing by elements, ping-pong approach
Issue	Issue	Issue	Issue
Why A should win	Rules	Rules	Rules
mix of rules, application, elements	Why A should win	Application	Application
Why B should win	muddle of elements	Why A should win	Element 1
mix of rules, application, elements	Why B should win	Element 1	Sentence by sentence switch between sides.
Conclusion	muddle of elements	Element 2	Element 2
	Conclusion	Element 3	Sentence by sentence switch between sides.
		Why B should win	Element 3
		Element 1	Sentence by sentence switch between sides.
		Element 2	Conclusion
		Element 3	
		Conclusion	

Creating an argument for both sides is, of course, an improvement on arguing only one side. It is more thorough. However, each of these four common models of organization has problems both in terms of scoring points on an exam and establishing good structures and habits for life as an attorney.

The models range from worse (left) to better (further right). Both Model 1 and Model 2 are poorly structured. There is little format to keep the student from generally devolving into stream of consciousness. The student is likely to repeat themselves and thereby lose points. The student is also likely to waste time by stopping to wonder about what to do next. Model 3 and Model 4 aren't terrible, but those models are also not likely to create the strongest arguments or win the most points in the scoring rubric. Model 3 invites repetition and circling through the facts, which is likely to waste time and lower the score. Model 4 may be able to check the boxes on a rubric for the most part, but is, frankly, very annoying to the reader. It is the ping-pong motion that comes from arguing one side for one sentence then moving to the other side on the next sentence — rinse and repeat endlessly. Bouncing from side to side with each sentence tends to frustrate the reader and invite a sense that the student does not really have an in-depth grasp of the situation.

Effective structure:

Use tests to structure your application. Break the key rule down into elements (or factors, or terms of art, or components of definitions). Now create a miniature IRAC (an irac) for each element.

If your rule for adverse possession requires hostile, continuous, visible appropriation for 15 years, then you know to structure your application in terms of four elements: hostile, continuous, visible, and 15 years. Give each of these elements a separate paragraph. Pretend each element of a rule creates a miniature issue question that is formed by asking whether there is evidence for this element in the facts.

i   Do the facts demonstrate hostility?

r   Provide rules that define or explain hostility.

a   Apply the hostility rules. If there are facts to do so, argue both sides.

c   Conclude as to whether there was or was not hostility.

Now move on to the next element, continuous, and create another miniature irac. The miniature iracs together form the application of the overall IRAC. What this ends up looking like might be called a nested IRAC approach:

IRA irac irac irac C

This approach is organized, requires little tweaking to be used in a motion or brief in actual practice, presents the student as a stronger crafter of arguments, and maximizes catching all the points in the rubric. Here is what the ideal model looks like:

Model for Nested IRA(irac)C Arguing Both Sides

Issue

Rule (central or primary test)

Application

  issue — element 1
  rules — clarify element 1
  application
   arguments for side 1
   arguments for side 2
  conclusion — on element 1

  issue — element 2
  rules — clarify element 2
  application
   arguments for side 1
   arguments for side 2
  conclusion — on element 2

  issue — element 3
  rules — clarify element 3
  application
   arguments for side 1
   arguments for side 2
  conclusion — on element 3

Conclusion

This model can be tweaked for practice by adopting side one as your client's side and adding a rebuttal to the arguments that you raise for side two.

Creating Rule Blocks

Some rules easily lend themselves to the nested IRAC format. Others read more like a narrative and can be difficult to see as elements. The trick is to break these into components or, as this book terms them, rule blocks. These are the key pieces — often legal terms of art — that must be proven to establish your case.

Example:

Poaching is defined as intentionally killing a protected animal on state park lands, not during hunting season.

Then you have, by default, a five-part test:

1. *Intent*

2. *Kill*

3. *Protected*

4. *State park land*

5. *Not during hunting season*

You can then use these blocks in the place of a list of elements for proving poaching. Each block gets a miniature irac. Argue each block, covering both yes and no for each side.

Rule blocks are very useful for making sure that you write a thorough analysis and get all of the points possible for each issue.

Making Sure You Are Thorough with the Facts

1. Use all of the facts, not just the ones you like better.

Beginning law students rarely use all of the facts in a hypothetical, even when all of the facts can be used to support one or both sides of the argument and many of them are relevant to multiple elements of a rule. Part of this may be time constraints, but even when professors give questions that have no time constraint, this is usually still true. It can take practice to notice all of the facts within the hypothetical and to set up a checklist system (quickly) to make sure that the answer utilizes all the key facts at least once.

2. Squeeze the facts, but avoid speculation.

Use facts in the most powerful ways possible. Squeeze the facts for all of the possible detail and arguments, like getting the last bits of juice out of a lemon. There are a few strategies that help with squeezing the facts.

First, note opportunities to present facts in different lights. This means to use the fact given without changing it, but to represent it in a way that is more or less powerful depending on the side of the argument being written. Second, add ordinary life comparisons and items within the common knowledge of readers where appropriate.

Example:

Fact: The room is 10 feet by 10 feet.

Squeezed fact: The room is 100 square feet.

Squeezed fact: The room is 100 square feet, which is one-third the size of many New York apartments.

Remember that it is generally okay to use your basic knowledge of the way things work in the world, even if that information is not contained within the hypothetical. If it is common sense or a 10-year-old gets it, it is probably fair game. Thus, in a torts problem, if the problem says that the accident happened at night, you can use your commonsense knowledge of the world to note that visibility is likely reduced in darkness.

Be careful, however, not to speculate about situations or events that are not presented within the hypothetical. Do not head off on random tangents. Students often begin a long paragraph with the words "but if" and proceed to tell the professor how things might have been different if the facts had been different. Well, sure, of course there would be a different outcome with different facts. But the professor picked *these* facts. The grading sheet does not reserve points for musings about scenarios not raised in the hypothetical.

3. Spend extra time on pivotal facts.

Ask whether there is a fact that changes the outcome if interpreted in two different ways. A key part of the application should focus on the pivotal fact, if there is one. (Sometimes there is more than one.)

In property law, crops transfer with a sale of real estate if ripe and do not transfer if unripe. A hypothetical inviting the student to apply this rule might include facts that make it difficult to classify a crop as either ripe or not ripe. These are pivotal facts.

Example:

One crop is pumpkins, which do not all ripen at once and at the time of the sale 65% were ripe. A second crop on the farm is cucumbers, which take 75 days to ripen, but once ripe continue to produce new crops so long as the first crop is picked — at any given time there are both ripe and unripe cucumbers. The final crop on the farm is tobacco, which is ready to pick at any time after the first 90 days, but continues to get taller for 150 days provided that the weather accommodates growing — and the taller the crop the greater the income from the crop. Which, if any, crops transfer with the sale of the farm?

In the example here, each pivotal fact makes it difficult to accurately and simply describe the crop as ripe or unripe at one moment in time. And the rule is applied at one moment — the moment of sale. To answer a hypothetical in the most thoughtful manner, capitalize on the pivotal facts. Describe this fact as one that is pivotal, explain why it is pivotal and how it can be interpreted differently by the two sides of a dispute.

4. Do not group facts unless you have already used them individually.

Chances are pretty good that you are missing opportunities to fully squeeze all the energy out of the facts. Grouping may be useful for connecting to a rule generally, but it can also circumvent your efforts to use each fact for its full persuasive value. For this reason, it is most useful to group facts only after having used each one.

5. Do not assume that once you have used a fact on one side of the argument or one element, you are done.

Many facts do not definitively support one side or the other. For example, the size of an object may be big, but not *that* big. Rather than assuming that X size is big, ask yourself if you can use the fact both ways.

Facts also can be relevant to more than one element of a test. For example, in an adverse possession problem, the use of the garage only during winter is relevant to whether there is "continuous use," but also whether there is "visible use giving notice to the true owner."

Adding Layers to the Application: Case Comparisons

Once you are comfortable being thorough with a basic application of the rules to the facts, you can move on to add more layers to your application — i.e., increase its sophistication. The most important way to do this is to work with the facts of the cases that you read for class.

To properly apply rules, you should add case comparisons that will reinforce arguments built on the facts, as well as rebut potential counterarguments. The first step in good case comparisons is to make sure that you compare facts to facts, and *not* to compare conclusions to conclusions. That might seem obvious, but law students often make this mistake, and it may not be as obvious as you think. Consider the examples below:

Examples:

No   *This case resembles* Max v. Wilde *where there was also a nuisance.*

No   *This case resembles* Max v. Wilde *because in both cases the plaintiff was disturbed in his "use and enjoyment of his property."*

Yes   *This case resembles* Max v. Wilde *because in both cases the defendant operated an industrial facility in a residential neighborhood.*

When comparing cases, be sure to explain precisely why the facts are similar. This similarity is most persuasive if it can be connected directly to the rule or the reasoning behind the rule.

Examples:

No   *The situation here resembles* Smith v. Larsen.

Yes   *The situation here resembles* Smith v. Larsen *because in both cases the plaintiffs were disturbed by industrial smoke from a neighboring property.*

With those basics in mind, there are a number of particular techniques that you can use to develop a solid argument through case comparisons. The remainder of this section considers some of these in more detail.

1. In-depth analysis

If a single case matches especially nicely with your facts, you may want to write a paragraph that gives an in-depth comparison of the facts of the two cases.

Professors often use facts from a case in the textbook as a hypothetical, taking a central fact and tweaking it problematically. When reading exam questions, watch for hypotheticals that resemble the facts of a case you have read, but also differ in some central aspect. Narrow in on that different fact. How is it different from the case you read? Ask yourself how this fact may change the outcome of the case when the rule is applied.

Example:

In Smith v. Larsen, *the plaintiffs were disturbed by industrial smoke from a neighboring property. The company was located adjacent to a residential neighborhood and smoke continued all day, every day. The Smiths suffered from an increased number of sinus infections and asthma attacks after moving to the neighborhood of the Larsen Chemical Company. In the hypothetical, the*

Workmans similarly complain of exposure to industrial smoke from a factory. The factory in the hypothetical is located much further from the Workmans' property — about ¼ mile instead of adjacent. However, like the Smiths, the Workmans can demonstrate substantial changes to their respiratory health that are attributable to exposure to smoke. Despite the increased distance in the hypothetical between the two properties, the similarity in injuries and nature of the problematic conduct suggest that the court should view the two cases as more similar than different. Therefore, the court should rule in favor of the Workmans.

Notice that the example focuses on a single case for a full paragraph. The example highlights both similarities and differences in facts. Then the example explains why the similarities are more important than the differences. You can, of course, also reverse this process — it is often called distinguishing a case — to explain why a case should not be followed because the facts of the hypothetical are too different from the facts of the case.

Finally, if the facts are unfamiliar to you (i.e., not related to a case in the textbook), then you should still pay attention to any fact that is particularly problematic or difficult to classify in the context of the rule.

2. Duck, duck, goose

This technique is named for the children's game. Essentially, the idea is to use examples from cases to show what is typically within the rule and to emphasize that the current case does or does not fit the pattern. In other words: this is a duck, this is a duck, and this is a duck. This case is a duck/is a goose.

Example:

Courts have found bad faith where the insurer refused to replace burned toiletries, refused to provide the paperwork necessary to file the claim, or refused to answer phone calls regarding a claim. In the present case, where the insurer merely delayed in processing the claim by 48 hours, there is no bad faith.

3. Parentheticals on small points

Parentheticals are good for factual comparisons when one very specific fact is at issue — such as a length of time. This allows you to essentially line up the facts side by side. This can be used similarly to the duck, duck, goose approach to show that your case does or does not belong in the list. Alternatively, the list can be used to demonstrate the breadth or the narrowness of facts where a court has applied a rule.

Example:

John v. Richards Ins., *234 F.2d 364 (4th Cir. 1993) (where insurer delayed in paying a claim by 18 months, the insurer acted in bad faith);* Jacobs v. LINA, *453 F.2d 789 (4th Cir. 2001) (where insurer delayed in paying a claim by 12 months, the insurer acted in bad faith).*

4. Hyperbole

If you want to argue that your case does not fit under a legal rule, give the most extreme examples available in the case law of what does fall under the rule. Then say, "Defendant's conduct here does not rise to the level of _____."

5. Using law from other jurisdictions to argue for a new rule

You may wish to make a general statement and then follow it up with a string cite of parentheticals. The key here is to show that each of the cases aligns with your facts, so that you have a stronger argument for adopting the same holding as the other jurisdictions did on similar facts. If you have room to address the point, you could use more in-depth comparisons as opposed to the parentheticals approach.

Example:

You are in the Fourth Circuit. The Fourth Circuit has not addressed the applicability of federal drug statutes to Martians, but other circuits have.

While the Fourth Circuit has never specifically addressed the applicability of federal drug statutes to Martian non-citizens, numerous other circuits have addressed this issue and concluded that the statutes apply. See, e.g., R2D2 v. U.S., 298 F.3d 435 (1st Cir. 2018) (finding a Martian liable for possession of ecstasy); E.T. v. U.S., 436 F.3d 378 (2d Cir. 2017) (finding a Martian liable for possession of opium).

Each of these approaches could be used within the context of an exam, but they are not all equally easy to use. For example, you may not recall an entire group of cases that would enable you to write a list of parentheticals. To the degree that you recall the facts of cases, however, any one of these methods is a good approach to making a comparison. Beware, however, the pull of a comparison. For a hypothetical it is important to write a well-developed answer, not an answer that is persuasive for one particular side. Pushing one comparison may encourage you to not think in a balanced way about the two sides. The comparison is not a conclusion. It is just one more thing to add to the nested-IRAC structure that will improve your overall answer.

Adding Layers to the Application: Recognizing and Working with Spectrum Words

Students tend to treat some words as simple yes/no questions, when a litigator would see those words as complex questions involving a spectrum or a range from less to more. This book refers to these as spectrum words.

For example, a four-year-old girl who has been raised in very quiet family describes herself as loud because compared to everyone she spends time around, she is. In fact, her parents have told her that she is loud. But then she meets another family, who are loud. It turns out she is not accurately described as loud; she is just less quiet than the rest of her family. Quiet and loud cannot be well managed as yes/no questions. In reality, quiet and loud point to two ends of a spectrum.

With a spectrum word, how accurately you use the term depends on your recognition of the spectrum and your knowledge of its breadth. Consider how people use political labels (left, right, conservative, liberal) and social words (casual, reliable, quiet, introverted, studious, light drinker, social drinker). Sometimes someone represents themselves as studious, honestly believes they are studious, but if you have a broader perspective, then you recognize that studious is not a very accurate label for that person. These labels are contextual. A political liberal in America is a moderate in most European countries. How people use these labels depends on their expectations, their social context, and their life experience. Because these types of labels are common in everyday life, legal rules sometimes refer to them.

Students should notice these words within legal rules and recognize them as spectrum words, because a yes/no analysis is not persuasive in this context.

What are some spectrum words within the legal context?

Annexed. Adapted. Annoying. Unreasonable. Abnormally dangerous. These words abound in legal rules, particularly in the context of property and torts. But you also see them in a variety of statutory contexts. Spectrum words help to give legal rules some social flexibility.

How do you recognize spectrum words?

If a thing or person can be "kind of" or "a little" or "really" that, then it is probably a spectrum word. You can be kind of introverted. You can be a little quiet. You can be really conservative or liberal. You can be kind of annoying.

How do you work with spectrum words when applying a rule?

Remember that spectrum words are about context and the breadth of experience. Focus on those two things.

First, give the reader context. Bring in and emphasize factual details that provide context for the label. If the issue is nuisance and you need to establish whether the land use is unreasonable or not, tell the reader about the context. Is it a city, suburban, or a rural area? Are the surrounding properties businesses, other homes, farms, or a mix? What else is nearby? What was the area historically? Are there other features around that are loud/smelly/dusty or is this the only one?

Second, make the reader aware of breadth of the spectrum. You can use practical examples, other facts in the hypothetical, or case comparisons to do this. Give examples of something that is only slightly adapted and something that is substantially adapted. Tell what other features courts have found to be annoying enough to create a nuisance. Give examples of activities that are just a little dangerous versus abnormally dangerous. Provide the entire range, so that the reader can see where these particular facts fall on the spectrum.

Adding Layers to the Application: Policy, Theory, and History

A thoroughly constructed application also often speaks to the main narratives that weave their way through the common law. It is not so helpful to throw in big, undefined concepts like justice. However, specific information about policy, theory, or history can be useful in understanding the intent and purpose behind a rule that you are applying. For example, it can be very helpful to point out why some jurisdictions have chosen to adopt a good faith requirement for adverse possession (because otherwise the courts are rewarding trespasses).

The first rule of including policy, theory, and history is that this is the icing on the cake. Many 1L students who are accustomed to writing papers in history or philosophy want to jump immediately to the policy discussion and never actually apply the rule. This is a disaster for scoring well on a hypothetical because the scoring rubric will focus on the law and only secondarily on policy.

The second rule of including policy, theory, and history is to use them in measured doses to support specific points. A great way to do this is to add a sentence to support your sub-conclusions in those miniature iracs.

Example:

There is a trespass issue. You will have miniature iracs for entry, private property, intent, and remedies. Each of those will have a sub-conclusion, i.e., there is or is not an entry, there is or is not private property, the entry was intentional or unintentional, there should be an injunction or damages or both.

Your sub-conclusion could be: The neighbor repeatedly walking on Jane's driveway was intentional.

Or: The neighbor repeatedly walking on Jane's driveway was intentional. Recognizing this intent is imperative for protecting Jane, because historically trespass was created largely to protect the right to exclude others from private property.

Including a bit of policy, theory, or history with the conclusion further supports that conclusion. Sprinkling it in with your sub-conclusions of the miniature iracs ensures that it is discrete, specific, and distributed throughout your analysis.

How to Pull It All Together?

Everything in this chapter probably sounds totally doable. The only problem is that often students can learn and recall all of these techniques, but still not actually execute them on a hypothetical. Understanding the techniques is not the same thing as being good at executing them. In other words, this chapter has described skills, not just provided information.

It is critical to learn these skills through practice. Compare it to playing the piano. It can help to read a good book on technique, but you must actually practice techniques to learn them. That is why you have a whole workbook here with hypotheticals and scoring rubrics.

Writing an Application: A Checklist

Steps	Implementation notes
1. Create a structure to fill in.	* Use the relevant rules to generate a structure for re-sponding to the issue. * Relationships between the rules should be logical in this structure (i.e., exceptions come after the primary rule). * Break rules into bite-sized chunks (the list of elements or create your own rule blocks) to further organize the structure. * Add a pro/con side to each piece of the structure.
2. Work with the facts to ex-plain them in the context of the rule.	* Use all of the facts. * Align facts with the pro/con sides. Be aware that some facts could go either way. * Use facts for multiple elements or rule blocks when possible. * Use facts individually, rather than grouping, to ensure thoroughness. * Do not just recite the facts—explain why each fact is interesting, meaningful, and relevant in the context of an element or rule block. Not in the context of a con-clusion. * Squeeze all the possible usefulness out of the facts without speculating.
3. Use cases to elucidate rule/fact con-nections.	* Compare facts to facts, not conclusions to conclusions. * Include the court's reasoning to make it persuasive. * Use case comparisons to make persuasive arguments when you have spectrum words like "unreasonable" or "dangerous." * Remember to use case comparisons on multiple ele-ments or rule blocks and for both pro/con sides.
4. Use theory, history, or pol-icy to support arguments.	* Add information that supports a sub-conclusion on an element or rule block rather than a final conclusion. * Use information regarding purposes or intent of rules/statutes. * Repeat for pro/con sides when possible.

FOUR

Scoring Rubrics, Diagnosing Errors, and Correcting Errors

Scoring Rubrics as Secret Information

Professors use rubrics for a variety of reasons, but one of the most important is to ensure that they grade fairly and accurately. Unfortunately, most professors treat rubrics like a trade secret and do not release them to students.

Releasing scoring rubrics provides students with the opportunity to practice and self-grade. It also means students feel less anxiety. They know what an exam and a scoring rubric look like and what to expect in terms of the difficulty level.

How to Use a Scoring Rubric

Avoid grading immediately after you finish a hypothetical. (Take a break, take a walk, etc.) This is only because you are more likely to read the hypothetical filling in what you meant to say, rather than grading what is really on the paper. It is important to grade only what is on the paper.

Alternatively, it is a great idea to use this workbook with a study partner or small group. Trade papers and grade each other. Then you are certain you only grade what is on the page, not in your head. Also, this way you can grade immediately after the problem and have a discussion as well while everyone still remembers the prompt thoroughly.

In terms of how to do it, the best way is to skim the rubric in full, so you have a sense of what is in there and where. Then sit down with your answer in front of you and the rubric beside your writing hand. Read your answer sentence by sentence. At the end of each sentence, pause to check off anything you have accomplished on the rubric. Try to remember not to give yourself points if you just restated a fact rather than explaining its importance and connecting it to the rule. Finally, total your scores.

Compare your score. Remembering that law school grading is comparative, your own hypothetical score is only really meaningful in the context of the range of scores for a class. Most importantly, what is your score compared to the mean score? Obviously, you do not have this information in real-time for your classmates. This book provides some sample means at the end of rubrics to give you an idea.

What You Learn from a Scoring Rubric and What You Do Not

Once you have compared your score to the mean, you can also look to the scoring rubric to see what you did not do in your answer. This provides very specific information, i.e., you forgot certain rules, skipped using certain facts in this prompt, or missed certain connections between the facts and rule.

This does not tell you instantly your more thematic errors, or errors in technique. These errors are not specific to the rules and facts of this hypothetical. They are about *how* you responded to the hypothetical more generally. Here are the most common thematic errors that 1L students present:

1. Failure to spot issues

2. Many conclusions, little to no application

3. Fact errors or speculation goes off the rubric

4. Answer is too short, comparatively

You can use the scoring rubric to see these things, to a certain degree, but it takes a bit more effort. Chapter 20 focuses on diagnosing problematic patterns in answers. Refer to Chapter 20 regularly as you go through the hypothetical exercises in this book. It will help you to recognize those problems and provides specific strategies for tackling such problems.

Another method you can consider is to use a secondary rubric that is the same for every hypothetical: a rubric that lists good reasoning techniques. That is, it is not about the facts and the rules, but it is a rubric focused specifically on technique. This book includes such a rubric, but note that it makes the most sense in conjunction with the chapter on diagnosing errors.

Finally, thematic errors can be more difficult to see in your own work, so if you have a study partner or group, this is a great time to take advantage of their feedback.

Hypothetical Answer Techniques Rubric		
Answer Segment	**Requirements for Excellence**	
Issue	❖ Grasp the key problem in layman's terms.	
	❖ Use appropriate legal terms.	
	❖ Include relevant alternatives if applicable.	
	❖ Include the reason the question is "sticky."	
Rule	❖ State rules accurately.	
	❖ Include all relevant rules.	
	❖ State rules with precision.	
	❖ Explicate relationships between rules: exceptions, elements, burdens, etc.	
Application	❖ Identify the "sticky" — the reason the facts do not fit neatly within the rule.	
	❖ Organize the application by breaking the rule into blocks — elements or phrases if there aren't clear elements listed.	
	❖ Argue both sides for each rule block.	
	❖ Weight arguments roughly 50/50.	
	❖ Use all of the facts provided. Use them on multiple rule blocks when possible.	
	❖ Squeeze all of the energy out of facts.	
	❖ Avoid speculation.	
	❖ Use commonsense, real-world knowledge.	
	❖ Connect the fact with the rule (giving a why or an explanation) rather than reciting the fact.	
	❖ Compare the facts of relevant cases, especially where there are "spectrum" words like "unreasonable," "substantial" or "open to the public."	

Continued

Continued

Application	❖ Distinguish cases by pointing to key facts.	
	❖ Avoid being conclusory; explain why facts are meaningful, interesting, or important.	
	❖ Use public policy, but only after all evidence.	
Conclusion	❖ There is one.	
	❖ It is in the appropriate location.	
Macro	❖ Organize by IRAC.	
	❖ Within IRAC, categorize appropriately.	
Micro	❖ Organize opposing views by paragraph.	
	❖ Use paragraphs for a single purpose.	
	❖ Provide framing and a path/map for the reader.	

PART TWO **PRACTICE**

FIVE

Simple One-Issue Hypotheticals

Personalty versus Realty

Basic Rules of Improvements

Personalty (non-land items of property) may become part of the realty (land) by joining to the land. Such joined items are called improvements, meaning that they add permanent value to the land.

Generally, an item of personalty becomes an improvement when it has a significant association with the land. The significant association is often measured by three factors: annexation, adaptation, and intent. Annexation, actual or constructive, is the process of attaching the item securely to the land — embedding or enclosing it.

Adaptation refers to how the item is suited to this particular property alone or how the land/item is changed to fit them to each other. Courts find that adaptation is entitled to great weight, especially in connection with the element of intention. If the item is essential to the purposes of the building, it will be considered an improvement, even if it can be severed without injury to either item or realty.

Intent is the most important of the three factors and refers to the intent of the person placing the item as to whether it would be permanent or not. Intent may be inferred from the nature of the article affixed, the purpose for which it was affixed, the relationship of the party making the annexation, and the structure and mode of annexation. Any doubt as to intent is resolved against the proprietor if he annexed personally. Annexation can be evaluated in conjunction with intent because the method or extent of annexation can indicate the intent of the party annexing.

The question of improvements often arises because statutory rules rely on the distinction between personalty and improvements. Such statutes may use this distinction to determine many different issues, including tax liability, the ability to include items in a tax sale, whether items transfer with realty, whether a tenant can remove items at the end of a lease, and whether a plaintiff can maintain a personal injury suit against a landowner or member of the construction industry.

Outline of Basic Rules: Realty versus Personalty

I. Determining realty (improvement) versus personalty

  A. Test (factors, weighted)

    1. Annexation

      a. Clarify: there are two types of annexation: actual and constructive.

      b. Strong indicia: something is embedded or enclosed.

    2. Adaptation to the use or purpose

      a. Weight: this factor is entitled to great weight, especially in connection with the element of intention. Trump card: if essential to the purposes of the building, it will be considered an improvement, even if it can be severed without injury to either the item or realty.

      b. Clarify: definition: adapted means fitted to the use or purpose of the property. It is relevant if either the item or the realty was changed.

    3. Intent of the parties

      a. Weight: this factor is the "chief test," described as "paramount" or "controlling."

      b. Clarify: inferences: intention may be inferred from the nature of the article affixed, the purpose for which it was affixed, the relationship of the party making the annexation, and the structure and mode of annexation.

      c. Clarify: burden: any doubt as to intention should be resolved against the proprietor if he annexed personally.

      d. Clarify: interrelated rule blocks: the method or extent of annexation can indicate the intent of the party annexing.

The Playhouse Hypothetical

Time to read and write your answer: one hour.

John purchased a walk-in playhouse for his daughter, Gloria, for her birthday in August. The playhouse is approximately five feet tall and has a footprint of five feet by ten feet. The playhouse arrived on a trailer on wheels. Not knowing if the family would move in the future, John decided that it would be difficult to load and unload the playhouse from the trailer. He left the trailer on the wheels and simply used a few loose cement blocks to hold the trailer in place. John then built a set of two wooden steps up to the front door and planted lots of low shrubs and gardens around the playhouse. The plantings cover up the wheels, so they are not visible, and they also give the playhouse the "cute English garden" appearance that Gloria loves for her tea parties.

The City of Lex, where John and Gloria live, has a provision that taxes all "outbuildings," which are defined as "improvements to the real property." Historically this ordinance was created to tax farm buildings that were improvements to the property, including everything from barns to chicken coops and outhouses. This January John's tax bill included an additional "outbuilding" cost of $100 for the playhouse. John asks you if he can reasonably fight his new tax bill.

Answer this hypothetical using the structure provided on the next page.

Sample Structure for a Single-Issue Hypothetical Answer

Issue: Is the playhouse a taxable improvement to the property?

Rule(s): Fixtures are property that fits between realty and personalty. They have a light association with the land and remain easily movable. On the other hand, improvements are personal property that has transferred into realty. Improvements need a significant association or attachment with the land. To prove a significant association, you need to prove: (1) annexation (attachment), (2) adaptation (for particular business purposes or by changes to the land), or (3) intent.

Application:

[Optional sentence about why it is a sticky question.]

Paragraph one:

Discussion of why the playhouse is annexed/attached to the land.

Paragraph two:

Discussion of why the playhouse is *not* annexed/attached to the land.

Paragraph three:

Discussion of why the playhouse is adapted to the land.

Paragraph four:

Discussion of why the playhouse is *not* adapted to the land.

Paragraph five:

Discussion of why the playhouse was intended as an improvement.

Paragraph six:

Discussion of why the playhouse was *not* intended as an improvement

[Optional paragraph about policy/rule purpose/intent/theory/history.]

Conclusion: [one or two sentences]

Scoring Rubric for the Playhouse Hypothetical

Section			
Issue:	☑ Identify the key problem, at least in layman's terms: Is a tax payment appropriate? (2) ☑ Legal: Is the playhouse personalty or an improvement? (4)	6	6
Rules:	☑ Improvements need a significant association with real property. (3) ☑ Improvement is decided by a three-part, factors test: annexation, adaptation, and intent. (3) ☑ Annexation is the physical connection. (3) ☑ Adaptation means suited to purpose/use or altered to fit the land. (3) ☐ Intent is the most important and is measured at the time of placement. (3)	15	15

Application:	☐ Identify the sticky point: the playhouse retains wheels and has the ability to be moved quickly, but visually appears permanent. (2)	2	
	Annexation		
	Yes		
	☐ Planting shrubs means that the wheels can't roll, and the playhouse is somewhat enclosed. (3) 15 *M*	15	
	☐ Concrete blocks also enclose the wheels and prevent forward movement. (3)		
	☐ Wooden steps create a physical attachment to the ground via a bridge of sorts. (3)		
	☐ At 50 square feet, the playhouse is not easily moved except with equipment, which makes it attached to the land. (3)		
	☐ By covering the wheels, John made the playhouse appear to be permanently attached. (3)		24
	No		
	☐ Wheels allow the playhouse to be moved at any time, making it less attached. (3)	12	
	☐ The cement blocks can be lifted away to remove any enclosure. (3)		
	☐ The playhouse is on a trailer, so the size is workable for moving it. (3)		
	☐ The shrubs are not a permanent enclosure and may be moved or cut down. (3)		
	Adaptation		
	Yes		
	☐ The steps adapted the playhouse to this location by creating a bridge to the ground. (3)	6	
	☐ The surrounding plants created a special place on the land for the playhouse, fitting the land to the playhouse. (3)		

Continued

57

24
+ 12 36

Continued

Application:	*No*		
	☐ The playhouse is not attached by pipes or wires, the way that a mobile home would be, which suggests there is very little adaptation. (3)	9	
	☐ The playhouse can be moved with little or no damage to it or the land, which suggests any adaptation was minimal. (3)		
	☐ The steps are a minor addition and can be easily removed, which suggests any adaptation is minor. (3)		
	Intent		
	Yes		
	☐ John placed cement blocks and shrubs, suggesting a long-term intent for the playhouse to remain. (3)	6	
	☑ John built steps that made a more permanent entrance to the playhouse, indicating an intention for a long-term solution. (3)		
	No		
	☑ John left the playhouse on wheels because he knew he might move it. (3)	9	
	☐ John only visually made the playhouse look permanent, but nothing was installed too solidly, which suggests he intended a temporary placement. (3)		
	☑ John bought the playhouse as a gift, which indicates a desire to take it with the family if they moved. (3)		
Conclusion:	✓	3	
	Total		

Mean Score for sample law student groups: 51

Sample Answer to the Playhouse Hypothetical

Issue:

Whether the playhouse, which appears attached but could be moved with moderate effort, is a fixture or instead an improvement, which could be taxed as an outbuilding.

Rules:

Personalty can transform into a fixture or an improvement. A fixture is personal property that becomes slightly attached to realty, but can be removed with minimal efforts. To become an improvement, the personal property must be significantly associated with the realty. To determine whether personal property has been transformed into an improvement, cases look to annexation, adaptation, and the intent of the party who originally attached the item.

Application:

The playhouse does not fit neatly in the categories of fixture and improvement because the degree to which it is attached to the land and the degree to which it is easily severable are debatable. Additionally, from any distance the playhouse will appear permanent, but upon closer inspection it remains on wheels, which makes the playhouse reasonably mobile. As a result, the level of attachment or association with the realty is unclear.

The first question is the level of attachment. Attachment refers to how stuck, embedded, or enclosed the item is. By planting the shrubs, the father has ensured that the trailer cannot simply be pulled forward, thus enclosing the playhouse. Similarly, the concrete blocks and steps will prevent the trailer from moving until those are removed, increasing the labor necessary to detach the playhouse from its surroundings before the trailer could be moved. Visibly, the picture of the playhouse and the description of a "cute English garden," suggest that the playhouse is solidly nestled within the landscape, and therefore relatively attached. In addition, the steps have created a physical attachment of the playhouse to the ground (a bridge). The size of the playhouse is also relevant, measuring 50 square feet, and suggesting a certain degree of difficulty in moving the structure.

On the other hand, with respect to annexation, the playhouse remains on wheels, which makes the playhouse much more mobile than it would be if it had to be lifted onto a trailer to be moved. The cement blocks could have been fastened in place, but instead are loose, allowing them to be moved rather rapidly. While the playhouse is large, it is not such a size that really prohibits movement, because it did arrive via a trailer. Additionally, when compared to something like a mobile home, which might be an improvement, the playhouse is much smaller and more easily transported. Overall, a court would be more likely to find that the playhouse is not annexed.

In terms of adaptation, the court looks to whether the purpose or use of the item is fitted to the property and whether the item or the land is adapted to fit. Here, steps have been added to the structure to fit the current landscape. Additionally, it is notable to consider that while the wheels remain on the playhouse (it would be difficult to lift the 50-square-foot playhouse off the trailer), the surroundings have been created to conceal this fact. To a passerby, the playhouse will appear to be physically adapted to fit into the premises.

On the other hand, unlike a stone wall, the playhouse can be moved without destroying much of the value of the property, which suggests that very little has been adapted. Additionally, when compared to something like a mobile home, which might be an improvement, the playhouse would not require the many physical attachments to systems (such as electrical wires, plumbing, and sewer pipes). The playhouse can easily be used on another property and can be removed with minimal or no damage to it or the land. In addition, the playhouse remains almost entirely unchanged and on the trailer. The only possible change to the structure is the steps, which are minor and quickly removable without harming the overall structure. As a result, a court is more likely to find that the playhouse is not adapted to the land.

Finally, courts consider the intent of the party placing the object. The intent is the most important of the three factors. Here, the cement blocks and plantings suggest that the playhouse was meant for a long-term installation. Additionally, the steps created a permanent bridge to the property. On the other hand, the father indicated that he left the playhouse on wheels because he might move it later, indicating a desire to not make the playhouse a permanent part of the realty. His temporary solutions to hide the wheels further support the desire to leave the playhouse movable. The plantings were not created to make the playhouse immovable, but rather to cater to his daughter's aesthetic sensibilities. Perhaps most importantly, the playhouse was intended to be a gift to his daughter, which suggests that it would be moved with the family, should they change residences. For these reasons, facts support the conclusion that the playhouse was not intended as a permanent addition to the property.

Conclusion:

The playhouse is not an improvement, and therefore will not be taxable under the ordinance.

SIX

Skill Building

Understanding What Goes Wrong in Reciting Facts

Reciting Facts Does Not Get Points

One of the most common problems with hypothetical answers is that students just repeat the facts given. Normally, students at least recognize that some of those facts support each side of the argument and organize the list of facts accordingly. This is a form of legal reasoning and requires an understanding of the rule. It is, however, only rudimentary legal reasoning.

To write an application, you must connect the facts with the rules. Consider how this can go wrong.

Sample Bad Answer

(1) John does not have to pay taxes on the playhouse. (2) The playhouse is small, just big enough to walk in. (3) In fact, the playhouse is only five feet tall. (4) The playhouse is still on the same wheels that it arrived on. (5) There are blocks around the wheels just to hold it all down. (6) John did not really do anything to the playhouse except put two steps up to the door and add a few shrubs around it in the yard. (7) It is basically the same as when he bought it. (8) Because it is small and has not been changed, the playhouse is still just an item of personal property, so there can be no real estate taxes on the playhouse.

Annotation of Sample Bad Answer

(1) John does not have to pay taxes on the playhouse.

> *Problem:* This is a conclusion for the primary issue posed by the hypothetical. The conclusion begins the entire analysis, which might be acceptable in oral argument or a formal brief, but it is not a good hypothetical answer strategy. Remember that the best score will come from discussing both sides

Huge concrete piece of [illegible] in suits

of the issue thoroughly and using all the facts. This is much less likely to happen if a student begins with a conclusion.

Problem: Yes, there is another problem with just this first sentence. There has been no statement of the issue in legal terms. Even the conclusion states the question in terms of the practical outcome for the imaginary client: he does not have to pay taxes on the playhouse. That might be an issue in tax class, but definitely not in property class. What legal question must be answered to know whether or not the taxes should be paid? You must decide if the playhouse is a personal good (personalty) or a part of the realty (an improvement). This is the legal issue at the heart of the analysis, not whether he has to pay taxes. If you must answer one question to answer another, make sure to explicitly say what that underlying question is. Additionally, note that properly identifying the issue also involves using the proper terms of art: realty and improvement.

(2) The playhouse is small, just big enough to walk in.

Problem: This just restates the facts that are given: limited size and walk-in. Why is the size relevant to taxes? What rule are you applying?

If your response to those questions was to say, "Is not it obvious?" or "it was the annexation rule," try going back and rereading the first two sentences of the sample bad answer. What if the judge does not remember the rule, or worse, misremembers the rule? What if you are the judge's least favorite lawyer in the entire city and agreeing with you is the last thing she wants to do? Just restating a fact is not very persuasive unless someone is already on your side. And by definition, a judge is not.

Additionally, when scoring a hypothetical, a professor can only grade what you write — not what is in your head. When a student writes this type of sentence, they have already thought about the annexation rule, gauged how large the playhouse is, and concluded that it is small. But all that happens on the paper is that last step.

You might think that adding the description of "small" changes this into an application. But there is another way to think of this description: it is, in fact, less detailed than the fact pattern, which gave precise dimensions.

(3) In fact, the playhouse is only five feet tall.

Problem: This restates the specific dimension without connection to a rule, explanation, or context. Without thinking in terms of what annexation means, why is five feet meaningful? It is not. It is fantastical for a mouse and tiny for an elephant. If the reader does not know whether you are talking about mice or elephants, then the reader has no way to evaluate the simple fact that the playhouse is five feet tall.

(4) The playhouse is still on the same wheels that it arrived on.

Problem: It restates the fact. There is no connection to the rule. Why does it matter if it is on wheels or not?

(5) There are blocks around the wheels to hold it all down.

Problem: It restates the fact. There is no connection to the rule.

(6) John did not really do anything to the playhouse except put two steps up to the door and add a few shrubs around it in the yard.

Problem: This still restates the fact. Although this sentence is slightly evaluative ("did not really do anything"), it is a very fuzzy statement. What does it mean to "really do anything" or not? More importantly, why does it matter what he does or does not do with a playhouse in his yard?

(7) It is basically the same as when he bought it.

Problem: This is even worse than sentence (6). It is the second sentence in a row that very casually says he did not alter the playhouse. Both sentences contain words that give wiggle room: "really" and "basically." If the reader is skeptical, then she is now positive that he did a lot to that playhouse.

(8) Because it is small and has not been changed, the playhouse is still just an item of personal property, so there can be no real estate taxes on the playhouse.

Problem: The reader has reached the conclusion and does not agree, because she was not given arguments to support it. The reader was given evidence, yes, but without connection to a rule, explanation, or context.

QUICK EXERCISE
Skill: Recognizing Recited Facts

Flip back and reread the bad answer as it was originally presented in paragraph form. This is especially important if you initially read the bad answer and thought, "this is not so bad." If you had an ounce of sympathy, or felt the tiniest bit persuaded by that answer, go back now. Reread it again after having read the critiques. You should now see that it is a simple list of facts without rules or explanations.

Fixing the Recited Facts Problem

Take the first recited fact in the bad answer. What will fix it? Most importantly, what pattern can a student use to fix the problem of recited facts each time it occurs?

Bad answer sentence: The playhouse is small, just big enough to walk in.

Strategy to fix recited facts:

1. There are questions you can ask to draw out the additional information that should have been included or explained.

Always ask:

What rule am I applying? Is that clear to the reader?

Why is this fact interesting, relevant, or meaningful in light of the rule?

If you are struggling, you may also need to ask:

Why do I care? Why does this matter?

Is there a comparison I can make that will help the reader understand why this fact matters?

Is there a word that I have used to characterize the fact? (Here, it is "small.") Why should that characterization persuade a reader?

Is this fact relevant to any other rules related to this issue? (This helps to check and make sure you are using facts thoroughly.)

2. Provide the information you gained from the questions to the reader. Give the reader a rule or part of a rule and a reason why the fact matters in the context of the rule. You can do that in your own words, but if you have trouble, there are some quick formats that work. When in doubt, use this simple pattern to create sentences.

[Fact] provides evidence of [key rule or rule part], because _____.

[Fact] indicates [key rule or rule part] due to _____.

In terms of [key rule or rule part], there is sufficient evidence because [fact] indicates that _____.

[Key rule or rule part] normally requires evidence of _____. Here, there is [fact], which means _____.

Example of fixing a reciting facts problem in your answer:

Go back to the ineffective sentence from the bad answer.

Bad answer sentence: The playhouse is small, just big enough to walk in.

Now apply the strategy:

1. What rule are you applying? Why is size important in terms of taxes? The size of the playhouse is relevant because whether an item is a personal good depends on annexation, which is, in part, determined by the size and difficulty of moving the object. So, the relevant rule is the multi-part rule for defining personalty versus realty, and specifically the definition of annexation. And the reason "small" is relevant here is because "small" is easier to move than "big." These are the pieces of information you need to communicate in the answer.

There are, of course, many ways to communicate that information. If you are having difficulty creating sentences on your own, go on to step two.

2. Write some basic rule-fact connection sentences to replace the original.

Pattern: [fact] provides evidence of [key rule or rule part], because _____.

Sentence: The playhouse is small (only 5 feet by 10 feet), which provides evidence of annexation, because the playhouse is small enough to be moved to another location.

Pattern: [fact] indicates [key rule or rule part] due to _____.

Sentence: The size of the playhouse (5-by-10 footprint) indicates annexation because such a limited size object can be hauled to a new location.

Pattern: In terms of [key rule or rule part], there is sufficient evidence because [fact] indicates that _____.

Sentence: In terms of annexation, there is sufficient evidence because the 5-by-10 footprint indicates that the playhouse is movable.

QUICK EXERCISE
Skill: Fixing Recited Facts

There are four more recited fact sentences in the sample bad answer. Try the strategy given above to write a better version of each of these sentences. (Note: Remember this was a very short answer to the hypothetical. It is fine to use multiple sentences to replace a single one. This is frequently necessary to fix the recited facts problem.)

Sentences to fix: (3) In fact, the playhouse is only five feet tall. (4) The playhouse is still on the same wheels that it arrived on. (5) There are blocks around the wheels just to hold it all down. (6) John did not really do anything to the playhouse except put two steps up to the door and add a few shrubs around it in the yard. (7) It is basically the same as when he bought it.

QUICK EXERCISE
Skill: Recognizing Recited Facts

In reading your own work, it may take practice to recognize recited facts. First, you are quite likely to do it intermittently rather than continuously, and this can make it more difficult to spot in your answer. Second, it can be difficult to pick out the recited facts problem in the context of rereading your answer as a whole.

Strategy: Read sentences aloud and out of order. Simply close your eyes and drop a pencil point on the page to pick a single sentence. If your answer is organized in an IRAC format, which it should be, aim for the application section generally. Now read only that sentence. If the sentence just states an issue or a rule, try again. Select an application/reasoning sentence. When read alone, does the sentence make clear both what rule is being applied and why the fact mentioned matters? If the sentence makes both clear, then great, it is not a recited fact. If it does not, check the sentences before and after, because perhaps it is a longer explanation. If the rule and connection can't be found just before or after that sentence, you probably have a recited fact.

Note: This is also an exercise that could work well with a friend. Get a partner to do this workbook with you. Exchange answers to hypotheticals. You can score each other rather than yourself and diagnose problems such as recited facts in the other person's answer. It is often easier to see when reading someone else's work rather than your own, because your connections/explanations/unwritten steps are in your head already, whereas the other person's are not.

QUICK EXERCISE
Skill: Avoiding the Recited Facts Problem

One method of avoiding writing recited facts sentences in your application is to practice writing the fact-rule connection sentences. After writing your answer to one of the other personalty versus improvement hypotheticals, reread the hypothetical prompt. Take a blank document and write practice sentences: Pick a fact in the prompt. Then write a sentence using that fact, a rule about personalty versus improvement, and an explanation of why the fact matters in the context of the rule. Write 10 sentences. If you find that the recited facts problem continues, repeat this exercise with more sentences and other hypotheticals. Practice will correct it in time.

SEVEN

Extra Practice of Simple One-Issue Personalty versus Realty Hypotheticals

This chapter contains extra practice hypotheticals that cover only one issue: whether an item counts as personalty or realty. These additional practice problems provide an opportunity to practice without needing to learn new rules, allowing you to focus on good structure and thorough applications.

The Billboard Hypothetical

Time to read and write your answer: one hour.

Bill recently purchased Blackacre, a farm adjoining I-81, from Fred for $350,000. Farms of that size typically sell for $300,000 in that location. The property contains a billboard, which is not currently in use. The billboard's advertising space is 800 square feet. Steel billboards, such as this one, cost between $50,000 and $70,000 to build. It weighs between 7,000 and 10,000 pounds. The billboard was built by Fred, the prior owner of the property. Fred leased advertising space on the billboard for a monthly rental income.

The deed did not mention the billboard or make any reservations of it for the seller. Such billboards are occasionally, but not frequently, sold independently of the land and moved to another location. Moving billboards requires oversized semis and a special permit, but generally takes only about eight hours. The cost of moving a billboard is about $10,000. More commonly, the billboards remain permanently in one location and space is leased to one of many companies seeking such spaces.

Scoring Rubric for The Billboard Hypothetical

Section			
Issue:	☐ Identify the key problem in layman's terms: Does the billboard go with the sale of the farm? (2) ☐ Legal question: Is it an improvement or a fixture? (4)	6	
Rules:	☐ Improvements need a significant association with real property. (3) ☐ Improvements are decided by a three-part test: annexation, adaptation, and intent. (3) ☐ Annexation is a physical connection. (3) ☐ Adaptation means suited to the purpose or altered to fit the land. (3) ☐ Intent is the most important and is measured at the time of placement. (3)	15	
App.:	☐ Sticky points: Billboards are movable, but with effort and they are not often moved. Intent is not clear here. (3) ***Annexation*** *Yes* ☐ Moving requires not just a semi, but an oversized one, suggesting it is not easy to move the billboard. (3) ☐ Moving requires special permits, suggesting a strong attachment. (3) ☐ Moving is a substantial cost (10K), making it less likely someone would move a billboard. (3) ☐ Moving is potentially 20% of the full cost of building, which suggests that it is comparatively expensive to move it and thus it is more fairly viewed as annexed. (3) ☐ The billboard is 800 square feet, and such large items are generally attached. (3) ☐ A weight of 7–10K pounds would be difficult to move. (3) *No* ☐ A weight of 7–10K pounds can be moved by semis, so it is not strongly attached. (3)	3 18 12	

App.:	☐ Moving can be done in about eight hours, so it is not attached. (3) ☐ Billboards are sometimes sold/moved, so it is not strongly attached. (3) ☐ The cost of moving is much less than the building cost, so it is more likely to be moved than rebuilt. (3) **Adaptation** *Yes* ☐ The billboard must be secured to the ground, so the area around it had to be changed. (3) *No* ☐ Minimal changes seem necessary to the land, so there is little evidence of adaptation. (3) ☐ The billboard required no changes to attach it, so the item itself was not adapted. (3) **Intent** *Yes, intended to attach* ☐ The contract purchase price of property is higher than it otherwise might be, suggesting intent to include the billboard. (3) ☐ The billboard is difficult to move, so that may itself indicate a permanent placement. (3) ☐ There is no reservation in the deed, and that may reflect the intent to include it. (3) ☐ Billboards are more often not sold separately, so an intent to include is statistically more likely. (3) *Intended to be detachable* ☐ The purchase price is not as high as it might be if it were meant to include the billboard, so intent is more debatable. (3) ☐ The billboard is not currently in use, which may indicate preparation for moving it. (3) ☐ Compared to items in other cases, a billboard is definitely movable, it is just not very convenient to move it, so an intent to move it is reasonable. (3)	 3 6 12 9	
Concl.:		6	
	Total		

Mean Score for sample law student groups: 59

The Envelope Machine Hypothetical

Time to read and write your answer: one hour.

Russell Hawes, a Massachusetts physician, invented the envelope-folding machine. His machine was installed approximately four years ago at a company that manufactures paper products, Goddard, Rice & Company, in Hollins, Virginia. Goddard recently sold their land and building to Hubbard & Bent Co., which Goddard knew intended to repurpose the property for a sewing factory. The contract for the sale made no reservations and made no mention of whether or not the envelope-folding machine would transfer with the real estate.

The folding machine weighs several thousand pounds and covers floor space of about 10 by 20 feet. The machine is about four and one-half feet high. The motor of the machine is attached to the floor by lug bolts; however, the rest of the machine is not attached to any part of the building. The machine folds paper and manufactures envelopes. The machine has never been moved from the initial location of installation; however, similar machines have been moved from time to time in the same plant. Goddard treats these machines as personal property for tax purposes.

The Goddard company building was designed to house such machines as the envelope-folding machine, but the machine is not integral to the building's construction. When Goddard moved out of its old location in 1960, it moved several envelope-making machines from its old Roanoke plant to its new facility in Hollins.

The machine is certainly used in the business of making envelopes, which is the purpose for which the building was designed, but any machinery installed in the building (from a printer to a coffee maker) is probably used in the business. The building was designed for the purposes of making envelopes, and features of the building were built around the need to house such large machines. There is, however, no evidence that the building will be significantly deprived of its function as a factory-style building if the machine were removed. Removing the machine would not harm the machine itself in any way. Regarding the building, moving the machine would leave some very small structural impairments (holes in the floor from the lug bolts, scrapes on the door casings).

Scoring Rubric for the Envelope Machine Hypothetical

Section			
Issue:	☐ Identify the key problem in layman's terms: Does the machine transfer with the real property? (2) ☐ Legal question: Is it an improvement, personal property, or a fixture? (4)	6	
Rules:	☐ Improvements need a significant association with real property. (3) ☐ The test for an improvement is: annexation, adaptation, and intent. (3) ☐ Annexation is the level of physical connection. (3) ☐ Adaptation means suited to the purpose or altered to fit the land. (3) ☐ Intent is the most important, and it is measured at the time of placement. (3)	15	
App.:	***Annexation*** *Yes* ☐ The machine weighs several thousand pounds, making it difficult to move, which suggests it is strongly attached. (3) ☐ The machine covers 200 square feet, which suggests it is too large to be easily moved and therefore is strongly attached. (3) ☐ The machine is roughly 800 cubic feet in size, which suggests it is very large and difficult to move, making it strongly attached. (3) ☐ The machine is attached to the floor with bolts, which suggests it is fully attached to the building. (3) *No* ☐ While the machine is heavy, it is not too heavy to be movable, which suggests it is not attached. (3) ☐ There is no evidence that the machine is embedded, which suggests it is not attached. (3) ☐ The machine is 10 feet by 20 feet, which is not too large to be moved by commercial equipment, suggesting it is not attached. (3)	12 24	

Continued

Continued

App.:	☐ The machine is 4.5 feet tall, which suggests it is not too big to move and therefore is not strongly attached. (3)		
	☐ The machine is only attached by bolts, which are easily removed, making it not strongly attached. (3)		
	☐ The machine is not integral to the building, which suggests that it is not strongly attached. (3)		
	☐ The floor will only be slightly damaged by moving the machine, which suggests there is minimal attachment. (3)		
	☐ Such machines have been moved before within the building, so moving it is realistic. (3)		
	Adaptation		
	Yes		
	☐ The machine is attached to the floor via lug bolts, which means the machine has been adapted by adding the bolts. (3)	9	
	☐ The floor has bolt holes, which means it has been modified to accept the machine. (3)		
	☐ The building was designed to house the machines, so it was specifically adapted to the machines. (3)		
	No		
	☐ The machines are not integral to the building construction, which suggests any adaptation is minimal. (3)	12	
	☐ While the building was built to house large machines, it does not have to be envelope machines and the new company plans to use sewing machines, so this suggests the building is not specifically adapted to only envelope production. (3)		
	☐ The machine will not be harmed by moving it, which suggests there was no significant adaptation of the machine to the space. (3)		
	☐ The floor will only be slightly damaged by moving the machine, suggesting minimal adaptation. (3)		
	Intent		
	Intended to attach		
	☐ The machine has never been moved since installation, which suggests an intent for it to have been permanently installed. (3)	6	

App.:	☐ While similar machines have been moved in this very plant, they have not usually been moved very far, so the intent is likely that they remain within the building. (3)		
	Intended for it to be detachable		
	☐ Similar machines have been moved in this plant, suggesting an intent for all of the machines to be portable. (3)	12	
	☐ The machines are listed as personal property for tax purposes, which suggests the machines were intended to be detachable. (3)		
	☐ Goddard has moved machines between plants before, suggesting it would be willing to move them again. (3)		
	☐ The floor will only be slightly damaged by moving the machine, suggesting it was attached in such a way as to minimize damage if it were moved. (3)		
Concl.:		6	
	Total		

Mean Score for sample law student groups: 53

EIGHT

Simple Single-Issue Hypotheticals with Inter-Vivos Gifts

Rules Regarding Inter-Vivos Gifts

Inter-vivos gifts, sometimes just called gifts, allow personalty to change ownership without a written document that records or describes the transfer. A simple example of an inter-vivos gift is a birthday present.

To determine if there is a valid transfer of ownership, courts ask if (1) the donor had an intent to give the gift to the recipient, (2) whether the donor made a delivery of the gift to the recipient, and (3) whether the recipient accepted the gift. The test requires that the intent be to give a present ownership interest and to do so voluntarily and gratuitously. Normally, the intent must be permanent because the gift will become irrevocable. Some jurisdictions recognize a conditional gift, which means that the intent can be conditioned on the completion of some act. In those jurisdictions, the gift becomes final and irrevocable only once the condition is satisfied. Other jurisdictions, however, do not allow conditional gifts and would regard conditions as violating the requirement for a present intent to give ownership. The delivery can be actual or constructive and is evaluated in the context of what is practical or possible considering the nature of the item. Where a gift has value, you can presume acceptance by the recipient.

A valid gift creates an irrevocable transfer of ownership of the personalty. The recipient has the burden of proving the gift by clear and convincing evidence. Inter-vivos gifts are important for determining whether an item passes through a will or whether ownership of the item changed before someone died. Gifts can also transfer individual (or separate) property into marital property, which may be important for determining tax liabilities, among other issues.

Outline of Inter-Vivos Gifts Rules

I. Inter-vivos gifts

    A. Test (three elements, and-type test)

        1. Intent to give the gift

            a. Clarify: the intent must be to give a present ownership interest and to do so voluntarily and gratuitously.

            b. Exception: split: in some jurisdictions, it is okay if the intent is conditional. In that case, gifts become irrevocable when the condition is completed.

        2. Delivery of the gift

            a. Clarify: two types: delivery can be actual or constructive.

            b. Clarify: situational: delivery should be evaluated in the context of what is practical or possible considering the nature of the item.

        3. Acceptance of the gift

            a. Presumption: acceptance is presumed if an item is valuable.

    B. Burden

        1. The recipient has the burden of clear and convincing evidence.

    C. Outcome

        1. A valid gift creates an irrevocable transfer of ownership of the personalty.

Birthday Baseball Hypothetical

Time to read and write your answer: one hour.

Carmen purchases an autographed baseball on eBay to give to her nephew, Chad, as a present. The ad described the baseball as "signed by THE Mickey Mantel." Carmen paid $500.00 for the baseball after an internet search for approximate values. Carmen did not check the spelling of the baseball legend's name (Mantle, not Mantel), and did not notice that the seller's name was Edward Michael Mantel. If the ball is a forgery or fraud, rather than a baseball really signed by the baseball legend, it is worth about $3.00.

Chad is away at college on the day of his birthday, so Carmen simply e-mails him the link to the eBay listing. Because she is in a hurry and can't write more, the e-mail has no content except a subject line that says: "Happy Birthday." Carmen tells a friend, "We always celebrate Chad's birthday when he can make it home over spring break. We give our gifts then." Carmen suddenly passes away a week after the birthday in a car accident. The baseball is still in her possession. Chad has not replied to her birthday message. He did try to call his aunt when he got the e-mail, but when she did not answer the phone, he thought he would try again another time and later forgot.

Scoring Rubric for Birthday Baseball Hypothetical

Section			
Issue:	☐ Did Carmen make a valid inter-vivos gift of the baseball to Chad? (6)	6	
Rules:	☐ Valid gifts require intent, delivery, and acceptance. (3) ☐ Intent should be present and permanent. (3) ☐ Delivery may be constructive or actual and fitted to the circumstances or nature of the item. (3) ☐ Acceptance may be presumed for things of value. (3) ☐ The burden of proof falls on the recipient of the gift. (3)	15	
App.:	☐ Sticky points: The intent to give a present interest via e-mail is not clear and delivery is not actual, but might be constructive. (3) **Intent to give a present interest** Yes	3	
	☐ The baseball was purchased and intended as a birthday present and such gifts are generally given as of the day of the birthday. (3) ☐ Carmen e-mailed the link, communicating the contents of the gift, which indicates her intent to provide the gift as of Chad's birthday. (3) ☐ The e-mail has a subject line that says: "Happy Birthday." This communicates Carmen's intent to provide the gift at that time. (3)	12	

Continued

Continued

App.:	☐ Carmen writes the e-mail because she is unable to see Chad that day and so sends the e-mail to communicate her intent to give the baseball as his birthday present. (3)		
	No		
	☐ Carmen's e-mail is not clear about whether the intent is for the gift to take effect that day or as of the "celebration day" later on. The e-mail has no content except a subject line that says: "Happy Birthday," and so it is ambiguous. (3)	6	
	☐ Carmen acknowledges that normally the family "gives" the gifts after Chad's birthday, so that they can celebrate in person. This suggests that the gifts are not actually intended to be given until that day. (3)		
	Delivery		
	Yes via constructive delivery		
	☐ Hand delivery is not physically possible on Chad's birthday, so it is appropriate to substitute the ad photo/link. (3)	6	
	☐ The ad photo/link communicates the content of the gift itself (giving away any surprise), so it makes an appropriate substitute for a birthday delivery. (3)		
	No, constructive delivery is not effective here		
	☐ There is no actual, physical delivery of the baseball to Chad. (3)	6	
	☐ The baseball is in Carmen's possession at the time of her death, which may indicate no attempt to deliver yet. (3)		
	Acceptance		
	Yes		
	☐ Chad read the e-mail and called his aunt with the intent to "say thanks," which indicates that he had accepted the gift. (3)	6	
	☐ There is no evidence that supports the idea that Chad refused the gift. The facts suggest that he intended to say thanks, but did not have the opportunity to do so. (3)		
	No		
	☐ Chad did not actually respond to the e-mail to communicate acceptance of the baseball. (3)	9	

App.:	☐ Chad did not leave a voicemail message when he called his aunt, which means he did not actually communicate his acceptance to her. (3)		
	☐ Chad forgot to call her back, so he did not ever communicate his acceptance of the gift. (3)		
	Yes (via presumed acceptance)		
	☐ Carmen paid $500 for the baseball, which suggests that it is a thing of value for which acceptance can be presumed. (3)	9	
	☐ Carmen's search suggested that the cost was reasonable for an autographed ball, so if it is authentic, she paid market value, which is substantial. (3)		
	☐ If the baseball is authentic, then it does have a substantial market value, so it is a thing of value. (3)		
	No (presumption doesn't work here)		
	☐ A presumption of value is not appropriate where the baseball is likely a forgery given the misspelling and the name of the seller. (3)	9	
	☐ Any market value that the baseball would have is impaired by this history of its acquisition (potential forgery). (3)		
	☐ If the baseball is a forgery, it is only worth $3.00, which is not a significant value. (3)		
Concl.:		6	
	Total		

Mean Score for sample law student groups: 63

Sample Answer to Birthday Baseball Hypothetical

To determine property rights after Carmen's death, a court would test the validity of the potential inter-vivos gift to her nephew, Chad. A valid inter-vivos gift requires intent, delivery, and acceptance. The burden falls on the party claiming the gift. A valid inter-vivos gift is irrevocable as of the time of the gift.

The first question is about Carmen's intent. For a valid inter-vivos gift, the intent to gift should be a present intent to transfer a permanent interest. In this instance, Carmen did not purchase the baseball for herself. Instead, she purchased the baseball with a specific intent. The baseball was intended as a birthday present and such gifts are generally given as of the day of the birthday. Chad is not directly available on his birthday, so Carmen sends him an e-mail to communicate her wishes and her gift. When Carmen e-mailed Chad, she included a link, communicating the contents of the gift, which indicates her intent to provide the gift as of Chad's birthday. If she meant to give the gift later, she likely would not have given away the surprise of the gift's contents. Additionally, the e-mail has a subject line that says: "Happy Birthday." This greeting, when combined with the link/photo of the baseball, communicates Carmen's intent to provide the gift at that time.

With that said, some evidence suggests Carmen's intent is less clear. Her e-mail does not specifically say that she is gifting the baseball as of that moment. This is particularly less clear given that there is a planned "celebration day" that will take place later on where she will see Chad in person. Carmen acknowledges that normally the family "gives" the gifts after Chad's birthday, so that they can celebrate in person. The e-mail has no content except a subject line that says: "Happy Birthday," and so it is not particularly clear as to whether her intent is to give the gift as of that moment, or to simply wish Chad a happy birthday and to give the gift at the later date. On the whole, in light of the fact that Carmen gave away the surprise, it seems more likely that she meant to give the gift as of Chad's birthday.

Additionally, for Chad to have a valid gift of the baseball before Carmen's death, he would need to establish delivery of the item. Delivery may be actual or constructive, and delivery is considered in the context of the circumstances and the nature of the item itself.

In Chad's situation, there is no actual, physical delivery of the baseball. Indeed, the baseball is in Carmen's possession at the time of her death, which may indicate no attempt to deliver yet. However, hand delivery is not physically possible on Chad's birthday, so it is arguably appropriate to substitute the ad photo/link to establish a constructive delivery. The ad photo/link communicates the content of the gift itself (giving away any surprise), so it makes an appropriate substitute for a birthday delivery. E-mail is a way to give Chad a visual of the gift when no other delivery is convenient. In the circumstances, the e-mail is an appropriate way to constructively deliver the gift to Chad.

Finally, Chad must also establish that he accepted the gift. Normally, the recipient communicates acceptance of a gift, but acceptance may be presumed for things of value. Unfortunately, in this situation Chad did not actually respond to the e-mail to communicate acceptance of the baseball. Although Chad called his aunt, he did not leave a voicemail message, which means he did not actually communicate his acceptance to her. Indeed, Chad later forgot to call her back, so he did not ever communicate his acceptance of the gift before her death.

Chad can, however, make a reasonable argument that he attempted to accept in the circumstances. Chad read the e-mail and called his aunt with the intent to "say thanks," which indicates that he had accepted the gift. And there is no evidence that supports the idea that Chad refused the gift. The facts suggest that he intended to say thanks, but did not have the opportunity to do so simply because his aunt did not answer the phone when he called.

Additionally, Chad can also argue that his acceptance should be presumed because the baseball is a thing of value. Carmen paid $500 for the baseball, which suggests that it is a thing of value for which acceptance can be presumed. Carmen documented an appropriate cost for the baseball. Carmen's search suggested that $500 was reasonable for an autographed ball, so if it is authentic, she paid market value, which is substantial. If the baseball is authentic, which is possible despite the oddity of the ad, then it does have a substantial market value, which would mean that it is a thing of value. On the other hand, such a presumption of authenticity may not be appropriate where the baseball is likely a forgery given the misspelling and the name of the seller. Additionally, the market value would be impaired by the history of its acquisition with this strange ad that raises the possibility of forgery, so the baseball may not have much market value. If the baseball is a forgery in fact, then it is only worth $3.00, which is not a significant value. All in all, the baseball is more likely a forgery and therefore it is not appropriate to classify it as a thing of value. However, Chad did attempt to call his aunt to thank her and could document such a call if necessary, via phone records. This is a sufficient reason to accept that Chad did — by making the phone call itself — communicate his acceptance in the best way that he could in the circumstances.

Because Chad has a feasible argument supported by evidence for each of the three elements, a court may conclude that Carmen made a valid inter-vivos gift of the baseball to Chad.

NINE

Two-Issue Hypotheticals on Bailments and Buyers in the Ordinary Course of Business

Recognizing Interrelated Issues

Within most areas of law there are particular issues that are interrelated, meaning that if you have one issue you either must have or are likely to have the other. Obviously, with any issue there may be sub-issues or defenses or questions of remedies that will also be prompted by the facts. In addition to this, however, there are also independent issues that are simply likely to connect in a set of facts.

Within property law, one situation that normally triggers multiple issues is when one person holds rightful title (is the rightful owner) of an item, but another person currently has possession of the item. A bailment describes the relationship between two people when one of them owns the item and the other has temporary, rightful possession.

The issue of a bailment arises frequently with other property law issues. Whenever a person finds an object, that person is in an involuntary bailment relationship. When an inter-vivos gift fails, there is a bailment relationship between the two parties.

Because bailments so commonly arise in the context of other property issues, bailments make the perfect example for a hypothetical with two issues.

Rules for Bailments

A bailment occurs when one person has rightful, legal possession of property, but not title to the property. Bailments are common, everyday occurrences. A borrowed jacket or lawn mower creates a bailment. To create a bailment, there is a transfer of personalty with mutual assent. Mutual assent refers to the acceptance of the item in the context of the delivery. The legal consequence of creating a bailment is that the person receiving the property now has a legal duty of care.

Traditionally, the law divided bailments into three primary categories. The categories are based on who gets the benefit of a bailment. With a gratuitous bailment, all of the benefit goes to the person giving the object (bailor), none to the person receiving (bailee). The perfect example of this is when someone holds another person's jacket or purse while the other goes to the restroom. The recipient of the item in a gratuitous bailment is watching the item as a favor. Unsurprisingly, then, the duty of care for a gratuitous bailment is only slight diligence.

A second type is a depositary for hire or bailment for hire. In this type of bailment, the bailment occurs through a purchase relationship. In other words, the person giving the object pays the other person receiving to keep object safe. An example of this type of bailment would be a safe deposit box in a bank being used to keep photographs or stocks or bonds. Because both parties benefit in this scenario, this type of bailment is also called a mutual benefit bailment. The duty of care for a bailment for hire or mutual benefit bailment is ordinary care.

The third type of bailment is the opposite end of the spectrum from a gratuitous bailment. The third type of bailment is generally described as one that is "solely for the benefit of the bailee." This is, essentially, a borrowing situation. If a neighbor borrows a lawn mower, the benefit goes entirely to the person who is borrowing the item. This is a sole benefit bailment. In this situation, the duty is extraordinary care. This standard is also called liability for even slight negligence.

Some jurisdictions do not divide bailments into these three types. Instead, in these jurisdictions, the courts apply a simple standard of ordinary care to all types of bailments. The defendant would prove ordinary care by establishing his diligence in relation to the context.

When a bailment is established by the evidence, there is a rebuttable presumption of negligence on nondelivery or damage. This means that if the plaintiff can prove that he requested his item and it was not returned, then the court will presume negligence. The defendant must present evidence sufficient to prove care commensurate with the appropriate standard for the type of bailment.

A bailment may also occur without mutual assent in some circumstances. Courts refer to these as involuntary or constructive bailments. Such bailments may exist when an item is mislaid or left behind or when a package is incorrectly delivered to the wrong address. The duty of care for an involuntary bailment is ordinary care, so long as the recipient exercised dominion or control over the item.

Finally, bailments can also be divisible. This means that the recipient of the item might be responsible for a container but not its contents. The question for the court is whether the contents of a container were foreseeable by the recipient when he took custody of the container.

Type of Bailment	Gratuitous Bailment Sole Benefit of Bailor (Sitter Service)	Bailment for Hire/ Mutual Benefit Bailment	Gratuitous Bailment Sole Benefit of Bailee (Borrowing)
Who gets the benefit?	All benefits to bailor (giver)	Benefits to each — exchange of services	Sole benefit to bailee (recipient)
Duty	Slight diligence	Ordinary care	Extraordinary care; liable for even slight negligence

Outline for Bailments

I. Bailments

    A. Test (three elements, and-type test)

        1. Transfer

           a. Clarify: transfer means that possession (dominion and control) moves from one party to another.

        2. Personalty (i.e., not realty)

        3. Mutual assent

           a. Clarify: mutual assent is an acceptance within the context of the delivery.

           b. Exception: an involuntary or constructive bailment may occur without mutual assent. If the recipient assumes dominion or control over the item, there is a bailment. If so, the duty is for ordinary care.

B. Outcome rules

    1. A proven bailment means the recipient has rightful, legal possession of property, but not title to the property.

    2. A proven bailment means there is a duty of care.

        a. Jurisdictional split:

           i. All bailments create a duty of ordinary care.

           ii. There are different duties of care for three types of bailments.

               1. Gratuitous bailment is where all of the benefit goes to the person giving the object. Duty is slight diligence.

               2. In a bailment for hire (aka mutual benefit bailment) both parties benefit from the bailment. The duty is ordinary care.

               3. Sole benefit bailment is where all the benefit goes to the recipient of the item. The duty is extraordinary care.

C. Divisibility

    1. The defendant is only liable for foreseeable contents of a container.

D. Breach

    1. Presumption: there is a rebuttable presumption of breach on nondelivery or damage to the item.

    2. The defendant must prove that the standard of care was met.

E. Remedies

    1. The standard remedy is for damages or item value.

        a. Exception: divisible bailment

           i. The defendant is only liable for the container when the contents were not foreseeable.

Rules for Buyers in the Ordinary Course of Business

The doctrine of a Buyer in the Ordinary Course of Business (BIOCB) allows a buyer to have good title to personalty that was sold by a merchant who did not own the merchandise. This occurs most commonly in two situations. First, sometimes merchants sell goods that are subject to liens. Second, sometimes merchants accidentally make a sale of an item that was not supposed to be available for sale.

For a customer to be a BIOCB, there are a number of elements that must be established. The merchant must have the item by *entrustment*. Entrustment means that the goods are given by the owner to a merchant who deals in goods of the kind. The buyer must make a transaction (a sale, not a gift) in the ordinary course of business. The buyer must also act in good faith. Good faith is the combination of actual "honesty in fact" along with "the observance of reasonable commercial standards." The buyer should not know that the sale violates someone else's rights. If the customer meets each of these requirements, then the customer will have good title to the personalty.

Outline for Buyers in the Ordinary Course of Business

I. Buyer in the ordinary course of business (BIOCB)

   A. BIOCB test (three-part, and-type test)

      1. The merchant must have the item by entrustment.

         a. Clarify: entrustment means that the goods are given by the owner to a merchant who deals in goods of the kind.

      2. The transaction with the buyer must be a real transaction.

         a. Clarify: it must be an actual transaction (i.e., a sale, not a gift).

      3. The buyer must act in good faith.

         a. Clarify: good faith means honesty in fact.

         b. Good faith requires observance of reasonable commercial standards.

         c. Good faith means the buyer must have no knowledge that the sale violates someone else's rights.

   B. Outcome: if the customer meets each of these requirements, then the customer will have good title to the personalty against the original owner of the item.

Magic Mike's Used Cars—
Key Lottery Hypothetical

Time to read and write your answer: one hour.

Stanley enjoys taking his neighbor's mail, usually just for the fun of it, or more specifically for the opportunity to flirt with his neighbor when he returns it. Lisa, the neighbor, receives a "turnkey lottery entry" from Magic Mike's, a local used car dealership. Many recipients on the mailing list received keys; only a few keys opened "Magic Mike's Motor Car Lock," giving the key-holder a certificate for 25% off any car on Magic Mike's lot. The certificate expires in 48 hours. Stanley takes Lisa's key to Magic Mike's lot and the key wins a certificate upon presenting Lisa's key.

For his car purchase, Stanley chooses a lovely, pink Honda (priced at $20,000), pays his 75% of the car's list price ($15,000), and heads home. Magic Mike calls to tell Stanley that there has been a terrible mistake. Mike meant to sell the pink Honda, not the fuchsia one. The fuchsia car was dropped off by Jane on Monday morning. Jane wanted to have the speakers checked because one was not working correctly. Jane arrived at the dealership where she ordinarily had her car repaired, but the dealership was not open yet. Jane left the car at the dealership prior to business hours, leaving the key in the ignition. On prior visits, Jane had been asked to leave the car in such a fashion. When Jane left the dealership, she planned to call that afternoon and ask for the repairs, but she got busy at work and forgot. On Tuesday, Stanley purchased Jane's fuchsia car, which was valued $5,000 more than the pink one.

Consider the positions of (1) Stanley and (2) Jane.

Scoring Rubric for Magic Mike's Used Cars — Key Lottery Hypothetical

Section			
Issue:	Did Jane and the car dealership create a bailment and, if so, did the dealership breach that bailment?	6	
Rules:	☐ An effective bailment requires a transfer of personalty with mutual assent or constructive assent. (3) ☐ Mutual assent requires acceptance in the context of a delivery. (3) ☐ Jurisdictional split: There is a traditional three-tiered set of different duties of care based on the type of bailment. The modern rule says the duty is always ordinary care. (3) ☐ In an involuntary bailment, if the party exercises dominion, the duty is ordinary care. (3) ☐ If the item is not returned, then the courts presume negligence. (3)	15	
App.:	***Transfer*** *Yes* ☐ Jane left the car on the property of the dealership, so she no longer has possession of the car. (3) ☐ Because the car is on their property, the dealership at least has constructive possession of the car. (3) ☐ Having sold the car, the dealership had to take actual possession of the car by using the keys. (3) ***Personalty*** ☐ The item at issue is a car, which is a good/chattel and not land, so it is personalty, not realty. (3) ***Mutual assent*** *Yes* ☐ Jane left her car at the dealership following her usual procedure for repairs, which suggests the method is agreed upon. (3)	9 3 9	

Continued

Continued

App.:	☐ Jane left the car for the purpose of repairs, the business of the dealership, so this suggests their assent. (3) ☐ The dealership apparently used the keys, which suggests they did accept the car. (3) *No* ☐ No one took possession of the car from Jane, so there was no communication of an acceptance. (3) ☐ Jane failed to call, so she did not speak to anyone who might have accepted the car. (3) ☐ The dealership sold the car by mistake, suggesting they never properly accepted it for repairs. (3) **Involuntary bailment** ☐ Jane left the car on the premises, so even if there was no acceptance, it may create an involuntary bailment. (3) **Outcome rules applied** ☐ In a standard rule jurisdiction, there would be a duty of ordinary care, because all bailments get ordinary care. (3) ☐ In a jurisdiction with different standards of care, this looks like a mutual benefit bailment, because it is a business that benefits from cars being left there. So there would be a duty of ordinary care. (3) **Nondelivery** ☐ Jane did not get her car when she came back to pick it up, so the court can presume a breach of the bailment due to nondelivery. (3)	9 3 6 3	
Concl.:		6	
Issue:	Is Stanley a BIOCB for the car?	6	
Rule:	☐ An item acquired by fraud has a voidable title and an item acquired by theft has a void title. (3) ☐ When a seller has a voidable title, a buyer can get a good title if they meet the BIOCB test. (3)	18	

Rule:	☐ A buyer is a BIOCB when there is entrustment to a merchant of goods of the kind, a sale transaction, and good faith of the buyer with no knowledge that the sale violates the rights of another. (3) ☐ Entrustment means voluntarily giving the item. (3) ☐ Goods of the kind means goods that match the one involved in the problematic sale. (3) ☐ The parties must follow customary business practices in the transaction. (3)		
App.:	**Title of dealership** ☐ There was no theft by dealership. (3) ☐ A mistake is closer to fraud than to theft because there was no illegal intent to take. (3)	6	
	Good faith of the buyer *Yes* ☐ While Stanley misbehaved, it had nothing to do with the pink car problem. (3) ☐ Stanley's misbehavior relates to his neighbor, not the owner of the car or the sale of the car. (3) ☐ Stanley did not know that the dealership was selling the wrong car. (3)	9	
	No ☐ Stanley stole the key to participate in the promotion at the dealership, so his whole involvement looks a bit suspect. (3) ☐ Stanley used the stolen key to be able to get the car, so it is hard to argue good faith in the transaction for a thief. (3) ☐ Stanley was not the owner of the key used in the transaction, so he cannot have good faith in the entire transaction. (3)	9	
	Entrustment to a merchant *Yes* ☐ Jane left her car at the dealership voluntarily for the purposes of repair, which indicates willing entrustment. (3) ☐ Jane left her keys with the car, which allowed the dealership to take possession with her permission. (3)	9	

Continued

Continued

App.:	☐ Jane left the car at her usual dealership in the usual manner, which indicates her willingness to entrust the car. (3)		
	No		
	☐ Jane never spoke to anyone to actually transfer custody of her car, which makes the entrustment less clear. (3)	9	
	☐ Jane left the car in a parking lot with no one there and the lot open to the public, which suggests the entrustment did not really take place. (3)		
	☐ Jane forgot to follow up, which also suggests that she did not actually entrust the car. (3)		
	Goods of the kind		
	Yes		
	☐ The problematic sale was of a used car, and it is a used car dealership. (3)	3	
	Ordinary business practices		
	Yes		
	☐ There are no facts that suggest the dealership used anything other than ordinary business practices. (3)	3	
Concl.:		6	
	Total		

Mean Score for sample law student groups: 83

Sample Answer to Magic Mike's Used Cars — Key Lottery Hypothetical

Note: This sample answer is annotated with the structure of a proper answer in the nested IRAC format.

Issue 1: Stanley as BIOCB?

Rules: Whatever title an owner has, he can transfer that and no other. There is an exception for BFPs and BIOCBs, who may take full title even though the seller had voidable title. For a BIOCB, as a threshold matter you need entrustment to a merchant who deals in goods of that kind. Then the test is: good faith in the buyer, who has no knowledge that the sale violates the rights of another, and with respect to the seller, the purchase must be from a dealer of goods of the kind and with customary practices.

Application:

(i) First, we must address the threshold question of the type of title held by the dealership.

(r) True owners have a good title, thieves have a void title, and items acquired through fraud or other similar consensual acts have a voidable title.

(a) The dealership did not have title to the car because it was not, in fact, owned by the dealership, but rather held for repairs. The dealership did not, however, possess the item by theft, which would have created a void title in the dealer. The dealership had the car rightfully (for repairs), but simply mistakenly made the sale.

(c) There was no theft, only an accidental conversion, which looks closer to fraud than anything else. When an item is sold through such accidental circumstances, the title transferred was voidable.

If Stanley is a BIOCB, the voidable title can transform into good title, but this requires that Stanley act in good faith.

(i) First, Stanley must act in good faith.

(r) Good faith means honesty in fact and no knowledge that the sale violates the rights of others.

(a) Here, Stanley had stolen the key, which taints his activities that day. He would never have been able to purchase the car without having made a theft earlier that morning. His duplicity put him in the position of purchasing the car, which means there was not honesty in fact in his transaction. He was not the owner of the key that was used for the purchase. He was not even a valid possessor of the key; Stanley is a thief.

On the other hand, with regard to this specific transaction, Stanley acted honestly and had no knowledge of the ownership of the car. Stanley's theft of the key is not relevant to the particular problem of the sale of the wrong car. If you look only at the transaction with the wrong car, Stanley did not act in any way that is problematic.

(c) Overall, the facts more strongly suggest that Stanley had good faith vis-à-vis the wrong car problem.

With respect the merchant, for Stanley to be a buyer in the ordinary course of business, there must be an entrustment to a dealer of goods of that kind, and ordinary business practices.

(i) The first question regarding the dealership is entrustment.

(r) Entrustment means that the car is given to a merchant willingly, usually for a business purpose.

(a) Here, Jane left her car at the dealership within their parking lot, which suggests she was giving the car into their possession willingly. Jane left the keys in the car, which would allow the dealership to drive the car, thus also indicating her willing transfer of possession. Jane left the car at her ordinary dealership and did so with the intention of seeking repairs, suggesting an entrustment for repair purposes.

On the other hand, Jane never actually spoke to anyone at the dealership about her car when she left it, which makes entrustment less certain. Jane left the car in a parking lot that was open to the public before business hours and did not leave her keys with any individual, suggesting there was no clear transfer of the car to the dealership. Jane even forgot to follow up later, so she never even requested the repairs, which suggests that she did not actually entrust the car for repairs.

(c) On the whole, Jane's intention was to give the car to the car dealership for repairs, thus there was entrustment.

(i) The entrustment must also be to a dealer of goods of the kind.

(r) A dealer of goods of the kind are in the same commercial family as those that are deposited.

(a) The item entrusted was a car and the party holding the car was a used car dealer.

(c) This indicates that the party was a dealer in "goods of that kind."

With respect to the requirement of ordinary business practices, Stanley purchased a used car at a used car dealer. There are no facts indicating business practices, so you have no reason to assume any deviation from usual business practices.

Conclusion: Stanley satisfies the BIOCB requirements and has title to the car.

Issue 2: Bailment of car with dealership?

Rules: A bailment is created with a transfer of personal property and mutual assent; a bailment creates a duty of care. Some jurisdictions use a duty of reasonable/ordinary care in the circumstances for all bailments. Some use a three-tiered standard, with bailments for hire creating a duty of ordinary care. On nondelivery, there is a rebuttable presumption of negligence.

Application:

(i) For the owner to create a bailment, she must have transferred the personalty to the dealership.

(r) Personalty is non-land property. Transfer refers to a change of dominion and control.

(a) Here, Jane left the car (non-land property) with the dealership for repairs, creating a voluntary relinquishment by Jane, which took place on the property of the dealership and in the fashion to which Jane was accustomed.

(c) Jane transferred (delivered) the property to the dealership.

(i) To create the bailment between the dealership and the owner, there must also be mutual assent.

(r) For mutual assent we are looking for an acceptance in the context of a delivery of the goods.

(a) Jane left the car at her usual place of repairs, which is necessary for the repairs to take place; this suggests that Jane transferred the car with the assent of the dealership. Additionally, Jane did so by following a procedure she had used before with the dealership, which suggests not only her voluntary relinquishment, but also suggests an implicit acceptance of the vehicle.

On the other hand, no one was present at the dealership to take possession of the car, which suggests that no assent to the transfer occurred. Additionally, Jane failed to call the dealership and notify them of the presence of the vehicle in the parking lot, and therefore she never fully secured the dealership's assent to conducting the repairs. Finally, the fact that the car was later sold to another person suggests that no one at the dealership really accepted the car for repairs and put it on the books in such a way.

(c) Given that Jane was following a prior procedure of the dealership, there probably was mutual assent.

(i) Once you have determined that a bailment exists, it may be necessary to determine the type of bailment to determine the duty of care owed by the bailee.

(r) If a statutory scheme exists, all bailments may create a duty of ordinary care. Without a statutory scheme, it is necessary to determine the type of bailment. The most likely type of bailment in a business context is a bailment for hire, which creates a duty of ordinary care. A bailment for hire requires that, along with transfer and mutual assent, there was consideration or mutual benefit.

(a) Here there was mutual benefit. The owner left the car to get it repaired, which would benefit her. The dealer planned to repair cars left in such a way and to receive compensation for those services, which would benefit the dealer.

(c) Because there was voluntary transfer, mutual assent, and mutual benefit, there will be a duty of ordinary care. This is true both under the common law scheme and the statutory scheme.

Conclusion:

There is no need to determine at this stage whether the dealership breached the duty of care. The dealership failed to redeliver; negligence is presumed.

Jane's damages are for the value of her car. It is irrelevant that Stanley paid less than the value of her car for the vehicle.

TEN

Skill Building: Undoing Muddled Elements

Avoiding Muddling the Organization

Organization matters because if a professor cannot find relevant parts of the anticipated arguments, then she cannot give the student credit for them. Professors generally try very hard (likely more than judges do when reading a muddled brief) to find the necessary pieces. Still, a student is more likely to score well if an answer is well organized. Additionally, judges may not be so lenient in looking for your good arguments. Good organization puts things where the reader expects to find them.

The primer section of this book speaks more to organization, but here is a brief summary as a refresher: There are a variety of methods of organizing an argument. In terms of hypotheticals, the most effective method is to organize by the elements. If they are in a neat list according to the courts, then you can just use that list. (For the purpose of exams, the order does not matter. If you are writing a brief, use the same order that the courts use unless the evidence supporting your case is very unevenly distributed across the elements.)

For example, the courts often list the elements of adverse possession: actual, open and notorious, continuous, exclusive, adverse or hostile, and continuing for the requisite statutory period. You can simply organize this issue by writing a paragraph for each element.

If the court opinions do not create a list of elements, you can generate your own through rule blocking. In other words, take a rule that reads as a sentence, not a list, and break that rule into components or blocks.

For example, trespass might be described by the court in this way: Trespass occurs when there is an intentional or unintentional and unauthorized entry onto the real property of another, harming the plaintiff's right of exclusive possession. While this is narrative in style and structure, you can break it into a list of requisite elements, i.e., the rule blocks. Trespass = [intentional or unintentional] + [unauthorized] + [entry] + [real property] + [plaintiff in exclusive possession]. Once you have these rule blocks, you can treat them just like a list of elements and organize by creating a paragraph for each one.

Bad Answer

(1) The billboard might or might not transfer with the real estate of the farm when it is not mentioned in the deed, depending on whether the billboard is personalty or realty. (2) Originally, the billboard was purchased and set to create another source of income on the farm. (3) The billboard was originally personalty, but once on the farm had to be secured to the ground to stand effectively. (4) By securing the billboard to the ground, the owner/seller annexed the billboard to the land. (5) In this process of placing the billboard, there must have been some attachment at the base of the billboard to fit it to the land. (6) Depending on the circumstances, this may also have been an adaptation. (7) When the seller later decided to sell, the billboard remained in place throughout the listing period, which may indicate that it was permanently secured to the ground.

(8) On the other hand, the item was a billboard and is a billboard, so it does not seem to have changed much in character. (9) This indicates that any adaptation must have been minimal. (10) While the billboard is attached to the ground so it can stand, it could also be transferred by truck if unattached. (11) This suggests that any annexation was minimal and temporary. (12) Adaptation also requires that the item be essential to the land or business in some way and a billboard is not a standard piece of equipment for a farm like a barn is. (13) The billboard was attached to the ground instead of leaving it on a trailer, and this suggests an intent for the billboard to remain.

QUICK EXERCISE
Skill: Rewriting a Bad Answer to Internalize Good Structure

To get better at organizing your arguments, it is crucial to practice good structure. One way to do this is to try reorganizing answers that are less than great. You have seen an outline of good structure.

Can you fix this bad answer before this chapter breaks down what is wrong with it and revises it for you? Try annotating the bad answer by recognizing the function of each sentence. What does each sentence do regarding the argument? Which element does each sentence speak to? On which side? Does the sentence give a rule, state an issue, or (worse) restate a fact without adding context? Before you proceed to the annotation of the bad answer and the revised version of it, try both annotating the bad answer to note the function of each sentence and then reorganizing them.

Untangling the Bad Answer

First take a look at the purpose of each of the sentences in bare form.

1. The billboard might or might not transfer with the real estate of the farm when it is not mentioned in the deed, depending on whether the billboard is personalty or realty. *Purpose:* **issue statement.**

2. Originally, the billboard was purchased and set to create another source of income on the farm. *Purpose:* **intent element**

3. The billboard was originally personalty, but once on the farm had to be secured to the ground to stand effectively. *Purpose:* **annexation element**

4. By securing the billboard to the ground, the owner/seller annexed the billboard to the land. *Purpose:* **annexation element**

5. In this process of placing the billboard, there must have been some attachment at the base of the billboard to fit it to the land. *Purpose:* **annexation element**

6. Depending on the circumstances, this may also have been an adaptation. *Purpose:* **adaptation element (speculative)**

7. When the seller later decided to sell, the billboard remained in place throughout the listing period, which may indicate that it was permanently secured to the ground. *Purpose:* **annexation element (maybe intent?)**

8. On the other hand, the item was a billboard and is a billboard, so it does not seem to have changed much in character. *Purpose:* **adaptation element**

9. This indicates that any adaptation must have been minimal. *Purpose:* **adaptation element**

10. While the billboard is attached to the ground so it can stand, it could also be transferred by truck if unattached. *Purpose:* **annexation element**

11. This suggests that any annexation was minimal and temporary. *Purpose:* **annexation element**

12. Adaptation also requires that the item be essential to the land or business in some way, and a billboard is not a standard piece of equipment for a farm like a barn. *Purpose:* **adaptation element**

13. The billboard was attached to the ground instead of leaving it on a trailer, and this suggests an intent for the billboard to remain. *Purpose:* **adaptation element**

Another way of thinking about it is that the paragraphs look like this:

Issue statement, intent element, annexation element, annexation element, annexation element, adaptation element, annexation element (maybe intent?)

Adaptation element, adaptation element, annexation element, annexation element, adaptation element, adaptation element

Does that really make sense to a reader?

The reader is meant to evaluate adaptation, annexation, and intent. Three different questions. This is difficult to do when the information for those three questions is alternated in shifts.

If you look back at the narrative and ask what the organization actually is, you find that it is primarily organized by the two sides of the case: evidence for, evidence against. Additionally, there is a somewhat chronological organization: the evidence is presented in the order that it occurred. Chronological might be useful in some legal drafting situations, but it is not particularly helpful when there is a list of elements to meet or not meet.

A Revised Answer

Issue: (1) The billboard might or might not transfer with the real estate of the farm when it is not mentioned in the deed, depending on whether the billboard is personalty or realty.

With respect to the question of annexation, (3) the billboard was originally personalty, but once on the farm had to be secured to the ground to stand effectively. (4) By securing the billboard to the ground, the owner/seller annexed the billboard to the land. (5) In this process of placing the billboard, there must have been some attachment at the base of the billboard to fit it to the land. (7) When the seller later decided to sell, the billboard remained in place throughout the listing period, which may indicate that it was permanently secured to the ground. (10) While the billboard is attached to the ground so it can stand, it could also be transferred by truck if unattached. (11) This suggests that any annexation was minimal and temporary.

Regarding adaptation, (8) the item was a billboard and is a billboard, so it does not seem to have changed much in character. (9) This indicates that any adaptation must have been minimal. (12) Adaptation also requires that the item be essential to the land or business in some way, and a billboard is not a standard piece of equipment for a farm like a barn.

In terms of intent, (2) originally, the billboard was purchased and installed to create another source of income on the farm. (13) The billboard was attached to the ground instead of leaving it on a trailer, and this suggests an intent for the billboard to remain.

Unpacking the Revisions

There are minimal changes. The sentences are now grouped according to the three elements. The revision changed a few words (these are italicized) at the beginning of sentences to indicate the issue statement and the three relevant elements. This creates context for the reader and guides their way through the three questions of annexation, adaptation, and intent. For the same reason, the revision also added a couple of words to indicate weighing the two sides. Finally, the revision omitted sentence six, which was speculative and unhelpful.

This kind of organization also has another great use for writing hypothetical answers. Looking at the three paragraphs of the revised answer, it is immediately clear in a second's glance that there is much more extensive evidence (more points) for element one than for elements two or three. This is a quick indication that one or both of two problems are happening: (1) the student does not thoroughly use all of the facts provided or (2) the student prefers one side and omits the other.

QUICK EXERCISE

Skill: Recognizing How an Answer Is Going Wrong Using Color-Coding

Review an answer that you have written to one of the personalty/realty hypotheticals. Print a hard copy. Gather three colors of highlighter or colored pencil. Give each color an element designation: annexation, adaptation, and intent. Write them down so you can't get them confused. Now reread the answer, using the highlighters to mark the purpose of each sentence. You should now see whether or not you are organizing by element effectively.

There is a second step to this process. Next look at the three colors to see if you have an equal amount of each of them. If not, then you are either not using the facts thoroughly or preferring one side and omitting and/or neglecting the other side. Notice that without the element-by-element organization, it can be very difficult to see these two problems unless you print the answer and color-code it. That is a 10-minute solution to a two-second problem. It is much more effective to practice organizing by elements.

Linking Argument Paragraphs Effectively and Elegantly

Students sometimes say that they are anxious when writing exams because they feel like their paragraphs are, well, ugly. They ask for ways to connect and organize their paragraphs that feel both smooth and simple. What students are really asking for are navigational signals that tell the reader when you are switching between sub-issues (like annexation, adaptation, and intent).

It is highly strategic to connect your argument in ways that provide navigation signals for your reader. It is like using *first*, *second*, and *third* to connect your points, but with a bit more elegance and detail. The revised answer above italicizes these navigational signals for the reader. Research demonstrates that readers recall information better when writers use navigational signals. Therefore, this type of organization is great for success in writing briefs and motions. In the context of exams, navigational signals help your professor understand and follow your argument.

Here is a chart of examples of smooth and simple navigational signals for readers.

Navigational Signals for Switching Sub-Issues

Regarding	In terms of
With respect to	As to
On the issue of	Concerning
As far as ____ goes	On the topic of
Apropos of	As for
About proving	When it comes to
On the subject of	On the question of
For the matter of	As to the problem of
Regarding determining	In the case of
As far as ____ is concerned	Thinking about
Turning to the issue of	Moving to the question of
Regarding proving	To evaluate
To determine	Applying the rules for
Evaluating the question of	Insofar as ____ is concerned
As to the extent of	As to the degree of
In terms of assessing	Appraising

Avoid Organizing by Facts

Sometimes students want to organize the discussion by the facts, almost in a list format. In other words, they focus on one fact and what it means, then another fact and what it means.

Example:

> *The size of the billboard is important to determine whether it is personalty or realty. The billboard is large enough to need to be secured strongly to the ground, creating an annexation. On the other hand, the billboard could be moved by a semi, which suggests it is movable and probably not annexed. The size of the billboard, however, suggests that it was intended to be a permanent addition to the farm. It would be difficult to unsecure it and put it back on a semi.*

The paragraph that follows would likely pick another fact, such as the nature of the land as a farm and then evaluate that fact in terms of both intent and adaptation.

What happens, of course, when you organize by fact is that the evidence for each element (annexation, adaptation, intent) is spread all over the discussion. The example paragraph includes both annexation and intent, but if there were more elements, a fact-based organization could be even more complicated.

For a professor these can be the hardest exams to grade. It is difficult to find the pieces and link them to points on the rubric. It is also difficult to tell if the student understands the rules or elements and how they work, because there is never a sustained discussion about any particular rule or element. In short, this is not advisable as an exam strategy.

QUICK EXERCISE

Skill: Organizing by Element

Try this the next time you do a hypothetical for practice. (You can re-do an old one or save this until you do the next one in the book.) Before you start writing in your blank document, create headings for Issue, Rules, Application, and Conclusion. Within the Application section, create headings for each of the elements. In other words, if you are rewriting a personalty versus realty hypothetical, it should look like this:

Issue:

Rules:

Application:

    Annexation

    Adaptation

    Intent

Conclusion:

Now as you write the hypothetical answer, organize your thoughts under these headings. This may come relatively easy to you or it may be hard. You may need to take a little more time at first. It may be something you must practice repeatedly, but it is worth it. Many students continue to use this method as they write their exams.

ELEVEN

Choosing Your Issue between Inter-Vivos Gifts versus Gifts Causa Mortis

Some issues or causes of action fit similar fact patterns. As a result, a plaintiff may be able to sue under two different causes of action or theories of liability. For an exam, the important thing is distinguishing when to fully discuss only one issue or both. This chapter addresses two types of gifts, inter-vivos and gifts causa mortis, which provides a good example for sorting out when to argue one or both issues. After discussing the basic rules for gifts causa mortis, this chapter returns to the problem of choosing between or choosing both issues.

Basic Rules for Gifts Causa Mortis

A gift causa mortis is a special type of gift made in anticipation of death. The gift causa mortis is important because this type of gift may be subject to debtors and taxes when an inter-vivos gift might not be. Additionally, this type of gift is incomplete — and therefore revocable — during the donor's lifetime. Finally, should the donor recover from the illness or pass the moment of peril safely, the courts consider the gift to be voided. In other words, to complete a valid gift causa mortis the donor must die of the anticipated illness or peril.

The gift causa mortis requires intent, delivery, and apprehension of death. The gift is revocable until the final requirement (death) is met.

The intent should be an intent to make this type of gift: a gift in the prospect of death. The intent should be that the title vests conditionally on death. There does not need to be an express condition, but rather it may be inferred from the surrounding circumstances.

Delivery is essential and should vest the donee with possession (dominion and control). However, constructive delivery suffices. It is enough that the donor provides some means of accessing or obtaining the personalty or gives the gift to an intermediary.

The donor must have an apprehension of death. An illness or "impending peril" is sufficient. Some courts have questioned whether intentional acts of the donor create an apprehension of death as traditionally understood. These courts reason that if the action that would cause peril is at the donor's choice, then there is not a true apprehension of death, because the donor can readily abandon by his or her own choice the action that brings about the risk.

The burden of proof is on the donee (the person claiming the gift was valid). When compared with inter-vivos gifts, the courts require a higher standard of proof, because such gifts are subject to a higher danger of fraud. Proof should be "most clear."

Outline of Basic Rules for Gifts Causa Mortis

I. Gift causa mortis

   A. Test (Four-part and-type test)

      1. Intent

         a. Clarify: intent should be that the title vests conditionally on death.

         b. Clarify: inference: there does not need to be an express condition of death, but rather it may be inferred from the surrounding circumstances.

      2. Delivery (actual or constructive)

         a. Actual: the giver must provide the donee with possession (dominion and control).

         b. Or constructive: it is sufficient that the donor provides some means of accessing or obtaining the personalty or gives the gift to an intermediary.

      3. Apprehension of death

         a. Clarify: the donor must have knowledge of a coming risk. An illness or "impending peril" is sufficient.

         b. Clarify: depending on the jurisdiction, an intentional act that creates risk may not be sufficient to create an apprehension of death.

4. Death

   a. Clarify: to finalize the gift, the giver must die of the expected illness/peril. Survival voids the gift.

B. Burdens

   1. The burden of proof falls on the recipient.

   2. There is a higher standard of proof because such gifts are subject to a higher danger of fraud. Proof should be "most clear."

C. Outcome rules

   1. Gifts causa mortis may be subject to creditors and taxes when an inter-vivos gift might not be.

   2. The gift is incomplete — and therefore revocable — during the donor's lifetime.

Choosing One Issue or Choosing Both

To begin the analysis, consider how the elements of the two tests align and diverge. If reduced to the basics, an inter-vivos gift requires intent, delivery, and acceptance (presumed for things of value). A gift causa mortis requires intent, delivery, apprehension of death, and the death of the donor. The two tests look rather similar, except for the circumstances of a potential death approaching.

Analyze the two sets of elements looking for any elements that fall into three particular categories. The categories are (1) overlapping, (2) divergent, and (3) circumstantial.

Overlapping elements are elements that are identical in both tests. Here, delivery is defined in the same way in both tests. Delivery is a fully overlapping element. That means that facts supporting one test will equally support the other.

Divergent elements are ones that are nearly impossible to satisfy at the same time. If one test required only actual delivery and the other accepted only constructive delivery, then the element would diverge in the two tests.

Finally, some elements can align circumstantially. This means that a situation might satisfy the element, but does not really matter for the purposes of the other test. In other words, the facts are meaningful in one test, but only circumstantial in the other. This generally occurs when one test has additional elements that are unrelated to the second test. In the case of gifts, gifts causa mortis have two elements that are unrelated to inter-vivos gifts: apprehension of death and death. If someone is ill and at risk of dying, he or she might still make gifts that have nothing to do with dying (inter-vivos gifts).

This is an important moment to pause to consider the importance of precision in the law. At first glance, it would be easy to believe that inter-vivos gifts overlap almost entirely with gifts causa mortis. The reasoning would be that acceptance is generally assumed, and the only two elements are intent and delivery, which are both elements of the gift causa mortis. With more precise reasoning, this is not really correct. The intent elements differ substantially. An inter-vivos gift requires the intent to be to transfer a present and permanent interest. On the other hand, the intent for a gift causa mortis should be based on the apprehension of death and therefore conditional. After examining these two intents, the appropriate conclusion is that they are different intents. The two elements are diverging, not overlapping.

So how does the analysis of the elements indicate which test to run or whether to run both tests if two issues appear somewhat similar? The key is to specifically examine the moments of divergence. The diverging elements would be the reason that you would choose only one test. So, to choose both tests, there has to be a way for the diverging element to intersect through ambiguity. In other words, the rule for when to do both tests is when all elements are either overlapping or circumstantial, except for one or two that are divergent but capable of an intersecting ambiguity.

An intersecting ambiguity means that there is a factual situation where the plaintiff could make a plausible argument for each of two divergent elements. When looking at the two types of gifts, the donor would have to have an intent that was fuzzy or ambiguous. The intent would have to be partially based on a risk of death, but also partially independent of that risk. In other words, the intent would need to be somewhat conditional on death and somewhat irrespective of the risk of death. It is appropriate to execute tests for both issues where you spot a fuzzy circumstance that would allow the two types of intent (a divergent element) to intersect.

Notably, this is thinking that takes a bit of time. Generally, too much time for a law school exam. An important part of exam preparation is to front-load this type of thinking about issues that are likely to overlap and what types of factual situations would lend themselves to an ambiguity that unites otherwise diverging elements.

Finally, there is a safety check of sorts that can go with this analysis. When reading a hypothetical, ask whether there are facts that are relevant to one or both sides of each element on each test. If there are facts (on either side) for all elements of a particular test, then discuss both issues in full. Execute a nested IRAC analysis of both issues. In such situations, if a professor has provided the facts, chances are there is an intersect or ambiguity that you are not seeing.

Checklist for Reasoning: Step-by-Step Reasoning for Choosing One Issue or Both

1. Outline basic tests of the two issues. Be precise.
2. Identify important divergences
   - Note and set aside those elements that are circumstantial or overlapping.
3. For two issues to be candidates for simultaneous causes of action/issues, all elements must be either overlapping or circumstantial except for one or two that are divergent.
4. Looking at the divergences, identify whether there is potential for ambiguity.
   - Is there a circumstance where an ambiguity could make it possible to meet either test? Note this is about possibility, not about likelihood.
   - If there is an intersecting divergence, execute both tests.
5. Redundancy check: Ask whether there are facts available that address each element of both issues.
   - Note this is not a pass/fail execution of the test. The question is whether there are any facts that you might use if you had to discuss one side or the other.
   - If there are facts to work out both sides of an element, chances are good that there is an intersecting ambiguity that you have not recognized.

The Jet-Propelled Car Hypothetical

Time to read and write your answer: one hour.

Marshall has been selected to test-drive an experimental new jet-propelled car. Marshall's life insurance company canceled his policy when they discovered his new venture; they said that he was intentionally putting himself in an "ultra-risky" situation. Marshall is concerned about the substantial risk to his life during the drive, but he also has enormous confidence in himself and in the design team. Marshall says, "Yeah, I know, it could squish me. But hey, I'm a genius behind the wheel, so maybe I'm the better bet."

In the week before the test drive, Marshall contacts his niece, Kala, and asks her to come by the house. She is away at school and can't make it before spring break. He explains on the phone, "I've got this test drive coming up. Anyway, there was this ring your grandmother left to me and I've always thought she would want you to have it." He continues, "It's a girl's ring anyway. Way too small for me." Marshall tells Kala that seeing as she is at school, he is going to leave the ring in the safe for now, but will tell his wife Maria the code. Marshall also promises, "I will send you a photograph, so you know what you are looking for in the safe." Kala thanks Marshall and wishes him a safe drive.

Marshall forgets to send the picture to Kala. He writes the code in lipstick on the mirror in the bathroom he shares with his wife, but does not indicate what the code is for.

Marshall dies during the test drive.

Scoring Rubric for the Jet-Propelled Car Hypothetical

Section		
Issue:	Is there a valid gift causa mortis of the ring?	6
Rules:	☐ The donor must intend to make a gift. (3) ☐ The intent should be conditional on death. (3) ☐ The donor must apprehend death. (3) ☐ Apprehension may be inferred from the circumstances. (3) ☐ The gift must be delivered. (3) ☐ Constructive delivery is acceptable. (3) ☐ Death must occur to make the gift irrevocable. (3)	21
App.:	***Intent*** *Conditional* ☐ When Marshall contacts Kala he wants to see her immediately and begins his conversation with her by citing the test drive. These facts suggest that his motivation in making the gift is the upcoming drive. (3) ☐ Marshall makes the call to Kala in the context of the upcoming drive and with the insurance agency having canceled his policy, which suggests he made the gift thinking of death. (3) *Not conditional* ☐ Marshall describes the ring as a family piece, which may mean that he would give it to his niece whether or not he died in the crash. (3) ☐ Marshall says that he "always thought" the grandmother would want Kala to have the ring, which suggests that his intent is perpetual and not contingent on the possibility of a crash. (3) ☐ Marshall apparently has no desire to keep the ring as he describes it as "a girl's ring" and "way too small." (3)	6 9

Continued

Continued

App.:	**Apprehended death**		
	Yes		
	☐ Both "experimental" and "jet-propelled" sound dangerous. Combining the two is even worse, so there seems to be an imminent risk of death. (3)	15	
	☐ Marshall was "selected" to drive so he must be in this business and that suggests he understands the level of risk. (3)		
	☐ Marshall's life insurance company canceled his policy, which indicates that there is a substantial level of risk involved. (3)		
	☐ The insurance company described the situation as "ultra-risky," suggesting that a reasonable person would apprehend death in this situation. (3)		
	☐ Marshall acknowledges that the car could "squish him," which suggests he realizes that the level of risk is significant. (3)		
	No		
	☐ Marshall said the car could "squish" him. The statement is ambiguous and does not make it clear that Marshall really thinks he could die. (3)	9	
	☐ Marshall has discounted the risk of the new car because he is relying on his own skills. To the degree that he honestly believes he is a genius, he may not believe that he would be likely to die. (3)		
	☐ Marshall suggests that he is "the better bet" in this situation, which suggests it is more likely than not (in his mind) that he will survive the test drive. (3)		
	Apprehension split: Is it okay if the act creating the risk is intentional?		
	☐ Marshall can choose not to do the test drive. Thus, he has the option to fully avoid the risk of death at any time up until the drive begins. Because he can control his own safety by refusing to drive, he does not have a true apprehension of death. (3)	6	
	☐ Because there is no illness or external circumstance, the risk is fully within Marshall's sole control, which limits the possibility that he is apprehending death in the traditional sense. (3)		

App.:	*Delivery*		
	Direct delivery		
	☐ There is no direct delivery of the ring. (3)	3	
	Constructive delivery		
	☐ Marshall asked to see Kala immediately and presumably would have done so if she had been available. Thus, when she was not, he fitted his actions for delivery to the circumstances. (3)	12	
	☐ Kala is at school and it appears she cannot return for an extended time (the next vacation), so Marshall is unable to make a direct or actual delivery. (3)		
	☐ Marshall tells Kala a location where he will leave the ring, which is a verbal attempt at delivery. (3)		
	☐ Marshall gives the code to his wife, so that Kala can get to the ring, thus facilitating a later delivery. (3)		
	Failure of constructive delivery		
	☐ Marshall could have given the code directly to Kala but chose not to do so. (3)	12	
	☐ Marshall puts the code in a haphazard place with no indication of what it is, which suggests he did very little to ensure a safe delivery of the ring. (3)		
	☐ Marshall told Kala he would send a picture so she would "know what" she was "looking for in the safe." This suggests that there is more than one ring in the safe and that without the picture, Kala does not know which ring Marshall meant to gift. (3)		
	☐ Marshall died, so if the gift is proven, then it is irrevocable. (3)		
Concl.:		3	

Continued

Continued

Issue:	Did Marshall make a valid inter-vivos gift?	6	
Rules:	**Elements of inter-vivos gift** The donor must intend to make an irrevocable transfer. (3) The intent must be to create a present interest. (3) The donor must deliver the gift. (3) Constructive delivery is acceptable. (3) The recipient must accept the gift. (3) Courts presume acceptance for things of value. (3) There is a split of jurisdictions on the validity of conditional gifts. In some jurisdictions they are valid when the condition is completed. In other jurisdictions, the condition violates the intent to create a present interest, so the gift is void. (3)	21	
App.:	**Intent** *Conditional* ☐ When Marshall contacts Kala he wants to see her immediately and begins his conversation with her by citing the test drive. These facts suggest that his motivation in making the gift is the upcoming drive rather than a more general motivation to make the gift. (3) ☐ Marshall makes the call to Kala in the context of the upcoming drive and with the insurance agency having canceled his policy, which suggests he made the gift thinking of death. (3) *Not conditional* ☐ Marshall describes the ring as a family piece, which may mean that he would give it to his niece whether or not he died in the crash. (3) ☐ Marshall says that he "always thought" the grandmother would want Kala to have the ring, which suggests that his intent is perpetual and not contingent on the possibility of death. (3) ☐ Marshall apparently has no desire to keep the ring as he describes it as "a girl's ring" and "way too small." (3)	6 9	

App.:	*Delivery*		
	Delivery here is identical to the above analysis, so no points for repeating it.		
	Acceptance		
	No, actual		
	☐ The facts do not specifically say that Kala communicated her acceptance. (3)	3	
	Yes, actual		
	☐ Given that Marshall arranged for a mechanism for delivery, that suggests Kala had made it clear to him that she would accept the gift. (3)	3	
	Presumed acceptance		
	☐ The gift is a ring and jewelry generally has a market value, so acceptance can be presumed. (3)	6	
	☐ The gift is also a family piece, which means it would likely have value to Kala specifically and be worth keeping in the family. (3)		
Concl.:		3	
	Total		

Mean Score for sample law student groups: 129

Sample Answer to the Jet-Propelled Car Hypothetical

The ring may be a gift causa mortis. To prove a gift causa mortis, the recipient has the burden to prove the donor intended to make the gift, delivered the gift, apprehended death, and died of the impending threat.

First, the recipient must prove the appropriate intent existed. For a gift causa mortis, the intent should be to make a gift in anticipation of a potential death. This intent then is conditional on the death, as opposed to a general intent to gift a present interest. Marshall's words may suggest that he has this type of conditional intent. Marshall contacts Kala, asking to see her immediately, which suggests some urgency and begins his conversation with her by citing the test drive. These circumstances suggest that the motivation behind the gift is the risk of the test drive. Additionally, Marshall makes the call to Kala in the context of the upcoming drive and with the insurance agency having canceled his policy, which suggests he made the gift in light of the potential risk to his life from the test drive. On the other hand, Marshall is not entirely clear about the nature of his intent.

Marshall describes the ring as a family piece, and if the piece is a family heirloom, he may intend that his niece have it in all circumstances. In other words, it may mean that he would give it to his niece whether or not he died in the crash. Marshall says that he "always thought" the grandmother would want Kala to have the ring, which suggests it is a family heirloom meant for Kala in any circumstance. Finally, Marshall apparently has no desire to keep the ring as he describes it as "a girl's ring" and "way too small," so he may mean for Kala to have it in all circumstances, not just because of the test drive and its risks. The timing is very persuasive for suggesting that Marshall was motivated by the upcoming test drive.

Second, Kala must establish that Marshall apprehended death. Apprehension may be inferred from the circumstances surrounding the alleged gift. Some circumstances suggest that Marshall did, in fact, apprehend death. Marshall describes the test drive as "experimental" and involving a "jet-propelled car," which suggests a highly dangerous enterprise. Marshall appears to be a driver (someone in the business), so he probably understands the risks of a jet-propelled car. Even if he did not understand the risks, he should have known them when his life insurance company canceled his policy. The insurance company described the situation as "ultra-risky," suggesting that a reasonable person would apprehend death in this situation. Finally, Marshall acknowledges that the car could "squish him," which suggests he has acknowledged that the level of risk is significant. His statement, however, is rather flippant and unclear as to how serious he saw the risk to be. Indeed, Marshall discounted the risk of the new car, citing his own skills. To the degree that he honestly believes he is a genius, he may not believe that he would be likely to die. Marshall suggests that he is "the better bet" in this situation, which suggests it is more likely than not (in his mind) that he will survive the test drive.

Even if Marshall does realize the level of risk, the courts may not be willing to consider this type of risk as meeting the test. Traditionally, apprehension of death involved an ongoing illness or impending threat (such as war or natural disaster). The common theme was that these circumstances were outside the donor's control. Here, Marshall can choose not to do the test drive. Thus, he has the option to fully avoid the risk of death at any time up until the drive begins. Because he can control his own safety by refusing to drive, he does not have a solid apprehension of death. Because there is no illness or external circumstance, the risk is fully within Marshall's sole control, which limits the possibility that he is apprehending death in the traditional sense. A court might conclude that he could not apprehend death in this type of voluntary situation.

Kala must also establish that Marshall delivered the ring. She can meet this test by establishing either actual or constructive delivery, which is evaluated circumstantially. There is no direct delivery of the ring. However, there may have been constructive delivery. Marshall asked to see Kala immediately and presumably would have done so if she had been available. Thus, when she was not, he fitted his actions for delivery to the circumstances. Kala was at school, preventing an actual delivery. Marshall tells Kala a location where he will leave the ring, which makes a verbal attempt at delivery and facilitates later delivery. Marshall gives the code to his wife, so that Kala can get to the ring, thus facilitating a later delivery.

This is, however, a somewhat removed mechanism of delivery. Marshall could have given the code directly to Kala but chose not to do so. Then Marshall put the code in a haphazard place with no indication of what it is, which suggests he did very little to ensure a safety delivery of the ring. Marshall told Kala he would send a picture so she would "know what" she was "looking for in the safe." This suggests that there is more than one ring in the safe and that without the picture, Kala does not know which ring Marshall meant to gift. This jeopardizes the specificity of the gift.

Kala must establish that Marshall died. The rule is that he must have died of the impending illness or threat that motivated the gift. Here, Marshall died during the test drive, which was the impending threat.

In the end, it is not terribly clear that Kala has established a gift causa mortis claim to the ring.

Kala may, however, have a second opportunity to prove a gift. Kala could prove an inter-vivos gift. An inter-vivos gift requires intent, delivery, and acceptance.

The primary rule for intent is that the donor must intend to gift a present, permanent interest. Such an intent is absolute rather than conditional. Marshall may have had such a permanent intent. Marshall describes the ring as a family piece, which may mean that he would give it to his niece whether or not he died in the crash. He states that he "always thought" the grandmother would want Kala to have the ring, which suggests that his intent is permanent. Additionally, Marshall apparently has no desire to keep the ring as he describes it as "a girl's ring" and "way too small." A jury could find that Marshall intended to gift a permanent, unconditional interest.

Other facts, however, suggest that Marshall's intent may have been conditional. When Marshall contacts Kala, he wants to see her immediately and begins his conversation with her by citing the test drive. These facts suggest that his motivation in making the gift is the upcoming drive.

Marshall makes the call to Kala in the context of the upcoming drive and with the insurance agency having canceled his policy, which suggests he made the gift thinking of death. If a jury found that Marshall's intent was conditional, the outcome would depend on which jurisdiction considered the claim. Some jurisdictions hold that a condition violates the intent requirement, and therefore there was no valid gift. Other jurisdictions choose to write out the condition, so to speak, and interpret the gift as permanent, whether or not the condition is met. Finally, a smaller group of states allow conditional gifts, and therefore would find the gift conditioned on Marshall dying and the condition would be met at his death, making the gift permanent.

Delivery for inter-vivos gifts should be actual or constructive, which is precisely the same as the requirement for gifts causa mortis. See analysis above, which suggests that the constructive delivery fails.

Finally, for an inter-vivos gift, there must be acceptance. Acceptance is presumed for things of value. Here, there may or may not be actual acceptance. The facts do not specifically say that Kala communicated her acceptance. However, given that Marshall arranged for a mechanism for delivery, that suggests that Kala had made it clear to him that she would accept the gift. In either case, there is also a good argument for presuming acceptance. The gift is a ring and jewelry generally has a market value, so acceptance can be presumed. The gift is also a family piece, which means it would likely have value to Kala specifically.

In the final evaluation, the intent, which may be conditional, would prevent the gift from being valid in some jurisdictions. The delivery here may not be effective. In light of those two problems, it is less likely that Marshall made an effective inter-vivos gift.

TWELVE

Private Nuisance and Adding Case Comparisons to the Analysis

Rules of Private Nuisance

Private nuisance law provides a remedy for a neighbor who makes life uncomfortable on the properties nearby. Nuisance sits on the line between property and tort. It might be called a tortious interference with property. In short, it is a property-tort.

The thing that sets nuisance apart from tort law is that the problematic behavior arises specifically from land use. In other words, if you set up a mad drum concert on a street corner you may be breaking various laws, but you are not creating a private nuisance. If, however, you set up a concert on your own lawn, you may be creating a private nuisance.

Both landowners and leaseholders can sue for nuisance. Additionally, there are no requirements in terms of the location of the plaintiff's property; it need not be adjacent or adjoining, only impacted by the defendant's property.

The statute of limitations for nuisance begins to run with the creation of the nuisance. And the statute of limitations tends to be, comparatively, short: usually two to three years. However, if the nuisance continues, then every continuation gives rise to a separate claim.

To prove a nuisance, the plaintiff must establish a substantial and unreasonable interference with the use and enjoyment of land. In some jurisdictions, plaintiffs demonstrate this interference by proving the land use is either intentional and unreasonable or abnormally dangerous. Courts evaluate unreasonableness contextually. The plaintiff should demonstrate a significant harm. Intent in this context is the intent to do the act, not the intent to cause the harm.

In some jurisdictions unclean hands may be an affirmative defense to nuisance. The defendant must then prove that there was some similar or related reprehensible conduct on the part of the plaintiff. In other words, the allegedly unclean conduct must be directly related to the subject matter being litigated. Additionally, the defendant must have been injured by the conduct. Note: Some jurisdictions allow unclean hands only as an equitable defense to an injunction or abatement order.

If the plaintiff establishes the prima facie case, the court will award legal damages (monetary compensation). When there is a continuing nuisance, and the statute of limitations has passed for the original creation, some jurisdictions will only consider equitable remedies, not damages.

There are two possible equitable remedies: injunction and abatement. Abatement refers to an order to remove the nuisance. Generally, to get an abatement order, the plaintiff must establish that the alleged danger or annoyance is sufficiently serious to justify abatement. Injunctions generally prevent future behavior. Both injunctions and abatement orders are discretionary. For injunctions, courts balance various factors fitted to the context, such as the social utility of the defendant's actions, the impact on the community, the benefit to the plaintiff of granting an injunction, and the impact on the defendant's property rights.

There are also defenses that a judge can consider when determining equitable remedies. These include defenses ordinarily available in situations of equity. The most common is laches or unreasonable delay in filing by the plaintiff that is prejudicial to the defendant.

Outline of Private Nuisance Rules

I. Private nuisance
   A. Procedural bars
      1. Statute of limitations
         a. Statutes are typically short (two to three years).
         b. Exception
            i. A continuing nuisance renews the claim on each occurrence. Courts may limit plaintiffs to equitable remedies if the statute of limitations has passed since the first occurrence.
   B. Test:
      1. Split: plaintiff must establish substantial interference with the use and enjoyment of property, creating significant harm.
      2. Or (Restatement): plaintiff must prove interference either:

  a. Intentional and unreasonable
    i. Clarify: unreasonable is evaluated contextually.
    ii. Clarify: the intent required is the intent to do the act, not to cause harm.
  b. Or abnormally dangerous
  3. Plaintiff must prove a significant harm.
C. Affirmative defenses
  1. Unclean hands
    Test:
    i. Defendant must prove that there is similar or related reprehensible conduct on the part of the plaintiff.
    ii. Defendant must have been injured by that conduct.
D. Remedies:
  1. Legal damages
    a. Damages are awarded as a matter of right, if the prima facie case is proven.
  2. Equitable remedies (discretionary)
    a. Available remedies
      i. Abatement
      Test: is the injury sufficiently serious to require removal in the eyes of the court?
      ii. Injunctions
      Balancing test:
        1. What is the social utility of the defendant's actions?
        2. What would be the impact on the community of granting an injunction?
        3. What is the benefit to the plaintiff of granting an injunction?
        4. What is the impact on the defendant's property rights of granting an injunction?
    b. Defenses to equitable remedies
      i. Standard equitable defenses such as laches are available.
      Test: was there unreasonable delay in filing suit, causing prejudice to the defendant?
      ii. Unclean hands (see above)

Case Notes for Private Nuisance

Here are some short case summaries to provide you with an opportunity to practice case comparisons as you do the next hypothetical.

Pestey v. Cushman, 259 Conn. 345 (2002).

Plaintiffs sued a neighboring dairy farm arguing private nuisance. The plaintiffs based their claim on the offensive odors from the farm, which included a 42,000-square-foot barn, a herd of dairy cows, and a manure pit. The air around the farm smelled acrid or burnt and of sulfur and sewage due to a manure "digester" machine. The smells were strong enough to disrupt the plaintiffs' sleep. Nuisance found. The jury awarded damages, and the Supreme Court affirmed.

Blue Ink v. Two Farms, Inc., 218 Md. App. 77 (2014).

Plaintiffs, a drive-in movie theater, sued the neighboring gas station. The theater sued for the cost of building a fence to block out the lght from the gas station at night. The gas station has a convenience store and parking spaces illuminated by pole-mounted lighting. The store also has a variety of lighted signs advertising products. The court found that the lights might be an annoyance for a movie theater in particular, but the lights failed to meet the test for an unreasonable and substantial interference, such as would be experienced by the ordinary person.

Nuisance not found. The Court of Appeals affirmed the trial court's grant of a motion for judgment notwithstanding the verdict.

Schiller v. Mitchell, 357 Ill. App. 3d 435 (2005).

The plaintiffs sued their neighbors for private nuisance, alleging that the neighbors maintained 24-hour surveillance with cameras on the plaintiffs' property. The defendants then used the surveillance to make frivolous reports of violations of the homeowners' association code. The court did not find that the cameras made an invasion into the space of the plaintiffs' property and therefore were not a private nuisance. The Court of Appeals affirmed dismissal.

Sorcerer's Flower Hypothetical

Time to read and write your answer: one hour.

Greer Kennedy, a noted expert in rare and heirloom flowers, lives next door to the Speedwell family (Veronica, Ranunculus, and their son, Fennel). A wide stream that cascades into small ponds separates the two properties. According to the deeds, the property line dates back to the 1700s and is the stream itself, making the center of the stream the dividing line between the two neighboring properties, which are in a rural Virginia village called Aster. Greer chose this property because it has excellent, rich soils, along with plenty of fresh spring water from the stream. Additionally, her property contains both a meadow area where she can plant sun-loving plants, and a shady area along the stream where she can grow her shade-loving flowers, such as the Helleborus.

Along the banks of the stream, in the shade of the trees, Greer planted several types of Helleborus, including the Helleborus Orientalis, and a recently developed experimental hybrid known as Madame Lemmonier. Greer planted her first Hellebores when she bought the property five years ago, but only in the last two years introduced the new experimental hybrid. Hellebores are a member of the Ranunculaceae family, whose members are frequently, but not always, extremely toxic. Hellebores were traditionally known as the sorcerer's flower because, according to folk legend, a sorcerer could use the powder of the dried plant to become invisible.

The toxicity of the plant, however, is not a matter of folklore. (One commonly known member of the family is Aconitum, or Monk's Hood, which has caused a number of documented accidental deaths just from handling the plant.) The roots are extremely toxic, containing a strong emetic that is fatal if ingested. Additionally, the liquid oils of the plants, found in both the leaves and the seeds, are toxic, causing severe skin burns following prolonged handling of the leaves or seedpods. Finally, airborne particles from the plants have been associated with eye and nasal irritation, but only in persons who are particularly sensitive to the plants. Helleborus orientalis is known to be one of the more toxic varieties; little is known about the toxicity of Madame Lemmonier because it is a newly developed hybrid.

Greer has only planted the Helleborus plants on her side of the stream. However, Helleborus plants self-seed quite easily and due to the wind, some seeds have drifted to the Speedwell side of the stream and grown there. Because the flowers are rather beautiful, the Speedwells have continued to let the plants grow for the past four years. Seeds may drift on the wind or on the stream water to neighbors further away, but there is no direct evidence of this yet — it remains only a probability.

During the eclipse, Fennel Speedwell, who is six years old, along with two school friends collected and opened the seedpods of the Helleborus plants on their side of the stream, apparently out of curiosity. Not knowing of the toxicity of Helleborus plants, the Speedwell parents did not discourage the activity. All three children suffered severe blistering on their hands, resulting in emergency room visits and a week during which they were largely unable to care for themselves due to the painfulness of their injured hands.

Do not consider trespass claims.

Scoring Rubric for Sorcerer's Flower Hypothetical

Section		
Issue:	☐ Are the Helleborus plants a private nuisance to the Speedwell family? (6)	6
Rules:	**Procedural** ☐ There is a short statute of limitations (two to three years). (3) ☐ Continuous behavior resets the clock, but there is a jurisdictional split as to what remedies are available (i.e., only equitable remedies or both equitable remedies and damages). (3)	6
	Basic test ☐ A nuisance requires an invasion of another person's use and enjoyment of property. (3) ☐ The plaintiff must show significant harm. (3) ☐ In Restatement jurisdictions, actions should be either "intentional and unreasonable" or "abnormally dangerous." (3) ☐ Unreasonableness is measured by the social and geographical context of the activity. (3) ☐ Compensation is automatic if a case is proven, but an injunction is discretionary. (3)	15

Rules:	**Abatement**		
	☐ The remedy of abatement is discretionary, and the court will weigh the seriousness of the defendant's injury. (3)	3	
	Factors for injunction		
	☐ Impacts on the community, such as loss of jobs (3)	12	
	☐ Impacts on the defendant's property interests (3)		
	☐ Benefits of stopping use to the plaintiff (3)		
	☐ Benefit of use/product to the public (3)		
	Laches		
	☐ Unreasonable delay in filing is a defense, particularly for equitable remedies. (3)	3	
App.:	**Procedural: statute of limitations**		
	☐ More than three years have passed since the experimental flowers were planted, so the initial act is no longer within the statute. (3)	9	
	☐ Flowers are still growing and creating seeds, so there is a continuing nuisance that resets the clock for the statute daily. (3)		
	☐ Self-seeding plants means there are always new plants and therefore potentially new nuisances. (3)		
	Unreasonable interference with the use and enjoyment of property		
	Yes, on the basis of property use		
	☐ Feeling unsafe outdoors would logically change (and diminish) the use of the plaintiff's property. (3)	3	
	Yes, on the basis of health concerns		
	☐ Toxic plants create a risk of health impacts, including burns, which place immediate neighbors at risk. (3)	27	
	☐ Children may not understand the risk. (3)		
	☐ Originally neighbors would have had to trespass to touch the plants, but seed drift has brought the poisonous plants outside the original property where they were planted. (3)		
	☐ Airborne dissemination makes the risk to people greater. (3)		

Continued

Continued

App.:	☐ Greer is planting one type known to be extremely toxic and another with unknown toxicities, which increases the risks. (3) ☐ Plants are near the property boundary, which increases the risk to neighbors. (3) ☐ Plants near the boundary increase the risk of seed spread, which increases the risk of injuries. (3) ☐ Children have been injured, so the risk is not simply hypothetical. (3) ☐ The injuries required hospitalization, so the risk is not minor. (3) ☐ ***Case comparison:*** Physical dangers to children are much more inappropriate to context in an area with homes when compared to parking lot lights in a commercial area. *Blue Ink v. Two Farms, Inc.*, 218 Md. App. 77 (2014). (3)		
		3	
	No, on the basis of property use		
	☐ There is no known change to the plaintiff's property value, and no permanent change as plants are easily removed. (3)	3	
	No, on the basis of health concerns		
	☐ There is no evidence of death from this plant except by ingestion of roots, which is unlikely to happen by accident. (3) ☐ The potential health impacts require touching, which requires action on the part of the person injured. (3) ☐ Risk is minimized by the difference in reactions. (3) ☐ The plant is only dangerous when seeding or with roots, making exposures less likely. (3)	12	
	Showing of significant harm		
	Yes		
	☐ The toxic plants create a risk of health impacts, including burns, which places immediate neighbors at risk. (3) ☐ Greer is planting one type known to be extremely toxic and another with unknown toxicities, which increases the risk. (3) ☐ Children have been injured already, so the risk is clear. (3)	15	

☐ The injuries required a hospital visit, so the risk is not minimal. (3) ☐ The injuries required recovery time and care, which suggests the injuries were substantial. (3) ☐ *Sample case comparison:* Injuries that require immediate hospital visits are more significant than waking at night due to smells. *Pestey v. Cushman*, 259 Conn. 345 (2002). (3)	3	
No ☐ There has been no permanent injury. (3) ☐ The children will not touch the plants or seeds again after this experience so the problem will not reoccur. (3) ☐ With unknown toxicities, some plants may be entirely harmless. (3)	9	
Abnormally dangerous *Yes* ☐ Toxic plants have a risk of health impacts, including burns, which place immediate neighbors at risk. (3) ☐ Originally neighbors would have had to trespass to touch the plants, but seed drift has brought the poisonous plants outside the original property boundaries. (3) ☐ Airborne dissemination makes the risk to people greater. (3) ☐ Greer is planting one type known to be extremely toxic and another with unknown toxicities, which increases the risk. (3) ☐ The plants are located near the boundary, increasing the risk of seed spread, which increases the risk of injuries. (3) ☐ Touching the plant parts sent children to the hospital. (3)	18	
No ☐ You must touch the plants (a lot) to be harmed. (3) ☐ Many plants are poisonous; this is not unusual. (3) ☐ Is this any worse than a bad case of poison ivy? (3) ☐ Most people do not touch plants (a lot). (3)	12	

Continued

Continued

	Remedies: injunction		
	☐ Greer works with rare and heirloom flowers, so it is important to maintain those plants for future generations. (3)	9	
	☐ The appropriate growing area is by the creek, so the plants may not be able to be relocated. (3)		
	☐ The plants are already in a "rural village," so farming is appropriate to the context. (3)		
	Remedies: abatement		
	☐ The severity of the children's injuries suggests abatement is appropriate. (3)	6	
	☐ There has been a single incident of injury within five years, which suggests abatement is not necessary. (3)		
	Remedies: defenses: laches		
	☐ The neighbors waited five years to file suit, which means the plants and the garden were well-established. (3)	6	
	☐ The risk, however, may be different over time because there are new varieties and the toxicity varies. (3)		
Concl.:		6	
	Total		

Mean Score for sample law student groups: 137

Sample Answer to Sorcerer's Flower Hypothetical

The Helleborus plants may create a private nuisance. Private nuisance generally has a short statute of limitations, such as two to three years. There is an exception for continuing nuisances, which reset the clock, although in some jurisdictions this will limit remedies to only equitable ones.

Here, the first plants were planted five years ago, which is beyond the statute of limitations. However, the plants are self-seeding, which means there are more plants and thereby more toxicity risks with each growing season. The self-seeding should reset the clock annually via the continuing nuisance doctrine. Additionally, the plants continue to exist every day, establishing a continuing nuisance that would renew daily. Finally, the plaintiff could split the claim in two causes of action — one for the original type of plant (which may be subject to the statute of limitations), and a second for the new experimental hybrid, which was planted more recently and possibly within the statute.

If the plaintiff overcomes procedural hurdles, she will need to provide evidence to establish the prima facie case for nuisance. A private nuisance exists where there is an interference with another person's use and enjoyment of land. The interference should be either intentional and unreasonable or abnormally dangerous. In either case, the plaintiff must establish significant harm. When the case is proven, the plaintiff is entitled to damages, but injunctions and abatement remain a matter of discretion.

To establish an unreasonable interference, the plaintiff must prove that the defendant's conduct would be unreasonable as judged by the ordinary person. Unreasonableness is measured within the neighborhood context.

A number of facts support a conclusion that there was an unreasonable interference. Once children have been harmed by playing outdoors, a reasonable person would be less likely to continue to allow the children to play outdoors. Fear would cause the plaintiffs to use their property less, thus reducing its effective size and value to them. Additionally, the plaintiffs can cite specific injuries and risks of continuing injuries that result from simply being a neighbor. The plaintiffs have already had to have a hospital visit as a direct result of Greer planting the Helleborus plants.

Additionally, on a continuing basis, the toxic plants create a risk of burns, a risk that may be especially high for children who would be likely to play outside and touch natural objects. Young children likely would not understand the risk of the plants, and therefore could be injured by the existence of the traveling seeds.

Originally, the children would have had to trespass to touch the seeds, but with wind and a stream at the property boundary, the seeds will drift onto other properties and already have. These two modes of potential travel for the seeds increase the risk that the seeds may injure someone.

The defendant has planted one type of Helleborus that is known to be extremely toxic and she has planted others whose toxicity level is unknown because they are newer hybrid plants. These unknowns increase the risk. She has planted the plants near the property boundary, which makes the seeds more likely to travel outside her own property and interfere with her neighbor's land. Additionally, if children cross over the boundary, they are immediately near the toxic plants.

The facts do not suggest that there is a fence, or sign, or anything else that would warn someone of the dangers of the plants. Within the context of family homes where small children reside, toxic plants bring special risks. The plants are not particularly appropriate to the neighborhood. Unlike the situation in *Blue Ink v. Two Farms*, where the defendant constructed a gas station with bright lights in a commercial area, here Greer has created a specialized farm with toxic plants in a neighborhood where children play outdoors.

With that said, some evidence would not necessarily support a finding of an interference. There is no evidence of a change in property value, or a change in the use as a residence. The plants can be easily removed if necessary, which means it is difficult to argue that there is a permanent harm to the value or use of the property. While toxic, the plants are not fatal except by eating the roots, which is extremely unlikely. Even small children rarely dig up plants and eat the roots. The plants are only dangerous at certain limited times of the year (when seeding) and at that time still require touching. That means the plaintiffs must take an action themselves that helps to cause the injury and must do so within a very limited window of time. Finally, not all people react in the same way to the plant and many would have a minimal reaction. In this way, growing Helleborus is not particularly different from having poison ivy at the edges of a farm. All in all, the Helleborus plants show at least some level of interference, but it may not be a significant level.

The plaintiffs must also establish that there are significant harms that result from the alleged interference. Here, the Helleborus plants bring with them a risk of health impacts, including burns, which place immediate neighbors at risk. Indeed, there are already injuries that have resulted from the plant seeds. These injuries were significant enough to require a hospital visit. Additionally, after the hospital visit, the injuries required a long recovery period and extended care. These harms are amplified by the continuing risk of further exposure. At least one type of the plants is very toxic, and the point of Greer's work is to experiment with plants whose toxicity level is unknown. Thus, more than one type of the plants may be toxic.

These harms are again amplified by the existence of the garden at the edge of the property where water and wind are likely to move the seeds, exposing the neighbors to the plants. Comparatively, these injuries and risks of future injuries are significant. For example, in *Pestey v. Cushman*, the court found a nuisance when the plaintiffs only cited repeatedly waking at night due to smells, but did not note any injury requiring hospitalization.

Greer can maintain that there has been no permanent injury in the situation to date. Additionally, having learned about the toxicity of the plants, her neighbors will be more careful in watching their children in the future and the children should now know better than to touch the plants. Additionally, with lots of varieties, many of the varieties should do the children no harm at all if touched, thus reducing the risk of injury in the future even if the children did touch the plants again. Finally, the toxic variety is only toxic by touch during the seeding period, which is a very limited time of the year, so most of the time there is zero risk. Although there are these limitations to the risk, given that the children have been injured, it is likely that the court would find a significant harm.

As an alternative to proving that a harm is unreasonable, the plaintiff can argue that the land use is an abnormally dangerous one. Here, Helleborus plants create a risk of important health impacts, including burns, which place immediate neighbors at risk. Wind and water make sure that this risk moves out into surrounding properties as the seeds move. It is unlikely that the risk would remain contained on Greer's property alone given that the seeds can be airborne. Greer has planted one variety that is known to be extremely toxic and she is experimenting with hybrids that may also be toxic. She has placed toxic plants at the edge of her property, which encourages the seeds to spread and therefore increases the risk of injury, which may include hospitalization just from touching the seeds.

With that said, it does take quite a bit of exposure to cause harm. You must touch the seeds a lot to create the toxic reaction. Most people do not spend extensive amounts of time touching random seeds outside. Additionally, Helleborus plants are hardly unusual in being toxic to humans. Many types of plants, including houseplants, are highly toxic if consumed or if one certain part of the plant is touched. The reaction that occurred in this situation is not particularly worse than a bad case of poison ivy. It is possible, but unlikely, that a court would find that growing the Helleborus plants is abnormally dangerous. Given, however, that the court is likely to conclude that there is an unreasonable interference and a significant harm, the court is likely to find that there is a nuisance. In such a case, the court would compensate the plaintiffs.

However, there is an affirmative defense that Greer may raise: unclean hands. The unclean hands defense requires similar conduct from the plaintiff that has damaged the defendant. The flowers now grow on the plaintiff's property as well. And this has been true for a number of years. The plaintiffs have not only not removed the plants, but in fact, have been enjoying their beautiful flowers. Finally, all of the plants self-seed, so the plaintiffs' plants would be sending their seed back to Greer's land on the other side of the creek. In this situation, the plaintiffs did not understand the toxicity of the plants or the risk of injury until very recently. However, the test for unclean hands does not require knowledge, only similar conduct and injury. Given that the plaintiffs have been growing the flowers on their own property cooperatively for years, the court should conclude that there were unclean hands.

In terms of equitable remedies, the plaintiff is likely to ask for abatement, because only the removal of all of the plants would be effective given their self-seeding nature. In deciding whether to issue an abatement order, the court will consider the seriousness of the injury to the plaintiff's rights. Here, the plaintiff's family members were injured enough to require a hospital visit and ongoing care, which suggests a serious injury. On the other hand, there is no permanent damage, which limits the seriousness of the injury. Finally, the children are unlikely to do this again, so the injury may be a one-time occurrence, which argues in favor of viewing the injury as less serious.

If the plaintiffs seek an injunction, the court has discretion even on finding a nuisance to decide whether or not to issue the injunction. The court considers a variety of factors related to the plaintiff, the defendant, and also the larger community. The court may consider such things as impact on the community, the benefit of the land use to the public, the impact on the defendant's property interests, and the benefit to the plaintiff of issuing the injunction. Here, Greer is carrying out important work that is scientific. Her work is related to maintaining rare and heirloom flowers, so not just any flowers will do. Her work, as such, will involve the healthy biodiversity of the planet. Society benefits from the work that Greer does. Additionally, flowers are aesthetically pleasing, and society benefits from the availability of a variety of flowers. Greer has not intentionally chosen the boundary of her property, but instead put the plants in the area where they are most likely to thrive — beside the creek in the shade. In light of this, it may not be feasible to allow Greer to continue her work, but to move the plants more toward the center of her property. Greer has already chosen a "rural village" for her work, so she has already intentionally moved her work away from population centers such as cities or suburbs. She has chosen an appropriate context. On the other hand, without the injunction the risk to neighbors, and particularly children, will continue. If the plant seeds move across the village, that risk will grow and at some point, the process may be very difficult to stop. This risk, however, seems less interesting in light of the sheer number of wild plants and ordinary garden flowers that are quite toxic. Given the value of her research and the commonness of toxic plants, a court would likely refuse to issue an injunction.

Additionally, Greer would argue that the plaintiffs committed laches, because they waited for five years before filing the claim. That was five years of growing time and a significant amount of research time, which would be lost if the plants were destroyed and the research discontinued. If the plaintiffs protested earlier, Greer may have relocated herself before investing five years of research time and funding. These factors suggest that Greer was substantially damaged by the delay in filing. The plaintiffs would argue that they did not actually delay if one regards the situation in terms of their awareness of the danger, which only recently presented itself with the injuries. The court would probably conclude that there was no delay given that most people do not understand the toxicity of plants in detail.

THIRTEEN

Skill Building: Adding Depth to an Analysis

Types of Useful Case Comparisons

The primer covered the basics of writing solid case comparisons. It began with the basic advice to not be conclusory. Compare facts with facts. Even better, make sure to explain why you see those facts as similar. Because it is often not fair to assume that the reader sees those facts just as you do.

Additionally, the primer suggested a variety of different ways that you can go about a useful case comparison. Here is a short version of that list:

1. In-depth analysis

   If a single case matches especially nicely with your facts, you may want to write a paragraph that gives an in-depth comparison of the facts of the two cases.

2. Duck, duck, goose

   Use examples from cases to show what is typically within the rule and to emphasize that the current case does or does not fit the pattern.

3. Parentheticals on small points

   Parentheticals are good for factual comparisons when one very specific fact is at issue — create a list of cases highlighting just one fact for each case.

4. Hyperbole

If you want to argue that your case does not fit under a legal rule, give the most extreme examples you can find of what does fall under the rule (using case examples). Then say, "Defendant's conduct here does not rise to the level ____"

5. Using law from other jurisdictions

You may wish to make a general statement and then follow it up with a string cite of parentheticals.

In writing a case brief, you should use most if not all of these methods of making case comparisons, depending on what relevant case law you have available. In an exam, on the other hand, a comparison is likely to fall solely into the first of these categories, because you often do not have access to extensive outside materials.

Case Comparisons on Exams

It is not unusual for case comparisons to be abundant during class discussions, but to pull a disappearing act when it comes to the exam. Either in the rush of time constraints or not recalling the facts of the cases effectively, students often simply omit the case comparison. Or the student might write, "This is like the baseball in *Popov v. Hayashi.*" The problem is that the student does not tell the reader why the cases are alike.

The idea of a case comparison is to help your reader see the facts of the case at hand through your lens, not their own. Ideally, a case comparison answers two key points: (1) specifically, how the hypothetical and case facts are similar, and (2) why those facts are particularly interesting, meaningful, or useful in the context of a rule.

Shaping Comparisons: Sorcerer's Flower Example

Take the Sorcerer's Flower Hypothetical, which used hellebores to create a situation of poisoning via touch. If you search case databases for nuisance cases that involve plants, you will find a large number of results. A quick scan of these cases will easily demonstrate that a plant might or might not be a nuisance, depending on the plant, as well as the context or circumstances.

It is easy to create a comparison using one of the many cases:

Example 1

The hellebores, like the tall grasses in Rodale Press v. Emmaus Borough, *were not a nuisance.*

This case comparison is appropriate in terms of the narrow facts (plants compared to plants). It is also a terrible comparison for two reasons. First, it does not say anything about the court's reasoning. Why were the plants not a nuisance in *Rodale Press*? Second, from the search, you already know that it will be easy to rebut this comparison by providing a case that says a plant can be a nuisance.

To improve the comparison, you need to add specificity about the facts.

Example 2

The hellebores are experimental plants, which, like the experimental tall grasses in Rodale Press v. Emmaus Borough, *are not a naturally occurring nuisance.*

This comparison is much more specific. There are many plants in the world; experimental plants are rare. Is it a good case comparison? No. This comparison is only useful if the court based its reasoning on the experimental nature of the plants. (The court in *Rodale Press* did not.) While Example 2 adds specificity to the facts, it still neglects the "why." There is no reasoning.

It does not help to add specificity to nonrelevant facts. You could talk about the sizes of the two properties. The hellebores are planted on a small piece of realty with a family home; the tall grasses grow on acres of property owned by a publishing corporation. How do you decide what facts to highlight? It goes back to the "why" that was missing from the first comparison example above. You must answer the why to be persuasive. Should you talk about the sizes of the two properties? To answer the question, you ask whether that fact was important to the court in making its decision.

That means, to make a good comparison, you need:

- A specific fact
- That is relevant (i.e., one that is persuasive to the court)
- That is the same for both cases
- And the court's conclusion has to be the one you want. (On the exam, this matters only so you can make a comparison to support both sides and fully develop your argument.)

Example 3

In Rodale Press v. Emmaus Borough, *the court concluded that an experimental area of tall grasses that was useful was not a nuisance within the meaning of a weed control ordinance. In coming to this decision, the court extensively reviewed the many social benefits for the environment of the experiment. Similarly, the hellebores are both ornamental and a part of a scientific experiment; the plants are useful to society, which suggests that they are not a nuisance.*

Example 3 provides a specific comparison of the facts: two useful and experimental plants, but also adds the court's emphasis on social benefit (i.e., the plants' usefulness) as a main reason why the plants were not a nuisance. Example 3 is much more persuasive as a case comparison.

Courts do not typically simply list the facts and choose an answer. Some facts are given more attention than others. Some are ignored entirely and never make it into the court's opinion. The court focuses on the facts that it regards as determinative for the issue at hand and generally says something about why those facts are interesting or useful. Your job in making a case comparison is to do the same. Tell the reader why the fact is interesting or useful.

QUICK EXERCISE

Skill: Making Effective Case Comparisons

How much time have you actually spent making case comparisons on paper? Probably not a lot. Maybe you have written a couple in legal writing class. Doing this correctly is a skill that can be developed by practicing. So you need some practice. Continue using the Sorcerer's Flower Hypothetical. Go to your favorite system for searching case law. Run a search (all jurisdictions) based on one of the other key facts in the hypothetical: the plants are poisonous. Search "nuisance and poison." You will get numerous results. Pick a few of these cases. Skim them quickly and then write a comparison with the Sorcerer's Flower Hypothetical facts. By narrowing the search to poison, you have a specific and relevant fact that is likely to be present in both cases. (Ignore any cases that mention poison only in passing, rather than having it as a fact.) Remember the list of useful case comparisons. You want a pair of specific, relevant facts, and a "why" for the court's reasoning. By narrowing the search to poison, you have a specific and relevant fact (and one you can skim for quickly). Your job is to find a "why" for the court's reasoning.

FOURTEEN

Public Nuisance and Extra Practice with Private Nuisance

Rules of Public Nuisance

Public nuisance encompasses a broad number of claims and is often said to elude "precise definition." The common theme is a substantial interference with a right common to the public. Public nuisance does not require that the interference come from use of private property. In other words, one could create a public nuisance on public property.

The right common to the public may be defined in two ways. First, there is a common right to such basic things as public health, safety, peace, comfort, and convenience. Additionally, there is a common right to all public property, and thus a nuisance occurs when there is interference with common access. Thus, public nuisance includes interference with public places or with the rights or well-being of an entire community.

Because the claim is so broad, when courts examine the alleged interference, they fit the inquiry to the circumstances and consider a variety of factors. Factors include the reasonableness and nature of the activity and whether it is fitted to the context, as well as the harm created and the nature of the right impinged.

Public nuisances may be either intentional or negligent in some jurisdictions, but others require that the defendant act knowingly. In either case, the defendant's actions must be the cause of the harm. Additionally, the defendant should have actual or constructive notice of the problematic activity.

Typically, governments bring public nuisance claims on behalf of the impacted community. An individual can, however, bring a public nuisance claim in some circumstances. The general requirement is that the plaintiff has a peculiar or special injury. Some jurisdictions note that the injury must be different in kind or type rather than just degree. Other jurisdictions will allow a claim based on degree, provided that the difference in degree is marked.

Finally, there are some activities or structures that are designated as nuisances per se. These require no proof of the harm or the context, but are nuisances under any circumstances and in any location. These are generally defined by common law or statute and include such activities as prostitution, operation of a brothel, and structures blocking rivers or roadways. The unique nature of nuisances per se means that proving the existence of the structure or activity is sufficient to establish the nuisance.

Outline of Rules for Public Nuisance

I. Public nuisance

  A. Clarify: definition: Public nuisance is a broad concept with no "precise definition."

  B. Test

    1. Is there substantial interference with a right common to the public?

      a. Rights common to the public

        i. There are public rights to health, safety, peace, comfort, and convenience.

        ii. There is a common right to all publicly designated open property.

      b. Interference

        i. The court will fit the inquiry to the circumstances.

        ii. Factors

          1. Reasonableness and nature of the activity

          2. Whether the activity is fitted to the context

          3. Harm created

          4. Nature of the right impinged

        iii. There is no requirement that interference come from use of private property.

2. Mindset
   a. Split:
      i. Courts require action that is intentional or negligent in some jurisdictions.
      ii. Other jurisdictions require knowing action.
3. The defendant must be the cause of the harm.
4. Notice
   a. The defendant should have actual or constructive notice of the problem.
5. Exception: nuisances per se are defined by statute or common law and do not have to pass this test.

C. Standing
   1. Governments may bring claims on behalf of a community.
   2. Individuals have standing if they have a peculiar or special injury.
      a. Split:
         i. Some jurisdictions require that the injury be different in kind or type rather than just degree.
         ii. Other jurisdictions allow a claim based on degree, provided that the difference in degree is marked.

Renaissance Faire Hypothetical

Time to read and write your answer: one hour.

All their other business ventures (gym, real estate, and restaurant) having failed, the Browns have decided to start a renaissance fair, Olde World.

Olde World is located just outside of Las Vegas in a semi-developed area with mostly houses and a few businesses. Olde World, which has been operational for three years, contains a collection of artisans who practice traditional trades such as broom making, wood carving, and outdoor blacksmithing, along with many other employees who dress in costume and fill the streets to create the medieval atmosphere.

The blacksmithing operation is conducted in a largely traditional fashion — it involves a hot, charcoal-burning fire that continues throughout the park's opening hours. At night, the fire is not put out entirely, but rather "stoked" to continue a slow burn through the night, making morning start-up easier. The fire is in a small cottage with a short chimney — in the traditional style — which stops at about seven feet. The blacksmithing process produces voluminous amounts of smoke and airborne ash (with occasional sparks) from the burning charcoal. While there are relatively few active blacksmithing operations in Las Vegas at the moment, outdoor fires and outdoor brick ovens with open fires are, in fact, quite common, because they are a part of local Native American culture, which has been imported into the suburbs.

One of Olde World's closest neighbors is Evangelical Church (notably not fans of the Browns' lifestyle and beliefs). Evangelical Church is located immediately west of the park and within 50 linear feet of the blacksmith shop. The Evangelical Church pastor is desperate to shut down Olde World. He says the smoke is noxious and it is giving his buildings a gray cast due to the ash blowing against the building and creating smudges. The pastor accounts his monetary damages to be $5,000 per year for pressure washing his white building, and an "unimaginable" amount for the metaphorical tarnishing of the church.

Locate all legal issues and analyze. Do not address trespass.

Scoring Rubric for Renaissance Faire Hypothetical

Section			
Issue:	Does the renaissance faire create a private nuisance that interferes with the church property?	6	
Rules:	**Basic rules** ☐ Nuisance requires an invasion of the use and enjoyment of land. (3) ☐ The plaintiff must show significant harm. (3) ☐ In Restatement jurisdictions, the act must be "intentional and unreasonable" or "abnormally dangerous." (3) ☐ The defendant must be the cause of the interference. (3) ☐ Nuisances are evaluated contextually. Consider "all of the circumstances of location," along with effect and impact on neighboring businesses. (3)	15	
	Remedies rules ☐ Compensation is automatic if the prima facie case is proven, but an injunction is discretionary. (3)	3	
	Factors for injunction ☐ Impacts on the community, such as loss of jobs (3) ☐ Impacts on the defendant's property interests (3) ☐ Benefits of stopping use to the plaintiff (3) ☐ Benefit of use/product to the public (3)	12	
App.:	**Causation** Yes ☐ There is no evidence of another source for the smoke or ash, so causation is logical. (3) ☐ Discoloration is a natural result of ash touching an object. (3)	6	
	No ☐ The weather/wind pattern would go away from the church, which makes causation less clear, despite the proximity. (3)	6	

Continued

Continued

App.:	☐ Others do build fires in the area, so the faire is not the only possible source, even if it is more likely due to proximity. (3)		
	Significant harm		
	Yes		
	☐ The discoloration has caused economic damages due to the need to wash the building, so there is a specific and quantifiable harm. (3)	18	
	☐ The discoloration is to a white building so it is very visible. (3)		
	☐ The cost of cleaning is $5,000 per year, which is not insignificant as an expense. (3)		
	☐ Sparks create a constant danger of fire, which is a danger to the health and well-being of people in the area and people within the church. (3)		
	☐ Continuing the fires at night means that sparks may fly and catch fire when no one is present at the church to notice the problem. (3)		
	☐ Fifty feet is not far away, which means that the church is quite close to the sparks, increasing the risk of a fire. (3)		
	No		
	☐ The harm can be remedied by annual washing, which suggests the harm is minimal; annually might be a reasonable washing time anyway. (3)	6	
	☐ The normal presence of open fires in this area may suggest that this is an expected activity and therefore the danger is not abnormal in this context. (3)		
	Abnormally dangerous		
	Yes		
	☐ Sparks create a risk of fire, which, given the potential loss of life and property, is abnormally dangerous. (3)	15	
	☐ Ordinary businesses do not produce sparks, which increases the risk of fire when this business is compared to others. (3)		
	☐ Businesses that do create fire risks (factories, etc.) would normally be forced to operate away from residential areas; this business looks more like those and less like a neighborhood business. (3)		

App.:	□ The desert context (with high winds and low water) amplifies the risk of fire from a flying spark. (3)		
	□ The sparks are low to the ground, which increases the chance of hitting flammable materials before the sparks go out. (3)		
	No		
	□ This is a desert, so there is plenty of dry sand and rocks where sparks will just burn out and nothing will catch fire. (3)	3	
	Intentional and unreasonable invasion of use and enjoyment		
	Yes		
	□ The pastor describes the smoke as "noxious," which suggests that the smoke/odor is making the outdoor areas uncomfortable for use. (3)	12	
	□ The sparks are a fire hazard, which puts the safety of the building at risk at any time, reducing the comfortable and quiet use of the property. (3)		
	□ The damage from discoloration is a bad metaphor for a church (which probably wants to give a message of hope and reassurance), and this makes the area even less comfortable. (3)		
	□ It is a semi-developed area, with a lot of residences, which suggests that Olde World is out of place. (3)		
	No		
	□ It is Las Vegas, which may mean that absolutely nothing is out of context. This area is semi-developed, which may mean there are other unexpected businesses. (3)	6	
	□ Other open fires in the neighborhood suggest that Olde World is not out of place for having one. (3)		
	Remedies		
	□ An injunction does not have to shut down Olde World, the court could just shut down the blacksmith part of the faire. (3)	12	
	□ The faire has some social utility because it creates jobs, as well as entertainment, but it is not critical (like a hospital or a school). (3)		
	□ Olde World offers a recreational opportunity, which is useful to the community and beyond because Vegas is a tourist destination. (3)		

Continued

Continued

App.:	☐ Olde World employs local people, which means it provides income to local people and supports the local tax base. (3)		
Concl.:		6	
Issue:	Did the same situation create a public nuisance? Is there a private right to sue for public nuisance?	6	
Rules:	☐ A public nuisance requires substantial interference with a right common to the public. (3) ☐ Rights common to the public include public health, safety, peace, comfort, and convenience. (3) ☐ Claims are evaluated contextually, given the nature of the activity. (3) ☐ A plaintiff must prove substantial harm. (3) ☐ Jurisdictional split: The mental state requirement may be intentional or negligent, or merely knowing. (3) ☐ The defendant must cause the harm. (3) ☐ The defendant should have actual or constructive notice of the problem. (3) ☐ Individuals may sue for public nuisance if they prove a special injury. (3) ☐ Jurisdictional split: Some courts allow a claim based on a more severe injury than other people, while other courts require the injury to be different in kind or type rather than just degree. (3)	27	
App.:	**Identify a right common to the public** ☐ Fire is a danger to public safety. (3) ☐ The smoke is a danger to public health. (3) **Unreasonable interference** Yes ☐ The smoke is "noxious," which impacts the use of neighboring properties. (3) ☐ Sparks are a fire hazard, which puts the safety of the public at risk. (3) ☐ The discoloration of buildings negatively impacts the appearance of the neighborhood. (3)	6 12	

App.:	☐ It is a semi-developed area, with a lot of residences, which suggests Olde World is out of place. (3)		
	No		
	☐ It is Las Vegas, which may mean that nothing is out of context. Additionally, this area is semi-developed, which may mean there are other unexpected businesses. (3)	6	
	☐ Other open fires in the neighborhood suggest that Olde World is not out of place for having one. (3)		
	Causation		
	Yes		
	☐ No evidence was given of another source, so causation is logical. (3)	6	
	☐ Discoloration is a natural result of ash. (3)		
	No		
	☐ The weather/wind pattern would go away from church, which makes causation less clear, despite the proximity. (3)	6	
	☐ Others do build fires in the area, so the faire is not the only possible source. (3)		
	Harm		
	Yes		
	☐ Discoloration has caused economic damage due to the need to wash the building, which provides a specific and quantifiable harm. (3)	9	
	☐ The harm is $5,000 per year for a single building, which would be multiplied over a neighborhood. (3)		
	☐ Sparks create a constant danger of fire, which is a danger to the health and well-being of people in the area. (3)		
	No		
	☐ The harm can be remedied by annual washing, which suggests the harm is minimal. (3)	9	
	☐ The normal presence of open fires in this area may suggest that this is an expected activity and therefore the danger is not abnormal in this context. (3)		
	☐ It is unlikely that discoloration happens very far from Olde World because the ash would float to the ground, so that would limit the impact and cost of cleaning. (3)		

Continued

Continued

App.:	Intent		
	Intentional		
	Specific		
	☐ The business would have no reason to intend to create the smoke in the neighborhood, so there is no specific intent. (3)	3	
	General intent		
	☐ The business does intend that the blacksmith operation be a part of the business, so there is a general intent. (3)	3	
	Negligent		
	Yes		
	☐ There is no evidence of anything done to prevent harms to neighbors, so there is no evidence of care with operations. Care might not be expected for the ash, but it should be for the sparks given the risk of fires. (3)	3	
	No		
	☐ There is no evidence that the blacksmithing part of the business operates in anything other than the standard way. Smoke and sparks are natural to the process of blacksmithing. (3)	3	
	Notice		
	Yes		
	☐ Smoke and sparks will be visible to the operators of the business. (3)	6	
	☐ A reasonable business owner would notice smoke and sparks and would note the fire danger, if only for their own business. (3)		
	No		
	☐ There is no specific evidence of a complaint made by neighbors or any attempt to notify the business. (3)	6	
	☐ There is no testimony that the business owners know of the problem. (3)		
	Special Injury		
	Different Type		
	☐ The fire danger is greater for the church, so it may have a different type of injury than the rest of the public, who only deal with the smoke. (3)	3	

App.:	Degree ☐ Discoloration is likely strongest near the facility, so the church may have a more severe problem than the business's other neighbors. (3)	3	
Concl.:		6	
	Total		

Mean Score for sample law student groups: 136

Sample Answer for Renaissance Faire Hypothetical

The Browns may be responsible for a private nuisance for (1) smoke and ash and (2) stray sparks. A private nuisance requires an interference with use and enjoyment of land with a showing of significant harm. The interference must be either intentional and unreasonable or abnormally dangerous. The first question is whether there was a significant harm. Significant harm is more than slight inconvenience or petty annoyance. (1) Regarding the smoke and ash, these cause discoloration to the church, which will require cleanup and cause the church to incur costs. Additionally, the smoke and ash that cause discoloration may also detract from the neighborhood's atmosphere of health and well-being, which may decrease property values as well as use and enjoyment. On the other hand, there is little information to establish how much smoke is released or how continuous the interference is, which would impact the significance of the harm. (2) Regarding the stray sparks, the sparks create the possibility of significant harm at any time because the sparks can cause a fire that may damage or destroy the church. On the other hand, this is only a risk of future harm, not a current harm. With respect to the ash and smoke and the stray sparks there is significant harm, or at least the potential for it.

The second question is whether there is intentional and unreasonable interference. Intention, here, is general, not specific, intent. The Browns intend to operate the faire because they have created it and run the business, which gives them a general intent to run the blacksmithing operation. The smoke, sparks, and ash are natural by-products of running that operation, and therefore there is a general intent to create those.

With respect to unreasonable interference, reasonableness is measured by the context of the neighborhood. The neighborhood is residential, which means that there should be no industrial land uses within the area. Without industrial land uses, there should not be smoke, ash, or sparks. Given that these would be odd in the neighborhood, they are more likely to be unreasonable for this location. The smoke damage is nothing like the scale of that in *Madison v. Ducktown*, but modern standards for a residential neighborhood are very different from a rural area at the turn of the twentieth century. The land in this area is also a desert, which means that all buildings are more subject to fire risk, which is especially problematic in a residential area. The smoke, ash, and sparks are unreasonable in this residential neighborhood. On the other hand, this is Las Vegas, and the city is just nuts, so there is a fair argument that nothing is out of place in Vegas.

With respect to abnormally dangerous, this is defined by a significant risk to life or the potential for serious injury. The smoke and ash are not inherently dangerous, but they carry with them the risk of sparks. Additionally, the sparks create a risk of fire, which can cause death or serious injury, and is a particular risk in a desert area. The sparks are inherently abnormally dangerous, at least in a desert residential area.

Because there are significant harms, and potentially interference that is either abnormally dangerous or intentional and unreasonable, there is likely a successful cause of action for nuisance for the church.

The Browns may have also created a public nuisance. A public nuisance is a broader category than private nuisance, incorporating general risks to public health and well-being. Courts define a public nuisance as an unreasonable interference with a right common to the general public. States usually bring the claim through the attorney general, but individuals can sue if they have a special injury. The first question is what right common to the general public applies here. The Browns have created smoke, ash, and sparks that are traveling some distance through the air, and bringing with them the risk of property damage, fire, and serious health consequences (injury or death from fire). Thus, the Browns may have endangered either air quality generally or public health.

The second question is whether there is an unreasonable interference. An unreasonable interference is determined contextually. Here, the Browns generate smoke, ash, and sparks, creating the potential for human injury or death. The risk of injury or death creates an unreasonable interference.

The third question is whether the church has a special injury. A special injury is an injury distinct from the injury to the public, usually not just in scale. The church members have the same risks as any other members of the public, but the church members may have a risk of fire due to proximity, whereas for most of the public, it will just be smoke and ash. The church members may have a special injury if they can prove a significantly different level of risk for fire due to the proximity. Because there is an unreasonable interference with the right to public health and good air quality, there is a public nuisance.

Grading Notes Regarding the Renaissance Faire Hypothetical

Making sure you are connecting facts to rules is an ongoing process for most students. Recheck this regularly. Here is a look at how it could go awry or work properly for one rule, the abnormally dangerous activities rule, for nuisance in the Renaissance Fair Hypothetical.

Rule—Abnormally dangerous activities create nuisances.

Relevant facts—Neighbor's blacksmithing creates sparks that cross the boundary on the wind. Only rarely do the sparks ever travel from neighbor's blacksmithing operation over to plaintiff's property.

Answer one—The neighbor's blacksmithing is a nuisance because it is an abnormally dangerous activity.

Score—No points. This is a legal conclusion. It assumes that blacksmithing is an abnormally dangerous activity. This answer does not prove that blacksmithing is an abnormally dangerous activity.

Answer two—(1) Neighbor's blacksmithing may create a nuisance. (2) Blacksmithing could be an unreasonably dangerous activity. (3) Blacksmithing creates sparks that cross the boundary on the wind. (4) On the other hand, in this case, the sparks only "rarely" travel across the property line. (5) It is unclear whether the facts given are sufficient to demonstrate an abnormally dangerous activity.

Score—Very few points. Sentences (1) and (2) serve as an introduction and foreshadow the conclusion of "maybe." Sentences (3) and (4) essentially recite the facts back. They do not apply the rule to the facts. The phrase "on the other hand" organizes the two facts into the opposing sides. That is the most reasoning that has been applied in this answer. The final sentence (5) gives a conclusion (maybe).

Answer three   Sparks from a neighboring property create a risk of fire. Sparks that travel on the wind elevate this risk even more. A risk of fire is dangerous to neighbors as well as public safety more generally, because fires endanger both property and personal safety. The airborne sparks make blacksmithing an abnormally dangerous activity. On the other hand, the sparks rarely travel across the property line, making the risk of fire a rare occurrence. While the risk is not happening regularly, the height of the risk (significant property damage and personal injury) remains each time a spark crosses. Even if the occurrence is rare, the potential risk is substantial and directly linked to the blacksmithing operation. For this reason, the neighbor's blacksmithing is a nuisance because it is an abnormally dangerous activity.

Score   Good. This answer connects the facts (sparks that fly on the wind) to the rule (abnormally dangerous things are automatically nuisances).

A Note About the Conclusions in These Samples

Answer three will score more highly than answer two because answer three chose one side rather than concluding "maybe." Because professors want to develop your analysis skills, they tend to write questions that are as evenly divided between the two sides as possible. In such instances, it does not matter which conclusion you choose at the end, so long as it is well-supported by your arguments. This is because there is not a "right answer."

With that said, some professors will write one-sided questions (or will write a single one-sided question out of three in an exam). Students may have difficulty recognizing the one-sided questions and the evenly matched questions. Therefore, the best strategy is to argue both sides as best you can with the facts you have, evaluating defenses and rebuttals. In the end, however, pick a side for the conclusion. If the professor created an equally weighted question, it would not matter which side you pick. If the question was one-sided, then you would be penalized for either an incorrect choice or a "maybe" answer. Therefore, your best strategy is to pick a side rather concluding "maybe."

Personal Amusement Park Hypothetical

Time to read and write your answer: one hour.

BlanK, a celebrated rap artist and multimillionaire, purchased a 500-acre farm in Virginia farming country to create a personal playground. BlanK's playground included an exotic animal zoo (none endangered, all legal), luxury swimming pools, and a mini amusement park built along the ridge of the Appalachian Mountains. One of the main features is a train that weaves through the entire enterprise, allowing BlanK and his guests to quickly access the estate's many entertainment features.

BlanK has been exploring alternative fuels (not necessarily more environmentally friendly, just more entertaining) for his train. Recently, his engineer developed a biofuel from a mixture of Kudzu and moonshine. Unfortunately, the mixture produces Z3 (a new chemical, not the BMW, regrettably) as a byproduct during the production process. The engineer does not know much about Z3, but he knows that it reacts with water to create an acid form that disintegrates other compounds. Also, he determines that Z3 is very similar to PGY, which is known to have connections to pancreatic cancer (at a rate of 1 per 10,000 with skin exposure). The engineer stored the Z3 in barrels, which he moved to the more remote areas of the farm.

Yesterday, Hurricane Andrew landed on the Virginia coast, pushing high winds and rains across the state. BlanK's farm was hit hard with both high winds and flood-level waters. The high water reached both his animals and the Z3 storage, spreading exotic animal manure and Z3 along the farm and down to two neighboring farms and to the James River. During the commotion, one poisonous lizard, Ralph, escaped and took up residence in the neighbor's garage.

Neither the EPA nor OSHA has set any standards for exposure to Z3, which has been previously unknown.

Locate all legal issues and analyze; discuss policy choices where appropriate. Do not consider trespass.

Scoring Rubric for Personal Amusement Park Hypothetical

Section			
Issue:	Is the personal amusement park a private nuisance to the neighbors?	6	
Rules:	**Basic rules** ☐ Nuisance requires an invasion of the use and enjoyment of land. (3) ☐ The plaintiff must show significant harm. (3) ☐ In Restatement jurisdictions, the act must be "intentional and unreasonable" or "abnormally dangerous." (3) ☐ The defendant must be the cause of the interference. (3) ☐ Nuisances are evaluated contextually. Consider "all of the circumstances of location," along with the impact on neighboring businesses. (3)	15	
	Remedies rules ☐ Compensation is automatic if the prima facie case is proven, but an injunction is discretionary. (3)	3	
	Factors for injunction ☐ Impacts on the community, such as loss of jobs (3) ☐ Impacts on defendant's property interests (3) ☐ Benefits of stopping use to the plaintiff (3) ☐ Benefit of use/product to the public (3)	12	
App.:	**Causation** *Yes* ☐ This is a new substance, so we are sure of its origin. (3)	3	
	No ☐ The manure smell is likely common in farm country, so that part is less clearly caused by the park. (3)	3	

App.:	**Significant harm**		
	Yes		
	☐ Exotic animal manure is smelly. (3)	15	
	☐ Exotic animal manure may contain germs distinct from those at other farms. (3)		
	☐ Z3 leakage requires a cleanup on the property. (3)		
	☐ Z3 is similar to another chemical that is toxic, so it may be a risk to the neighbors. (3)		
	☐ Z3 is similar to another chemical that is a carcinogen, so this increases the likelihood of future harm. (3)		
	No		
	☐ There is no current evidence of medical issues from Z3. (3)	9	
	☐ There is no clear evidence that Z3 has the same toxicity as the similar chemical. (3)		
	☐ There is no evidence that Z3 is a carcinogen, so there may be no risk at all. (3)		
	Abnormally dangerous		
	Yes		
	☐ Exotic animal manure is not an ordinary risk of community living. (3)	9	
	☐ Exposure to chemical spills is not an ordinary community risk. (3)		
	☐ Carcinogens and chemical experiments are more than the ordinary business risks. (3)		
	No		
	☐ Manure is not unusual as a farm risk due to germs. (3)	9	
	☐ Z3's risks are unclear, and it may not have the toxic qualities of the other chemical. (3)		
	☐ It is not clear that Z3 has same carcinogenic properties. (3)		
	Intentional and unreasonable invasion of use and enjoyment (contextual)		
	Yes		
	☐ A chemical leak is not normal in a farming community. (3)	12	

Continued

Continued

App.:	☐ Experimentation with chemicals is not normal in a farming community. (3)		
	☐ Manure is ordinary in a farming community, but not exotic animal manure, which has other risks of different types of germs. (3)		
	☐ Exposure to a potentially cancer-causing spill is not normal in a farming community. (3)		
	No		
	☐ Manure is common in a farming community. (3)	6	
	☐ Chemical pesticides and fertilizers are normal on farms, and some of those are toxic, so a toxic chemical is not out of place. (3)		
	Remedies		
	☐ A personal amusement park has limited social value. (3)	9	
	☐ The personal amusement park employs people, such as the engineer who is experimenting. (3)		
	☐ An injunction could require less than a full shutdown; it could require testing of Z3's safety and procedures for preventing future spills. (3)		
Concl.:		6	
Issue:	Is the personal amusement park a public nuisance?	6	
Rules:	☐ A public nuisance requires substantial interference with a right common to the public. (3)	27	
	☐ Rights common to the public include public health, safety, peace, comfort, and convenience. (3)		
	☐ Claims are evaluated contextually, given the nature of the activity. (3)		
	☐ A plaintiff must prove substantial harm. (3)		
	☐ Jurisdictional split: The mental state requirement may be intentional or negligent, or merely knowing. (3)		
	☐ The defendant must cause the harm. (3)		
	☐ The defendant should have actual or constructive notice of the problem. (3)		
	☐ Individuals may sue for public nuisance if they prove a special injury. (3)		

	☐ Jurisdictional split: Some courts allow a claim based on a more severe injury than other people, while other courts require the injury to be different in kind or type rather than just degree. (3)		
App.:	**_Identify right common to the public_**		
	Yes		
	☐ There is a risk to public safety from the toxin and spill. (3)	6	
	☐ There is a risk to public health from the toxin. (3)		
	_No_		
	☐ The project risks are guesses based on the risks from another chemical, so there is no clear evidence of risk. (3)	3	
	Unreasonable interference		
	☐ Z3 is potentially dangerous to humans, which impacts the use of neighboring properties. (3)	9	
	☐ A chemical spill limits land usage and interferes with the ability to safely use land. (3)		
	☐ It is a farm, so chemical experimentation is out of place. (3)		
	_No_		
	☐ The chemical spill is an invasion but may not be toxic. (3)	6	
	☐ Manure is ordinary in a farming community. (3)		
	Causation		
	Yes		
	☐ The new chemical has no other source, so it must originate from the park. (3)	6	
	☐ The exotic animals are unusual, and there is no evidence of another source for the manure. (3)		
	_No_		
	☐ Weather may have been a superseding event. But for the unusual weather, there would not have been a spill. (3)	3	
	Harm		
	Yes		
	☐ Cleanup will require funds. (3)	9	
	☐ If Z3 is as toxic as similar chemicals, then there is a risk to the public. Additionally, the chemical is now flowing in the James River. (3)		

Continued

Continued

App.:	☐ If Z3 is as toxic as similar chemicals, then there is a risk of cancer for the public. (3)		
	No		
	☐ The risks of Z3 are unclear, so there may be no harms. (3)	3	
	Intent		
	Intentional		
	Specific		
	☐ The engineer intentionally experimented to create a new chemical. (3)	6	
	☐ The spill was caused by weather, so there was no intent that the chemical escape. (3)		
	General intent		
	☐ The park is using the chemical as a part of their operations. (3)	3	
	Negligent		
	Yes		
	☐ There is no evidence of anything done to prevent harms to neighbors, so there is no evidence of care with operations. (3)	3	
	No		
	☐ Weather may be a superseding event or an act of god that made normal care not work to contain the chemical. (3)	3	
	Notice		
	Yes		
	☐ The engineer was aware of Z3 being similar to the toxic chemical. (3)	3	
	No		
	☐ The storm was not expected to cause a spill. (3)	3	

App.:	**Special injury**		
	Different type of injury		
	☐ The nearest neighbors have direct exposure when others would have only indirect exposure. (3)	3	
	Degree		
	☐ Exposure to the chemical will be highest nearest the park. (3)	3	
Concl.:		6	
	Total		

Mean Score for sample law student groups: 149

FIFTEEN

Skill Building: Understanding the Chronology of a Case

What Happens When There Are Sub-issues?

The purpose of this chapter is to give you a framework for organizing multiple sub-issues related to a single cause of action such as nuisance. This framework is important because using it will place information where your reader expects to find it. In other words, this is the order that courts use, so judges and professors expect to find information in this order. That can mean more points for you.

Additionally, this framework can be helpful when you feel overwhelmed by the number of sub-issues in a hypothetical. Sometimes it is hard for students to know where to get started. If you have a framework to quickly drop issues into, you can avoid both panicking and staring at the blank page.

Nuisance law works as a great example here because it can be a bit complicated. Put another way, there are lots of opportunities for sub-issues in a hypothetical.

There are public nuisances, private nuisances, and even statutory nuisances in some instances. If you narrow down to private nuisance, it does not really get any better.

Private nuisance law at its heart encompasses the interference with use and enjoyment of property. But nuisance law also will contain a variety of procedural rules. Procedural rules address things like how long you can wait to bring suit (the statute of limitations). Procedural rules also explain who has standing, or a right, to sue. For example, if a home is rented, does the plaintiff need to be the owner of the home or can the renter sue?

There are also some defenses that may be relevant to a nuisance claim. Some of these are generally available in civil cases: laches, unclean hands, etc. Others are specific to the issue of nuisance: the defense of coming to a nuisance.

When it comes to remedies, nuisance is more complicated than most issues. In civil suits, there are generally two possibilities: damages and/or an injunction (usually to stop some conduct or other). Nuisance adds a third option: abatement, which is the court forcing the defendant to correct the situation, usually by removing the offensive object. An injunction usually prevents further action, whereas abatement requires corrective action. If you prove the prima facie case for nuisance, you do not just get to select the remedy you prefer. There are additional rules that determine which remedy you get.

In addition to the prima facie case, this creates a list of eight potential sub-issues. And that is a conservative list for nuisance. In some jurisdictions, there could be more due to the existence of additional procedural rules or defenses.

Sample Bad Answer

Issue:

Whether Greer created a private nuisance with the unintentional spread of her experimental flowers onto the Speedwell family's property.

Rules:

To maintain an action for private nuisance, a plaintiff must demonstrate an unreasonable interference with the use and enjoyment of land. Some jurisdictions also require a demonstration that the conduct was intentional and unreasonable or abnormally dangerous. A plaintiff may obtain an injunction, an order for abatement, and/or damages.

Application:

1. Greer may have unreasonably interfered with the Speedwell family's use and enjoyment of their property. The spread of the Helleborus seeds created toxic flowers on the Speedwell property. As a flower expert, Greer would have known of the possibility of the flowers spreading by self-seeding. The Speedwells would need to remove the plants to get rid of the risk of exposure to the poisonous seeds. Because there are poisonous plants

on the property, the Speedwells could not use those specific portions of property without removing the toxic plants. In other words, the Speedwells could not use their property without potentially encountering the poison. Finally, as a plant expert, Greer would have known of the risk of the poison and did not alert her neighbors, even when she would have seen the plants spreading to the neighboring property.

2. The Speedwells own their property and therefore can remove the plants at any time. However, the plants on Greer's property will continue to self-seed. Thus, an effective remedy to this problem would potentially require both an abatement of the plants on Greer's property and an injunction to prevent her from planting this type of plant in the future.

3. The court must balance social utility and community interests as well as the benefit to the plaintiff and the interference with the defendant landowner's rights. Greer is trying to create new breeds of plants with her experimental hybrid. The creation of a new and useful (beautiful) plant is socially useful. Her impact on the Speedwells is unfortunate, but her actions are beneficial in terms of the larger community of flower growers in the world who always want new and attractive varieties. Greer bought this property specifically so that she could do her gardening here and she is a scientific expert. The court might give damages for the burns, but not give an abatement order or injunction. The kids aren't going to touch the plants again after getting blisters.

4. You could also argue that there was no unreasonable interference with use and enjoyment, as the Speedwells were still able to use and enjoy their land as they did on the day of the eclipse. Additionally, after this incident, the Speedwells are going to keep the kids from playing with the seeds. (And the kids may have learned their lesson, anyway.) The Speedwells enjoy the beauty of the flowers, so they are still getting enjoyment from their property, and even could be considered to have unclean hands because they now own land with self-seeding poisonous plants as well. The interference was just the injury, which is unlikely to reoccur. Furthermore, as the property is located in rural Virginia, it does not seem unreasonable for Greer to plant many types of plants on her property. Finally, Greer would be aware that there is extreme variance in toxicity of the Helleborus, and she may have had reason to believe the particular Helleborus she planted were not toxic.

5. Finally, Greer planted the first Helleborus flowers five years ago. This is beyond the standard statute of limitations of three years. Even more seriously, the Speedwells knew the flowers had spread to their own land and ignored it, so they may have committed laches by recognizing the invasive plants and failing to file suit for years.

Conclusion:

The evidence suggests that Greer will be found liable for private nuisance, and the court is likely to issue an abatement order.

QUICK EXERCISE
Skill: Recognizing the Organization of a Legal Argument

To get better at organizing your arguments, it is crucial to understand the purpose — in legal terms — of each portion of an argument. Before continuing to the next section, which debriefs the bad answer, make margin notes indicating the legal purpose of each portion of the argument. You can use the discussion that follows to see how accurate you are.

Analysis of Sample Bad Answer

The application contains five numbered paragraphs. Each has at least one distinct purpose within the legal argument. Here is what each paragraph analyzes:

1. Prima facie case for interference with use and enjoyment — Speedwell's side

2. Injunction

   Abatement

3. Injunction

4. Prima facie case for interference with use and enjoyment — Greer's side

   Unclean hands defense

5. Statute of limitations

   Laches

Initially, you should have already noticed that this bad answer organized the prima facie case by the two sides, rather than considering the evidence for each rule block necessary to prove a private nuisance. Even worse, the two sides are split apart by other sub-issues. This makes it more difficult to either evaluate the evidence as a reader or to make balanced arguments as a writer. You already know how to fix the prima facie case sections — organize by rule block.

This does not fix the problems, though. There are sub-issues here not covered by the prima facie case: abatement, injunctions, the statute of limitations, laches, and the defense of unclean hands. Where should those pieces of the argument go?

An Organizational Framework for Sub-issues

The best organizational framework for sub-issues is the one that will place information where your reader expects to find it. The order that courts generally use when writing an opinion is the chronological order of how the sub-issues would be raised during the life of a case from filing of the complaint to the final disposition.

That sounds a bit formal and complicated. It is not.

When a case is filed, the first thing that happens is motions to dismiss based on procedural issues. Then there is discovery, followed by the presentation of the plaintiff's claim. The defendant attempts to rebut, if possible, through cross-examination of witnesses. Then the defendant raises distinct defenses (i.e., defenses other than just rebutting one of the elements required for the cause of action). Finally, the court considers remedies. What does that look like as a framework?

STRATEGIES FOR SUCCESS

Chronological Case Format for Organizing Sub-issues

1. Procedural sub-issues (anything that avoids the merits of the claim)
2. The prima facie case (both sides)
3. Distinct/affirmative defenses
4. Remedies
   a. Legal
   b. Equitable

Revising the Bad Answer

Here is a better organization for the bad answer, using the chronological case format:

1. Procedural

   Statute of limitations

2. Prima facie case for interference with use and enjoyment — both sides

3. Defenses

   Unclean hands
   Laches

4. Remedies

   Injunction
   Abatement

To do this accurately, the trick is to make sure that you know how to characterize sub-issues. Otherwise, you do not know how to accurately place the sub-issues within the chronological framework. As you learn rules, pay attention to the subject matter type of the rule. Is it a procedural rule? A remedies rule? A rule about the prima facie case? These are things you need to recognize in order to understand the meaning of the rules.

SIXTEEN

Adverse Possession and Trespass

Rules for Adverse Possession

Adverse possession allows a neighbor to claim title to another's real property through continued use over an extended period of time. Elements of the claim vary across jurisdictions. Additionally, courts examine many of the elements contextually, fitting the expected behaviors to claim property to the type of property being claimed (i.e., actual or continuous possession of a forest looks different from that of a house).

Although the elements vary slightly, there are a core number of basic elements present in most jurisdictions. Actual and visible possession supports a claim for adverse possession. This element contrasts with the concept of constructive possession, which might occur symbolically or in another indirect way. Actual and visible possession focuses on the claimant acting in a way that would put a reasonable owner on notice. "Continuous" requires the claimant to be in regular possession of the premises, rather than merely exhibiting intermittent activities. Possession should also be exclusive, or not shared with others, especially the original owner.

Some jurisdictions require hostile possession. Hostile, however, has two very different interpretations. Hostile possession may refer to a mental state, meaning that the claimant must understand that the property belongs to someone else and still intend to claim it. The mental state requirement then aligns with bad faith. Alternatively, hostility may be interpreted as a neutral act requirement. In other words, in this interpretation hostility is not about mental state. Hostility simply requires actions that are inconsistent with the rights of a title owner, such as someone other than the titleholder paying taxes or insuring the property.

Some jurisdictions require that the claimant act under a claim of right. The claim of right requirement can also be interpreted both as a mental state requirement and as a neutral action approach. When interpreted as a mental state requirement, claim of right aligns with good faith. It means that the claimant should be occupying property that she believes she has the right to possess. The clearest way to meet this standard is by a mistake in the location of a boundary. Alternatively, the claim of right requirement can also refer to actions rather than mental state. In this interpretation, claim of right simply means exhibiting actions consistent with an owner of a property.

Because it is possible to interpret both claim of right and hostility in two different ways, some jurisdictions have both elements, using one to refer to a mental state and the other to refer to the neutral act requirements favored by that jurisdiction.

Possession must continue until it meets the state's statute of limitations. The statutes vary in length from seven to twenty years. If the original owner ousts (evicts by words or deeds) the claimant, then the possession is interrupted. Some jurisdictions note that the possession must be uninterrupted. Logically, though, this how a statute of limitations should work in the context of possession that is required over a period of years. An interruption simply resets the clock for the statute. There is one exception to the statute of limitations requirement. One possessor may meet the required number of years by adding her possession to that of a previous possessor. Property law refers to this as "tacking." Tacking is available only where there is privity between the two possessors and both possessors meet all of the other elements independently during their time periods. Privity comes from a contractual relationship such as a sale of property or another similar property relationship such as inheriting property.

Although the list of elements varies somewhat across jurisdictions, the full list is required in all jurisdictions. That means that if a claimant fails to prove one of the elements, the adverse possession claim fails.

Finally, permission of the original owner is a defense to adverse possession. If an owner can establish that the entry occurs by permission, then that entry will not support a later claim of adverse possession.

Rules for Trespass

Trespass occurs when there is an entry onto the real property of another, causing damages to the right to exclude. The entry must be tangible, although some jurisdictions recognize particulate/microscopic entry, if it is detectable. Trespass can be intentional or unintentional. Compensatory damages are available for either, but punitive damages are sometimes awarded for intentional trespasses. Injunctions can prevent future entries if they are anticipated.

Outline of the Rules for Adverse Possession

I. Adverse possession

    A. Test: and-type test, several elements

        1. Actual and visible

            a. Actual contrasts with constructive possession.

            b. Visible means actions that would put a reasonable owner on notice.

        2. Continuous

            a. Continuous means regular possession of the premises.

            b. Continuousness is not established where there are only intermittent activities.

        3. Exclusive

            a. Exclusive means that possession is not shared with others, especially the original owner.

            b. Hostile: split

                i.   In some jurisdictions, hostile is a mental state, meaning the party must claim another's property intentionally or have bad faith.

                ii. In other jurisdictions, hostility is a neutral act requirement, met by actions that are inconsistent with the rights of a title owner, such as paying taxes.

        4. Under a claim of right: split

            a. In some jurisdictions a claim of right is a mental state requirement: it means good faith, usually a mistake in the location of a boundary.

            b. In other jurisdictions, claim of right is about actions, not the mental state. It requires actions consistent with ownership.

        5. Statute of limitations

            a. Statutes vary in length from seven to twenty years.

            b. Ousting resets the clock.

      c. Exception: tacking

         i. Definition: tacking is adding one party's years of possession to that of a previous possessor to meet the statute of limitations requirement.

         ii. Test: tacking is only available if there is (1) privity between the two possessors and (2) both possessors meet all of the other elements independently during their time periods.

         iii. Definition: privity means a contractual relationship or similar rightful claim of both parties.

  B. Defenses

    1. Permission

      a. Definition: permission of the original owner defeats a claim of adverse possession.

Outline of the Rules for Trespass

I. Trespass

  A. Test

    1. Entry

      a. Split: degree or level of entry required

         i. Some jurisdictions require that the entry be tangible.

         ii. Other jurisdictions recognize entry by microscopic particles.

    2. Intent

      a. Intentional or

      b. Unintentional

    3. Entry must be made onto the real property of another.

II. Remedies

  A. Legal remedies

    1. Compensatory damages are available for all trespasses.

    2. Punitive damages are available only for intentional trespasses.

  B. Equitable remedies

    1. Injunctions may be available to prevent future entries if those are likely.

Gardens and Gazebos Hypothetical

Time to read and write your answer: one hour.

The Wythe family purchased their riverside farm from the heirs of Mr. and Mrs. Tyne, who had operated the farm and run a produce stand since 1948. In their later years (the last 10 years) Mr. and Mrs. Tyne had been ill and rarely left the farmhouse. The Wythe/Tyne farm is next door to the Dean farm, which also abuts the river.

There is a gazebo on a pier, which the Wythes have recently discovered (through a survey) is within the bounds of their land. The gazebo was built by the Dean family 25 years ago. The Deans and the Tynes were friends and often used the gazebo together until the Tynes became unwell. Because the Tynes have now passed away, no one is quite sure of the arrangement. There is no indication in the record that anyone knew the property was solely on Tyne land (as opposed to perhaps being on the boundary). There is evidence that the Deans individually used the gazebo — maybe three or four times a year — before the Tynes became unwell. No one remembers the Tynes using the gazebo individually.

The Deans are apparently only roughly sure of where the boundary line is. Nothing marks the boundary formally. The Deans do mow enough of the land that they mow past the entry to the pier/gazebo. The Dean family has used the gazebo to host about four summer parties per year since the Tynes became ill. In the warmer months, when the river is not frozen, their daughter reads there in the afternoon sometimes and — when their mother is not watching — the sons use the upper railing of the gazebo as a diving board. The Dean parents are too busy to use the pier and gazebo on a regular basis. In the winter months, when the river is frozen, one of the children occasionally builds a snowman there, but in general the pier is not used in this weather. For the last three summers, the Deans' daughter has been planting a few flowers near the edge of the pier.

Scoring Rubric for Gardens and Gazebos Hypothetical

Section			
Issue:	Is there an effective claim for adverse possession?	6	
Rules:	**Elements of adverse possession** ☐ Actual and visible appropriation (open and notorious) (3) ☐ Exclusive possession, especially excluding the original owner (3) ☐ Continuous possession, defined contextually (3) ☐ Hostile (bad faith or neutral acts of ownership) (3) ☐ Claim of right (good faith or neutral acts of ownership) (3) ☐ Intent is evaluated, but it is masked within elements of hostile or claim of right. (3) ☐ Claimant must meet the statute of limitations (7–25 years). (3) ☐ Permission defeats adverse possession. (3)	24	
App.:	**Actual and visible** Yes ☐ The claimant's predecessors built a gazebo, which the owner couldn't miss. (3) ☐ The gazebo is a permanent improvement to property, and therefore gives notice to the owner. (3) ☐ The claimants used the gazebo to host parties, giving notice via both noise and guests. (3) ☐ Claimant's children play in the gazebo seasonally, providing notice of the family's use of the property. (3) ☐ The claimants mowed the land up to the pier. (3) ☐ Claimants planted flowers, which were visible all summer. (3)	18	
	No ☐ If the gazebo was constructed as joint project, then existence of the structure is not notice of the neighbor's intent to claim the land. (3) ☐ Claimants only use the gazebo three to four times per year, so their use gives limited notice. (3) ☐ The boys hide their use, limiting any chance of giving notice of use. (3)	18	

App.:	☐ The girl only uses the gazebo sometimes, limiting any potential notice. (3)		
	☐ Almost all use is seasonal, which limits the possibility of notice. (3)		
	☐ Mowing is limited in its visibility because grass grows quickly. (3)		
	Continuous		
	Yes		
	☐ Because the pier gets ice and snow, it is reasonable to expect only seasonal use. (3)	12	
	☐ The claimants host three to four parties a year in summer, every summer, creating a pattern of regular use. (3)		
	☐ The claimant's children play there regularly (if not frequently) every summer. (3)		
	☐ The children occasionally use the structure in the winter. (3)		
	No		
	☐ A gazebo has a roof so it is a year-round structure, and we should anticipate year-round use. (3)	6	
	☐ Building a snowman there suggests that winter use is possible, the claimants just don't usually do it. (3)		
	Exclusive		
	Yes		
	☐ From the time of the Tynes' illnesses, only the Deans used the structure. (3)	6	
	☐ There is no evidence of any other neighbor using it. (3)		
	No		
	☐ The Deans and Tynes used it together until the Tynes became unwell, so they shared any possession with the true owner. (3)	6	
	☐ After the Tynes became ill, the Deans may have used it alone, but it is unclear how long that was. (3)		
	Statute of limitations		
	Yes		
	☐ The gazebo was built 25 years ago, so it meets the requirement in all jurisdictions, if the building was done by the claimant's predecessors without permission. (3)	3	

Continued

Continued

App.:	No		
	☐ If the gazebo was shared, exclusive use may be more recent and may not meet the requirement, depending on the state. (3)	3	
	Hostile and claim of right		
	Activities (neutral)		
	☐ The claimants mowed the land to the pier, so they did maintenance. (3)	9	
	☐ The family used the premises, which an ordinary owner would. (3)		
	☐ The claimants planted flowers recently, which is an embellishment and something an owner would do. (3)		
	Good intent		
	☐ The Deans and Tynes were friends so there probably was not a bad intent between the original neighbors. (3)	6	
	☐ The Deans only "roughly know" where the boundary line is, so they may be able to argue that they are acting based on a mistake. (3)		
	Bad intent		
	☐ The Deans knew the Tynes were ill, but kept using the structure. (3)	3	
	Permission		
	☐ Gazebo possibly built with permission (3)	6	
	☐ Arrangement for use unclear, no testimony (3)		
	Compare to cases		
	☐	3X	
	☐		
	☐		
Concl.:		3	
Issue:	Is there a trespass?	6	
Rules:	**Elements of trespass**		
	☐ There must be an entry across the boundary. (3)	9	
	☐ The entry must be into the property or possessory interest of the plaintiff. (3)		

Rules:	☐ The intent can be intentional or unintentional, but only intentional trespasses create the possibility of punitive damages. (3)		
App.:	**Entry to property** Yes ☐ The gazebo was built on another's land. (3) ☐ The parties and the play of the children indicate the use of another's land. (3) ☐ The neighbors planted flowers and mowed grass across the border. (3)	9	
	No intent to trespass ☐ Permission may have existed (at beginning) between the friends. (3) ☐ A traditional of cooperation between the two properties may indicate that there was no negative intent to trespass on the property of another. (3)	6	
	Intent ☐ Continuing to enter after the suit is filed suggests a negative intent to occupy the property of another. (3)	3	
Concl.:		6	
	Total		

Mean Score for sample law student groups: 117

Sample Answer to Gardens and Gazebos Hypothetical

To establish adverse possession, the plaintiff must prove actual and visible, hostile, exclusive, and continuous possession, under a claim of right, for the statutory period.

Statutes of limitations vary in different jurisdictions, but it is frequently 15 years. Here, both the gazebo and the general pattern of use have existed for 25 years, which would be sufficient in all jurisdictions. The only problem is that it is not clear how much use is individual or shared. This means that proof of the element of exclusivity may only begin 10 years ago when the Tynes became ill.

All elements must continue for the requisite period, so if there is not exclusivity for the period, then there is not a successful adverse possession. Ten years will meet the statute of limitations in only a few jurisdictions.

The plaintiffs must also establish actual and visible use or occupation of the property. Visible possession occurs when it is obvious that the true owner may be presumed to be put on notice. Here, there is a structure, the gazebo, so its construction and continued existence are a part of the occupation of the property, providing daily visibility on the property. The Deans used the gazebo to host parties, which also would have given notice of their claim through visibility. The Deans mowed the land up to the pier area, which gave visible notice of their claim by including the gazebo within their boundaries. The Deans also planted flowers in this area, which would also be visible not only during the planting, but on a daily basis (seasonally). Finally, the Deans have children who also play in the gazebo some of the time, providing additional notice of the family's claim.

The construction of the gazebo, however, was a joint project, so that suggests that the gazebo's construction and existence is not a visible statement of ownership by one family. While the Deans have used the gazebo individually, this is only on a few days of the year, which indicates both limited use and limited visibility. The children also use the gazebo either rarely or while attempting to avoid notice, which again limits visibility. All of the use of the gazebo is contingent on acceptable weather, so there would also be seasonal limits to visibility. In sum, this limited use is insufficient to create notice of an individual claim to the gazebo.

The exclusivity element requires that the possession and use is not in common with others. For the last 10 years, while the Tynes were ill, only the Deans used the gazebo. No one else used it, so there is good evidence of exclusive use for this time period. Prior to this, however, the use was generally shared with group events held for both families.

Continuous means that possession existed without interruption for the statutory period in full. While use of the gazebo would be limited by seasons and weather, there is evidence of continued use during the reasonable periods of use. The pier might not be usable in the winter, but there is continuous summer use of the property, including mowing, planting, and hosting parties. By doing these activities each year during the warm months, the Deans established their claim. However, the gazebo's use was only seasonal, when it could have been used in the other months. Building a snowman suggests that winter use was possible, but maybe just not preferred. This may be then considered an interruption of the possession each year as the Deans became less infatuated with the gazebo. In this context, however, the use is more fairly regarded as continuous.

Plaintiffs must also establish that their claim was hostile and/or under a claim of right. There is a split across jurisdictions as to how to interpret both hostility and a claim of right. In general, courts regard the requirement as one of good faith, bad faith, or neutrally as just indicating the usual kinds of use that an owner would make.

In a jurisdiction that regards the requirement as neutral, the Deans would simply use the same evidence and arguments that they did to establish visible and actual use of the property. The Deans would point to their use of the premises regularly and their maintenance of the land through mowing and planting flowers. This should be successful, unless the court is convinced that the seasonal nature of the activities limits their ability to indicate that the Deans were acting as owners of the property.

If the jurisdiction requires a good intent, then we must consider the relationship between the parties. The Deans and Tynes were friends. This dispute only arose after the death of the Tynes. This suggests that there was a good intent during the use of the property, and that when the joint construction project was built only on the Tyne land rather than at the border, this was likely a mistake. A mistake would indicate a good faith situation.

On the other hand, if the Deans must prove a bad intent, there may be some evidence of that. The Deans would have known that their friends were ill, but for 10 years continued to use the gazebo alone. This may suggest an intent to coopt the property for themselves.

Finally, there is the possibility of permission. Permission is an affirmative defense to a claim of adverse possession. Here, the gazebo was built as a joint project, which suggests that there was permission to build it, wherever it ended up vis-à-vis the property lines. Additionally, we do not have testimony that makes clear the nature of the individual use. Given that there was also joint use, the individual use may indicate that it was done with an understanding created when the gazebo was built.

Additionally, the entry of the Deans would create a trespass claim for the new owners. The Deans enter onto the property owned by the Wythes when they mow, plant grass, or use the gazebo. Each of these activities would create an entry. The gazebo and land up to it is by deed owned by the Wythes. Therefore, the Deans entered the real property of another family. The Deans did enter intentionally, and therefore, punitive damages may be available.

SEVENTEEN

Complex Hypotheticals with Multiple Issues

Prioritizing Issues and Managing Time

One of the most typical complaints of 1Ls is that they are too slow in writing hypotheticals. It is impossible to address all the issues thoroughly in the allotted time.

First, it is important to recognize that this is not unusual and that it is, in part, a function of the mandatory mean system normally used for grading in law schools. If professors want to give a range of grades, they need a range of scores. One of the easiest ways to ensure this is to give a difficult exam. If the exam is easy, everyone will do perfectly, and all end up with the B+ mean despite perfect performance. (This is the insanity of the mandatory mean system.)

Second, the hypothetical is unique to law school. In other words, unlike multiple-choice exams or essays that answer direct, discrete questions, you haven't practiced hypotheticals since elementary school. A very few people — usually fast-typing, good at memorization, highly organized people — are naturally fast at hypotheticals. Everyone else must practice to become faster. And law school does not offer many opportunities to practice.

The first solution to time management and hypotheticals is simple: If you keep practicing, you will get faster. With that said, because professors create difficult exams to get a range of scores, you very likely still will not finish at least some of your exams. For those situations, you need a strategy for prioritizing which issues to tackle first.

STRATEGIES FOR SUCCESS

Prioritizing Issues to Manage Time

How to do it:

1. When doing a hypothetical, make a list of all the issues you see. Write the list as you read the hypothetical. That is important. Do not try to remember them later. You can add, of course, if you see something you missed. But make sure that you write this list as you read the prompt. It is best to just write it down one margin on a blank piece of paper.

   Your list should group sub-issues with the relevant main issue. Under each main issue, make sure to write "basic test." This is your reminder to actually run the full test for, say, adverse possession (the six or so elements, depending on which cases you read). Without this reminder, you might skip to the sub-issues that are relevant to the hypothetical, such as permission as a defense and tacking to meet the statute of limitations.

2. Number your list in accordance with this rule: do the issues with the shortest lists of elements first. Then keep going and check them off your list, getting as far as you can.

Example list:

Adverse possession (3)

   Basic test

   Tacking to meet statute of limitations

   Permission defense

Trespass (1)

Nuisance (2)

   Basic test

   Unclean hands defense

   Injunction needed

Evil Eggs Hypothetical

Time to read and write your answer: one hour.

Ellerslie Farms, which has existed since around 1845, is situated just west of the last shop on North Main Street of Wellington, Virginia. Wellington is historically a small, rural farming town with a small population. There is a small downtown of about eight blocks by eight blocks that is otherwise surrounded by countryside.

Historically, Ellerslie Farms has raised sheep, chickens, and commercial quantities of green peppers and mint. Mild odors from these activities occasionally reached town, but never caused any complaints from residents or shop owners. This is unsurprising given that mint is a rather attractive scent. The last shop on North Main Street is a gourmet organic grocery operated by Cassie Olson.

Two months ago, the last generation of the Ellerslies passed away and the Evil Egg Corporation bought the property. Evil Egg Corporation has quickly eliminated all Ellerslie Farms products except for chickens, which it now raises by the hundreds of thousands to produce eggs. The company has hired 100 new workers, but the town's residents are still not big fans of the corporation. As a result of the new operations, the stench of over-occupied chicken coops slides into north Wellington every morning.

Olson's shop, being the closest business to the farm, suffers the most. Customers can be seen making faces as they step from their cars, particularly on foggy mornings. Additionally, when the wind blows, feathers from the farm blow all the way to Ms. Olson's shop where they — rather comically — plaster the front of the building and cover the organic herbs that Ms. Olson has for sale on metal racks in front of her shop.

Ms. Olson requested that Ellerslie Farms change its operations or mitigate the effects. She received no response.

After two months, she has lost patience. Ms. Olson is in the process of closing her shop, which she has contracted to sell to Alex Stockly. Ms. Olson intends to buy a property in another town and move her store.

When Ms. Olson purchased the Wellington property and moved in, the shop was empty — just floor, ceiling, and four walls. To provide an attractive display space, Ms. Olson had a local carpenter craft beautiful wood shelving units. The units appear to be built in to the walls of the store unless you look very closely. The shelving units have brackets on the back, behind the top molding, that allow them to be screwed into the wall so that they look like built-ins. There are only four screws holding each unit to the wall. The shelves were built within the store, so to get them out, Ms. Olson has to remove the front door of the store and then put it back on again. This gives just enough room to get the shelves out of the building. The contract for purchase of the property does not mention the shelving, which Mr. Stockly expects to stay, and Ms. Olson expects to move to her new store.

Scoring Rubric for Evil Eggs Hypothetical

Section			
Issue:	Do Evil Egg's chicken smell and feathers create a private nuisance?	6	
Rules:	**Basic rules**		
	☐ Nuisance requires an invasion of the use and enjoyment of land. (3)	15	
	☐ Plaintiff must show significant harm. (3)		
	☐ In Restatement jurisdictions, the act must be "intentional and unreasonable" or "abnormally dangerous." (3)		
	☐ The defendant must be the cause of the interference. (3)		
	☐ Nuisances are evaluated contextually. Consider "all of the circumstances of location," along with effect and impact on neighboring businesses. (3)		
	Remedies rules		
	☐ Compensation is automatic if the prima facie case is proven, but an injunction is discretionary. (3)	3	
	Factors for injunction		
	☐ Impacts on the community, such as loss of jobs (3)	12	
	☐ Impacts on the defendant's property interests (3)		
	☐ Benefits of stopping use to the plaintiff (3)		
	☐ Benefit of the use/product to the public (3)		

App.:	**Significant harm**		
	Yes		
	☐ Shop customers can be seen making faces, suggesting they do not like coming there, which may interfere with profits. (3)	15	
	☐ The feathers on the front of the building are comical, which may impact a business's reputation. (3)		
	☐ Feathers from a commercial chicken farm cover the organic herbs, making them not organic anymore. (3)		
	☐ Feathers on plants are probably aesthetically unpleasing and may deter sales. (3)		
	☐ Ms. Olson is in the process of closing her shop, which suggests a problem in business operations. (3)		
	No		
	☐ No facts are given that specifically support a loss of business, customers, or profits. (3)	15	
	☐ Moving a business does not necessarily mean profits were down. There is no proof of the motivation, so there is limited proof of harm. (3)		
	☐ Feathers on the windows are annoying, but do not stop a business from operating. (3)		
	☐ Feathers on plants do not prevent the sale of those plants. (3)		
	☐ Customers may be reacting to the smell, but we do not know that they are staying away, so it is not sufficient proof of harm. (3)		
	Abnormally dangerous		
	No		
	☐ There is no evidence of health impacts, just annoyance. (3)	3	
	Intentional and unreasonable invasion of use and enjoyment		
	Yes		
	☐ The chicken farm is commercial, not accidental, and smell and feathers naturally come with it, so it is intentional. (3)	12	
	☐ The feathers and smell are apparently causing someone to move their business, so this is not neighborly behavior. (3)		

Continued

Continued

App.:	☐ Having a smell from a chicken farm is not appropriate to context in a downtown area. (3) ☐ Feathers, again, are normal for farming, and are not reasonable in downtown. (3) *No* ☐ This is a rural community with many farms nearby so neither smell nor feathers would be unreasonable. (3) ☐ The farm has existed since the 1800s and is still a farm, so it is not an unreasonable activity in that place. (3) ☐ Any annoyance is minor and aesthetic. There is no proof of loss of business, so there is no unreasonable interference. (3)	9	
	Remedies		
	Monetary damages		
	☐ There is no proof of loss of business profits or a loss on the sale of the business, so there are no monetary damages established on these facts. (3) ☐ The need to move the business suggests the severity of harm to the right to use and enjoyment. The court can compensate for loss of that right. (3)	6	
	Abatement		
	☐ The need to move a business shows the level of harm and strengthens the argument to abate. (3) ☐ Abatement requires serious harm and here, there is limited evidence of serious harm when compared to other nuisances that have health impacts. (3)	6	
	Injunction		
	Impact on community		
	☐ The chicken farm is now a major local employer in a rural town, so there will be a loss of jobs and the tax base if it closes. (3) ☐ Due to the smell, the farm is not well-liked in town despite the jobs, so the community will approve of the improved smell. (3)	6	
	Impact on defendant's property interests		
	☐ Defendant bought a farm and is using it as a farm, so there is serious interference with the defendant's property rights. (3)	3	

App.:	*Benefit to the plaintiff of stopping the disputed use*		
	She could stop the plans to move if the court granted an injunction. (3)	3	
	Benefit of use/product to public		
	Chicken farms are a necessary part of modern life and create lots of eggs/chicken for consumption. (3)	3	
Concl.:		6	
Issue:	Do the smell and feathers create a public nuisance and particularly one that might be actionable by Olson as an individual?	6	
Rules:	☐ A public nuisance requires substantial interference with a right common to the public. (3)	27	
	☐ Rights common to the public include public health, safety, peace, comfort, and convenience. (3)		
	☐ Claims are evaluated contextually, given the nature of the activity. (3)		
	☐ A plaintiff must prove substantial harm. (3)		
	☐ Jurisdictional split: The mental state requirement may be intentional or negligent, or merely knowing. (3)		
	☐ The defendant must cause the harm. (3)		
	☐ The defendant should have actual or constructive notice of the problem. (3)		
	☐ Individuals may sue for public nuisance if they prove a special injury. (3)		
	☐ Jurisdictional split: Some courts allow a claim based on a more severe injury than other people, while other courts require the injury to be different in kind or type rather than just degree. (3)		
App.:	**Identify right common to the public**		
	☐ Comfort is a public right. (3)	3	
	Causation		
	☐ Commercial chicken operations commonly create smells and feathers, and there is no indication of another potential source, even though there are other farms in the area. (3)	3	

Continued

Continued

App.:	**Unreasonable interference**		
	Yes		
	☐ People are making faces, so they are not happy being in the town with the smell. (3)	15	
	☐ Feathers on all the buildings makes the town look ridiculous. (3)		
	☐ Feathers cover the organic herbs, ruining their organic designation. (3)		
	☐ Feathers on plants will not promote their sale. (3)		
	☐ Ms. Olson is in the process of closing her shop, which suggests a problem in business operations. (3)		
	No		
	☐ No facts were given to support a loss of business, customers, or profits. (3)	15	
	☐ Moving a business does not necessarily mean the business was not faring well. (3)		
	☐ Feathers on windows are annoying, but do not stop the business from operating. (3)		
	☐ Feathers on plants do not prevent sale of those plants. (3)		
	☐ There is no evidence of fewer customers to Ms. Olson's store. (3)		
	Harm		
	Yes		
	☐ A business is leaving town, so this is reducing the town tax base. (3)	6	
	☐ Making faces suggests it is uncomfortable to be outdoors in town, which substantially impacts people being in the town and doing business in the town. (3)		
	No		
	☐ Smells can be annoying, but there is no evidence of health consequences. (3)	6	
	☐ Ms. Olson has shown no decrease in profits. (3)		
	Intent		
	Intentional		
	Specific		
	☐ The chicken farm would have no reason to intend to create the noxious odors. They just want the product, so there is no specific intent. (3)	3	

App.:	*General intent* ☐ But the farm does intend to have gigantic chicken coops, so there is general intent. (3)	3	
	Negligent *Yes* ☐ There is no evidence of anything being done to prevent harms to neighbors. (3)	3	
	No ☐ There is no evidence of operating the chicken farm in anything other than the standard way. How could you stop a smell? (3)	3	
	Notice ☐ Ms. Olson asked the farm to address the smell and feathers. (3)	3	
	Special injury *Different type* ☐ Ms. Olson's shop has the same complaints others would have (smell and feathers). (3)	3	
	Degree ☐ The shop is closest to the farm, so the effects would be strongest there. (3)	3	
Concl.:		6	
Issue:	Did the Evil Egg Company trespass by allowing its feathers to enter onto the shop property?	6	
Rules:	**Basic test** ☐ Trespass requires an entry across the border, usually a tangible entry. (3) ☐ The entry must be into the property or possessory interest of the plaintiff. (3) ☐ Punitive damages are only available if the trespass is intentional. (3)	9	
App.:	**Entry** ☐ Feathers are entering Ms. Olson's property from the farm and covering plants and windows. (3)	3	

Continued

Continued

App.:	**Property** ☐ Her shop is real property (3) **Intent** ☐ Feathers are blowing, not thrown, so their entry is unintentional. (3) **Remedies** ☐ Monetary damages are appropriate, but not punitive damages because there is no intent to enter. (3)	3 3 3	
Concl.:		6	
Issue:	Are the shelves personalty, which remains with the seller after the sale, or realty, which transfers to the buyer with the sale?	6	
Rules:	**Basic rules** ☐ Improvements need a significant association with real property. (3) ☐ Improvement is decided by a three-part, factors test: annexation, adaptation, and intent. (3) ☐ Annexation is the physical connection. (3) ☐ Adaptation means suited to purpose/use, or altered to fit the land. (3) ☐ Intent is the most important and is measured at the time of placement. (3)	15	
App.:	**Annexation** Yes ☐ The shelves appear to be built into the walls and therefore look attached. (3) ☐ The attachment mechanisms are hidden, making the shelves look fully attached. (3) No ☐ The shelves are not built-ins and are movable. (3) ☐ The shelves can be moved out of the building with the minor adjustment of removing and rehanging the door. (3) ☐ Each unit is attached with only four screws, so it is minimally attached to the premises. (3)	 6 9	

App.:	**Adaptation**		
	Yes		
	☐ The shelves were custom-built for this store, so they are specific to this purpose. (3)	6	
	☐ The shelves were built within the store itself and are too big to get out without changes to the space. (3)		
	No		
	☐ The shelves were custom-built to be removable, so they are not specific to this location. (3)	6	
	☐ The shelves were built just small enough to fit out of the building if the door is removed, so they were sized to relocate, not to stay. (3)		
	Intent to remain		
	Yes		
	☐ The shelves were built inside the store itself, which suggests they were made as a permanent addition. (3)	6	
	☐ It is not possible to get the units out of the building without at least some change to the building itself. (3)		
	No		
	☐ The shelves were built specially with brackets so they could be removed. (3)	6	
	☐ The shelves were built to a size that could be removed with a minor adjustment, which suggests an intent to move them in the future. (3)		
Concl.:		6	
	Total		

Mean Score for sample law student groups: 149

Sample Answer to Evil Eggs Hypothetical

The first question is whether Olson can effectively sue Evil Egg for private nuisance due to the impact of the smell and feathers on her business and, if so, what remedies she can get.

Private nuisance is defined as an interference with the use and enjoyment of property, resulting in significant harm. The Restatement jurisdictions require either "intentional and unreasonable" or "abnormally dangerous." Unreasonableness is contextual. Besides money damages, two equitable remedies are available: abatement with proof of seriousness of injury, and injunctions, which are subject to the usual equitable balancing. For injunctions, the judge considers impact on the community and on the defendant's property interests, along with the benefit of stopping use to the plaintiff, as well as any benefit of the use/product to the public.

Olson has a variety of unfortunate interferences caused by Evil Egg. Her customers are not happy. They can be seen making faces, suggesting they do not like coming there, which is a negative impact for a business. The feathers on the windows are comical, which is not the look you are going for with an organic grocery. The feathers on the plants are aesthetically unpleasing. In addition, this is a commercial chicken farm, and feathers likely contaminate organic plants. The impacts are severe enough for Olson to relocate her business, so she feels them quite drastically.

With that said, there is limited evidence about her desire to relocate the business. There are no facts given to support a loss of profits. So we can't be entirely sure that her motivation is not just annoyance. She has not closed down the business, so any harm is insufficient to stop operation. It was a shop and still is a shop. Customers may not love the smell, but they are still coming to the shop. A lack of evidence of the severity of interference is problematic for Olson.

Additionally, in a Restatement jurisdiction, Olson could not establish that the farm is abnormally dangerous, because there is no evidence of health impacts from the farm.

Olson, may, however, be able to prove the other side of the Restatement test: intentional and unreasonable invasion of use and enjoyment. With respect to intent, this is a business, so the feathers and smell result from intentional acts. It does not matter that the intent is not for the smell to travel. As for reasonableness, Olson is moving, so that is one measure of how unreasonable the impacts are for her. Additionally, the horrible smell and feathers are present within a downtown area, which is unreasonable. That is appropriate for a farm, not a town, so it is not reasonable within the context.

On the other hand, the setting is rural Virginia in an area that has been a farming area for many years. Smells and feathers are standard. The town is entirely surrounded by exactly these types of things. This specific farm has existed since the 1800s and is still a farm, so it is not an unreasonable activity in that place. In fact, the farm fits right into the type of community that it is: rural farming. Finally, the feathers and smell are not pleasant. But they are aesthetic in nature, which limits their impact.

Olson could recover for interference with her use and enjoyment of land generally, but she hasn't introduced evidence to support lost profits. She may also want abatement or an injunction, although she already has a sale contract, so it may be too late for those to help her.

Regarding abatement, the need to relocate her business indicates the severity of the problem with the smell and feathers. However, we cannot be fully sure about why she is moving her business or that there was a loss of profits. When combined with the contract that she already has, this argues against abatement. Finally, abatement would be expensive and cost jobs to the community, so this makes the option less appealing unless there is significant evidence of harm.

Regarding an injunction that would stop future behavior, it has the same problems as abatement. There would be important community problems. There would be a loss of jobs. The farm produces eggs/chicken, so the farm is a useful part of our society. People in the community, however, would all benefit from the improved aesthetics if the farm shut down. Granting an injunction would shut down the entire business operations unless there is a way to stop the smell and feathers, and that may not be possible. So, if it means stopping operations, this is a significant impairment of the corporation's ability to use the property it purchased. The defendant bought a farm and is using it as a farm, so an injunction would be a serious interference with property rights. An injunction would stop the problem entirely for the plaintiff as well as for the other members of the town, so it would be a full remedy.

The second question is whether the feathers/smell also create a public nuisance, and whether Olson can sue as an individual, when usually it has to be a government suing.

A public nuisance requires a substantial interference with a right common to the public, such as public health, safety, comfort, etc., creating substantial harm. Like private nuisance, it is evaluated contextually, including reasonableness and nature of the activity. We must be confident that the defendant caused the harm. But jurisdictions differ on the level of intent required. It ranges from intentional to negligent to knowing. Defendants must have notice of the problem. And individuals can sue, but only if they have a special injury, which is defined as a different type and/or a different degree, depending on jurisdiction.

Here, the comfort of the public is at issue. There is no evidence to contest causation. The debate will be about the level of interference.

Some evidence suggests there is an unreasonable interference. Residents are making faces, so they are not happy being in the town with the smell. It is uncomfortable and annoying. Additionally, for Olson, it is embarrassing for her to have her business covered in feathers. For her outdoor products, it is also a deterrent to sales due to the aesthetics. It may also interfere with her organic status, which would undermine her business model as an organic grocery. These interferences are so severe that she is actually relocating.

Yet there is limited evidence to support an unreasonable interference. There are no facts given to support a loss of business. Her personal level of annoyance cannot dictate the standard of law, so it would be a much stronger argument if it were clear she was losing business. There is no evidence to suggest the business has stopped/reduced hours/closed at any point, so the interference is not enough to stop the operations of the shop. The feathers and smell are annoying, but do not stop sales to customers. Additionally, from the testimony we know there are customers, so that suggests a limit on the level of interference that has happened.

Regarding substantial harm, the loss of the business by relocation is the best evidence of harm. Additionally, the displeasure of people in the town with the company, despite the new jobs, suggests that there is a substantial reduction in the comfort level in the town. On the other hand, there is no evidence of other businesses leaving, just this one, for reasons that are not entirely clear. And the smells and feathers are aesthetic, rather than being a direct monetary harm, as far as we know.

In terms of intent, the business would have no reason to intend to create the noxious odors. They just want to operate their business, therefore there is no evidence of a specific intent to harm Olson or the town. There is a general intent or knowledge that the harm will occur by virtue of the operation of the farm.

There is no direct evidence of negligence in the operation of the business. Feathers and smells are standard for a commercial farm.

Regarding Olson's ability to sue as an individual for public nuisance, she does not have a different type of complaint that others in town would have for the smell and feathers. However, she does have the closest location to the farm, so she would have the highest degree of impacts. This means she would be able to sue in some jurisdictions, but not others.

The third question is whether the feathers create a trespass by the corporation onto Olson's store property. Trespass requires a tangible entry onto the property of others. Compensatory damages are by right on proof, but punitive damages are limited to intentional trespasses.

Here, there is a tangible entry by the feathers, which come from the farm and land on the shop regularly. The shop is real property; therefore, it is protected from trespass. There is no intent to send the feathers there, so this is unintentional trespass, not intentional. There cannot be punitive damages but there could be money damages if demonstrated. There is no evidence here to support a specific amount of money damages.

The fourth and final issue is whether the shop shelving is personalty or realty. For the shelving to be realty, it must be an improvement. Improvements need significant association with real property, which is tested by weighing three concepts: annexation (physical adhesion), adaptation (alteration or suited to purpose), and intent (most important and measured at time of placement of the goods).

For annexation, there is some evidence to suggest that the shelves are attached or appear to be. The shelves appear to be built into the walls, therefore look they look like a permanent part of the real estate and they were specifically built to look that way. The attachment mechanisms are hidden, making them look like part of the walls. On the other hand, the shelves are not built-ins, but instead are movable with minor effort. Shelves can be moved out of the building with a minor adjustment of removing and rehanging the door. Each shelving unit is attached with only four screws, so they are only very minimally attached to the walls. All in all, the shelves are not strongly attached to the premises, therefore there is no annexation.

On the topic of adaptation, there is evidence the shelves were specifically adapted to this shop location. The shelves were custom-built for this store, so they are specific to this purpose and location. Additionally, the shelves were, in fact, built within the store itself and are too big to get out without removing the doors of the store. On the other hand, the shelves were built with the design intended to create a removable shelf. And the shelves can be moved out of the building without disassembly.

The most important issue, though, is the intent of the person who placed the shelves. So, we must ask what Olson was thinking when the shelves were built. The shelving was built inside the store itself, which suggests an intent to leave them there. Indeed, you can't actually get them out of the building without removing the door and thus changing the building in some way. On the other hand, the shelves were built specially with brackets so they could be removed. This indicates a desire to be able to move them in the future. And the shelves were built to a size that could be removed once the door was off. This suggests that Olson intended to be able to move the shelves in the future if she moved her business or wanted to sell them separately.

EIGHTEEN

Supersize Hypos (No Estates Issues)

Important Note on Issues and Rules

Law schools in America are national in terms of recruiting students, but the law is a state creature in large part, especially for property. This means that property textbooks have cases from a variety of jurisdictions and try to teach central concepts, but there are, of course, splits in the law. Additionally, textbooks differ to some degree on the topics taught. It is important to get your rules for your final exam preparation from your own class notes and textbook. This book uses the rules that are most commonly taught, and in this chapter covers additional property issues, such as easements and covenants, that are also commonly taught, but have not been covered in the earlier chapters of this book. The purpose is to provide you with hypotheticals that are as exam-realistic as possible. Rules here are provided as a basic checklist, but you are likely to see a little variation in your own class.

Finally, in recent years, some classes have moved to not teaching estates. For this reason, this chapter contains only hypotheticals without estates issues.

The Prohibition Diary Hypothetical

Time to read and write your answer: one hour.

Professor Fraley's latest research project involves Prohibition-era Virginia. She focuses primarily on obscure connections to theories of democracy. But as we all know, she is very easily distracted by anything related to property. During the early summer, she and her two research assistants, Alexis and Jon, stumble upon a diary of a gangster's girlfriend listed on eBay. The gangster was "Rowdy" Joe Marina, owner of a local vineyard, which produced "medicinal" wine. Professor Fraley purchases the diary for $150. All three take turns reading it until one day, as Alexis holds it, the back cover loosens slightly to reveal — oh joy — a map! While Professor Fraley is overjoyed with a new map of any sort, Jon is quick to point out that it looks like a map to something in particular. Jon continues skimming the diary and concludes that the map indicates where the gangster was stashing a mixture of cash and gold coins.

By happy circumstance, the property where Rowdy Marina lived is for sale and Professor Fraley quickly switches her home purchase plans. Unfortunately, the map is not terribly clear, and your absent-minded professor is not to be trusted with operating heavy machinery, therefore she enlists her research assistants to help. Jon and Alexis operate small front-loaders to begin digging holes.

Unfortunately, the neighbors, who operate larger-scale farms, are less than thrilled about the digging enterprise, which creates vast amounts of blowing dust and the constant *hummm-whirrr-grunt* of machinery. The noises startle the cows who run, in fear, into the side of the barn at times, acquiring minor injuries. Professor Fraley installs fans with blowing red sheets to attempt to scare the cows away from property line.

The neighbors also complain that the students do not like to work during the hotter mid-day hours of August and instead, tend to work from 2:00 p.m. to 10:00 p.m., employing bright construction lights for the last two hours. Professor Fraley shrugs the neighbors away, saying, "This is a commercial operation. This has been a vineyard since the early 1900s. You bought property by a commercial operation and you knew it could mean construction at times."

Alexis and Jon finally locate a pair of metal trunks, but the trunks are near a stone fence at the edge of the property, which, according to the surveyor's map, is not on Professor Fraley's land. The stone fence, however, marks the treasure area as within the professor's land.

This area of the property contains a stone fence, more recently constructed, but meant to match the older fences of the property, as well as vines that a horticulturalist estimates are 12–15 years of age. After a trip to the courthouse, Alexis and Jon find the name of the person who owned the property 15 years earlier, Mr. Lode.

Lode says, "Yep, I put that fence there. Around July of 1998. I planted the vines later that fall. I think anyway. I have trouble remembering these days." He chuckles, "The neighbors never came to that area of the farm, ever. One day my nephew came to visit. He was in law school at the time and he joked that I could just take it over and extend the farm. After he left, I thought, why not? So, I put in the stone fence where I wanted it to be."

Professor Fraley opens the trunks to discover $100,000 in old bills and gold coins valued at $1.6 million.

Scoring Rubric for the Prohibition Diary Hypothetical

Section		
Issue:	Who is the legal finder of the treasure (i.e., who has first possession)?	6
Rules:	☐ Finder's law attempts to identify the "first possessor" and reward that person. (3) ☐ The relevant moment is when the item is "found" in a legal sense, i.e., when possession and control exist. (3) ☐ Finding may include discovery of the item or, if there is a container, knowledge of the contents. (3) ☐ Finding can also include removal from the area. (3)	12
App.:	Multiple possible times of finding: ☐ The moment of finding could be the discovery of the book and its purchase, but that does not seem to include knowledge of the treasure, and includes only possession of the book, not the treasure. (3) ☐ Alexis finds the map, but does not seem to know that it is anything other than a map, so it is unconnected to the possession of the treasure at that point. (3) ☐ Jon realizes the purpose of the map, so he is the first to connect the map to the treasure, but he does not know what the treasure is, so has no knowledge of the contents. (3) ☐ Professor Fraley purchases and owns the real property with an intent to retrieve the treasure, so she may constructively possess it as of the date of purchase. (3) ☐ Alexis and Jon dig up the trunk but do not open it, so they do not know the contents. (3) ☐ Professor Fraley opens it and it is only at this moment that someone knows the contents; she is the first one able to physically touch the treasure. (3)	18
Concl.:		6
Issue:	Who is the legal owner of the treasure?	6

Rules:	**Traditional common law rules regarding the place of finding**		
	☐ The finder of lost property in a public place acquires rights against all others except the rightful owner. (3)	12	
	☐ On private property, the presumption is that the real property owner constructively possesses everything on the property, so long as the owner is in actual possession of the real property. (3)		
	☐ If private property is open to the public, a finder gets possession unless the item is within actual control of the real property owner or the owner's agent. (3)		
	☐ Right of possession is not ownership; ownership remains with the true owner, if that person can be located. (3)		
	Characterizations of the object		
	Some jurisdictions use the nature of the object to determine who should have legal possession:	30	
	☐ Lost—finder gets possession (3)		
	☐ Mislaid—premises owner gets possession (3)		
	☐ Treasure trove—finder gets possession (3)		
	☐ The treasure trove rule usually does not apply to cash, but a minority of jurisdictions apply the rule to cash as well as coins. (3)		
	☐ Abandoned—title, not possession, goes to the first finder. (3)		
	☐ Abandonment is based on the circumstances of finding and the location, but not necessarily the passage of time. (3)		
	☐ Embedded—goes to the owner of the land where found (3)		
	☐ "Embedded" is defined as being within the earth or buried. (3)		
	☐ Statutes provide for eventual termination of the true owner's rights if the property remains unclaimed. Possessors then become title owners. (3)		
	☐ Stolen property has a void title. (3)		
App.:	**True owner**		
	☐ We know who the true owner was, so that person has title. (6)	9	
	☐ The true owner is now dead, but the court may be able to locate an estate or heirs. (3)		

Continued

Continued

App.:	**Nature of the location where the item is found**	
	☐ This is private property, not public, because Professor Fraley was able to buy it. (3)	6
	☐ The ownership of the exact place where the treasure was found, however, is unclear because of a potential adverse possession issue. (3)	
	Characterization of the object	
	☐ Given that there is a map, the property was buried intentionally to keep it safe. (3)	18
	☐ The placement was intentional, not accidental, so it was not lost. (3)	
	☐ The property was intentionally placed, and the owner failed to return for it, which means this resembles mislaid property situations. (3)	
	☐ Abandonment is unclear but possible because both the land and the diary were sold. (3)	
	☐ The property was buried in the earth, inside the trunk, so it may be embedded. (3)	
	☐ The property may fit the treasure trove category—at least the coin portion of it. (3)	
Concl.:		6

Issue:	Did the treasure recovery operation create a private nuisance actionable by the neighbors?	6
Rules:	**Procedural**	
	☐ There is a short statute of limitations (two to three years). (3)	6
	☐ Continuous behavior resets the clock, but there is a jurisdictional split as to what remedies are available (i.e., only equitable remedies or both equitable remedies and damages). (3)	
	Basic test	
	☐ A nuisance requires an invasion of another person's use and enjoyment of property. (3)	15
	☐ The plaintiff must show significant harm. (3)	
	☐ In Restatement jurisdictions, actions should be either "intentional and unreasonable" or "abnormally dangerous." (3)	

Rules:	☐ Unreasonableness is measured by the social and geographical context of the activity. (3) ☐ Compensation is automatic if a case is proven, but an injunction is discretionary. (3)		
App.:	**Unreasonable interference with use and enjoyment** *Yes* ☐ Farming is both residential and commercial, so lights and machinery are both appropriate and out of place. (3) ☐ Farming is normally a daytime activity, so the use of these at night is more out of place. (3) ☐ Front loaders are like tractors and other farming equipment (which are also loud), so they are not out of place. (3) ☐ Dust is more typical to construction than to farming, but farming will create some dust as well. (3) ☐ The treasure hunting operations caused injury to cows, making it unreasonable in a farming area. (3) *No* ☐ Lights are not typical to farms, so they are out of context. (3) ☐ This is a rural/residential area, so extensive machinery sounds, particularly at night, are out of context. (3) ☐ Cow injuries were minor and there is a process in place to mitigate. (3) **Intentional and unreasonable** ☐ Unreasonableness—see analysis above. ☐ The lights and machines were operated intentionally. (3) **Showing of significant harm** *Yes* ☐ Any neighbor would be annoyed by dust, bright lights late at night, and machinery. (3) *No* ☐ There is no proof of disruption of sleep or of farm activities. (3)	15 9 3 3 3	
Concl.:		6	

Continued

Continued

Issue:	Does the dust trespass on the property of the neighbors?	6	
Rules:	**Elements of trespass:** ☐ There must be an entry across the boundary. (3) ☐ The entry must be onto the property or possessory interest of the plaintiff. (3) ☐ The intent can be intentional or unintentional, but only intentional trespasses create the possibility of punitive damages. (3)	9	
App.:	**Entry** ☐ The neighbors complain of significant amounts of dust, so this suggests an obvious entry, and it can be touched, so it is tangible. (3) ☐ There may not be enough dust for it to count as a tangible entry, because there are only two machines operating. (3) ☐ Dust from the treasure hunters is unlikely to be that different from other farming operations, so it would be hard to distinguish entries. (3) ☐ Tangibility will depend on the amount and visibility. (3) **Property** ☐ Farm/private property, so yes (3) **Intent** ☐ Unintentional crossing of border, intentional machinery operation, so could be knowing (3)	12 3 3	
Concl.:		6	

Issue:	Did the prior owners of the vineyard who pre-date Fraley successfully adversely possess the land up to and including the stone fence?	6	
Rules:	**Elements of adverse possession** ☐ Actual and visible appropriation (open and notorious) (3) ☐ Exclusive possession, especially excluding the original owner (3)	24	

Rules:	☐ Continuous possession, defined contextually (3) ☐ Hostile (bad faith or neutral acts of ownership) (3) ☐ Claim of right (good faith or neutral acts of ownership) (3) ☐ Intent is evaluated, but it is masked within elements of hostile or claim of right. (3) ☐ Claimant must meet the statute of limitations (7–25 years). (3) ☐ Permission defeats adverse possession. (3)		
App.:	***Visible/actual*** ☐ The area in dispute is not small. It is 40 feet x 800 yards, so highly visible. (3) ☐ The stone fence is a permanent improvement to the property, so it creates consistent, permanent visibility of the claim. (3) ☐ A fence is a quintessential marker of ownership, and gives notice of the claim. (3) ☐ The vines are always visible. (3)	12	
	Continuous ☐ There is no evidence of ouster. (3) ☐ The vines and the fence are there at all times. (3)	6	
	Statute of limitations ☐ The vines have been in place for 12–15 years. (3) ☐ The fence has been in place since 1998, so more than 20 years. (3)	6	
	Hostile/claim of right ☐ There was no mistake here, so there is no good faith claim. (3) ☐ The interview shows that the former owner chose to possess adversely, so there is bad faith. (3) ☐ There are actions of a typical owner, including planting vines and building the permanent stone fence. (3)	9	
Concl.:		6	
		Total	

Scandals at the Art Gallery Hypothetical

Time to read and write your answer: one hour.

On April 1, The Muse, a contemporary art gallery in Alexandria, Virginia, paired with Furry Friends, an animal rescue society, for an evening of art, wine, and fundraising. The highlight of the event was a "bachelor auction" featuring local celebrities.

In advance of the event, Allison Stone, a young artist whose paintings had been valued at more than $500,000, dropped off four new, stunning works to display at the event. The assistant curator, Beatrice Loon, took the paintings from Stone, promising they would be on display for the big event.

Also, in advance of the event, The Muse complained to Pendleton Company, the owner of the gallery's space, that their security system, provided by the building, had been "on the fritz." Ellie Carson, curator and owner of The Muse, was particularly concerned because in recent months there had been a string of burglaries in their upscale neighborhood. Most were of jewelry shops, but there had been a recent attempt thwarted at another gallery. Pendleton Company did not return the calls and The Muse hired two security guards specifically for the night of the Muse & Furry Friends Bachelor Auction.

Unfortunately for Allison Stone, Beatrice Loon, the assistant curator, was, well, "losing it." Feeling jealous of the owner, Carson, and underappreciated, Loon sets out to spoil The Muse's reputation. First, Ms. Loon took one of Allison Stone's paintings, Masterpiece One, and mailed it to the Museum of Modern Art in New York. A note inside the box indicated that the work was intended to be "an anonymous donation." MOMA, in the process of expensive renovations, decided it needed the cash more than the new piece and sold it to Maria Teresa Lyon. Masterpieces Two and Three were properly hung in the gallery, but mislabeled with prices of "$50,000." Loon intended to take Masterpiece Four with her when she left before the gala, but in her haste, she forgot it by the back door.

The Muse & Furry Friends Bachelor Auction was the social event of the week for the Alexandria area. Within the first hour, Masterpieces Two and Three had already been sold to Senator Jackson, who asked to have them delivered the following day to his townhouse. After the closing of the event, robbers targeted The Muse, easily gaining entry, tying up the security guards, and removing both Masterpieces Two and Three, but not noticing Masterpiece Four, which they jostled on their way out, gouging a small hole in the canvas.

Masterpieces Two and Three were quickly sold on the underground market to Hidden Collector, who will not, of course, divulge his real name.

When Pendleton Company finally returns the gallery's calls, the company says that they had not fixed the alarm because they had learned it was in violation of a restriction in their deed. The company said it intended shortly to replace the device with a compliant system. The gallery is unhappy as the proposed system offers even less security than the existing one. The deed provision, created some 20 years before when the property was subdivided, reads "no property owner shall install either (1) exterior video surveillance cameras (which distract from the historical character of the neighborhood), or metal or wooden shutters or garage-style doors (which would distract from the character of the neighborhood and make the street dark and less inviting for shoppers).

Scoring Rubric for Scandals at the Art Gallery Hypothetical

Section			
Issue:	Did the artist create a bailment with the gallery?	6	
Rules:	☐ An effective bailment requires a transfer of personalty with mutual assent or constructive assent. (3) ☐ Mutual assent requires acceptance in the context of a delivery. (3) ☐ Jurisdictional split: There is a traditional three-tiered set of different duties of care based on the type of bailment. The modern rule says the duty is always ordinary care. (3) ☐ In an involuntary bailment, if the party exercises dominion, the duty is ordinary care. (3) ☐ If the item is not returned, then the courts presume negligence. (3)	15	
App.:	***Creation of a bailment*** *Transfer* ☐ The paintings were delivered to the gallery agent. (3)	3	

Continued

Continued

App.:	**Personal property**		
	☐ The paintings are goods, not land, so they are personalty, not realty. (3)	3	
	Mutual assent		
	☐ The delivery of the item was through a normal process known to both parties—dropping off for a sale. (3)	9	
	☐ The item was delivered to an agent. (3)		
	☐ Both parties benefit from this type of arrangement to show art, so this would be a mutual benefit or bailment-for-hire type. (3)		
	Liability for bailment: duty of care		
	☐ It is a mutual benefit bailment, so the duty of care is ordinary care at common law and under the modern rule. (3)	6	
	☐ The gallery must prove that there was no negligence because the bailment was established, and they could not produce the item. (3)		
	Negligence		
	☐ M1 was not at the show and the gallery could not locate it, so there is a good indication of negligence. (3)	18	
	☐ M1 might have sold, but if it did, it has not been delivered, which also suggests negligence. (3)		
	☐ M2 and M3 were not sold for the appropriate price, and the gallery does the pricing for the show and did not notice the problem, indicating negligence. (3)		
	☐ M4 was damaged, which indicates negligence. (3)		
	☐ The gallery is responsible for the actions of its agents. (3)		
	☐ The gallery had set up extra security. (3)		
Concl.:		6	
Issue:	Is the purchaser of M1 a buyer in the ordinary course of business?	6	
Rules:	☐ An item acquired by fraud has a voidable title and an item acquired by theft has a void title. (3)	18	
	☐ When a seller has a voidable title, a buyer can get a good title if they meet the BIOCB test. (3)		

Rules:	☐ A buyer is a BIOCB when there is entrustment to a merchant of goods of the kind, a sale transaction, and good faith of the buyer with no knowledge that the sale violates the rights of another. (3) ☐ Entrustment means voluntarily giving the item. (3) ☐ Goods of the kind means goods that match the one involved in the problematic sale. (3) ☐ The parties must follow customary business practices in the transaction. (3)		
	Type of title ☐ The painting was given to an agent of the merchant voluntarily, so there was no theft. (3) ☐ The agent was rogue and so was not acting within the normal job capacity. (3) ☐ Given the voluntary relinquishment, this looks more like fraud than theft, although the agent actually took the items. (3)	9	
	BIOCB test ☐ Entrustment was to an art gallery, which is a merchant dealing in goods of the kind. (3) ☐ MOMA is *not* a buyer, but instead a recipient of a gift. (3) ☐ MOMA's title depends on whether the acts of the gallery employee are better understood as theft or fraud. Given that the employee took a valuable painting and made it a gift intentionally, this sounds more like theft. (3) ☐ The employee's actions look a little more like fraud if we view the museum as an obvious place to find the painting and a place that would give it back. (3) ☐ MOMA is not a buyer and therefore cannot obtain a good title via the BIOCB test. MOMA has a void or voidable title, depending on whether the employee acted to commit a fraud or theft. (3)	15	
	BIOCB test and sale to Lyon ☐ For Lyon, the test is only potentially effective if the gift to MOMA is viewed as a fraud (and thus MOMA has voidable title) rather than a theft (making MOMA's title void) (3) ☐ Lyon acted in good faith and had no knowledge that the sale violates the rights of another—none specifically. (3)	12	

Continued

Continued

App.:	☐ Lyon bought the painting from a museum, which can be understood to occasionally sell artwork, if not regularly sell it. (3) ☐ There was a sale and that sale comported with the usual or customary practices of that type of business/industry. (3)		
Concl.:		6	
Issue:	Purchaser of M2 and M3 as BIOCB?	6	
Rules:	☐ As above		
App.:	☐ The artist delivered to the gallery, so there was entrustment. (3) ☐ The senator is not aware of issues with title, so he has good faith with respect to that. (3) ☐ The senator buys for one-tenth the normal price, so he should be suspicious, and this may indicate bad faith. (3) ☐ But there is no indication that the senator is an expert, so he may not understand that it was a very cheap price. (3) ☐ It is reasonable for a buyer to assume that the listed price at a gallery is a fair price for the item. (3) ☐ The senator made the purchase from a person who is in that type of business—a gallery. (3) ☐ There is a sale, and the sale comports with the usual or customary practices of that type of business/industry. (3)	21	
Concl.:		6	
Issue:	Did the Senator create a bailment of M2 and M3 with the gallery and was that bailment breached?	6	
Rules:	☐ As above		
App.:	**Creation** ☐ The bailment, if it exists, is a mutual benefit or "for hire" bailment, because of the commercial context. (3)	3	

App.:	*Transfer*	
	☐ The painting was already at the gallery and the senator left it with gallery after purchase for delivery. (3)	3
	Personalty	
	☐ The painting is a good, so it is personalty. (3)	3
	Mutual Assent	
	☐ Leaving a painting with the gallery for later delivery is an ordinary practice between the gallery and buyers. (3)	3
	Liability	
	☐ Ordinary care is required in this type of bailment. (3)	18
	☐ The paintings were secured within the gallery, so good care was taken. (3)	
	☐ The gallery employed two guards, so good care was taken. (3)	
	☐ But the alarm system was malfunctioning, so a lack of system care and maintenance may indicate negligence. (3)	
	☐ The gallery had knowledge of recent thefts, so would have known that it should be particularly careful of the alarm system. (3)	
	☐ The gallery could have refused to keep the paintings after purchase, but did not refuse bailment despite having knowledge of the system malfunction and neighborhood thefts. (3)	
Concl.:		6
Issue:	Is there liability of the landlord regarding the criminal acts due to the implied warranty of suitability/quality or the responsibility to secure against criminal acts?	6
Rules:	**Duty**	
	☐ A leased commercial property has an implied warranty of quality/suitability. (3)	9
	☐ The landlord is responsible for those within his/her control. (3)	
	☐ The duty of the landlord is for reasonable measures to secure areas under their own control against foreseeable criminal acts. (3)	

Continued

Continued

Rules:	**Factors to determine breach of duty**	21	
	☐ Foreseeability of the injury (3)		
	☐ Closeness of connection between defendant's conduct and injury suffered (3)		
	☐ Moral blame attached to defendant's conduct (3)		
	☐ Policy of preventing future harm (3)		
	☐ Extent of the burden (3)		
	☐ Availability and cost of insurance (3)		
	☐ Weighted: The most significant factors are foreseeability and extent of the burden to the defendant. (3)		
App.:	**Foreseeability**	9	
	☐ Reasonable measures would be those suitable to the neighborhood, which was posh. (3)		
	☐ Foreseeability of a break-in would be high given recent thefts. (3)		
	☐ Other thefts involved similar establishments, which suggests a higher degree of foreseeability. (3)		
	Closeness/connection	3	
	☐ The connection is direct: the failure of the security system allowed the entry of criminals and the theft. (3)		
	Moral blame	9	
	☐ The tenant notified the landlord, and there was no response, which increases blame. (3)		
	☐ Given that two guards did not manage to stop the theft, it is unclear that the alarm system would have done so in those circumstances, so perhaps blame is less clear. (3)		
	☐ No injuries were suffered. (3)		
	Extent of the burden	9	
	☐ The burden on the landlord was not extensive and the building already had the alarm system, it just needed a repair. (3)		
	☐ Changing the system would be expensive. (3)		
	☐ But they knew about the contract, and so they should not have to change the system. (3)		
	Insurance	3	
	☐ Insurance was available to both parties; costs either way are unknown. (3)		
Concl.:		6	

Issue:	Is the covenant enforceable, at least by the property owner if not the leaseholder?	6	
Rules:	**Creating an effective covenant** ☐ There must be notice of the existence of the covenant (either actual or constructive via recording). (3) ☐ The covenant must either satisfy the statute of frauds or meet the qualifications for an implied covenant. (3)	6	
	Test for a covenant to run with the land ☐ The covenant must be established with the intent for it to run with the land. (3) ☐ The covenant must touch and concern the land. (3) ☐ There must be privity, both horizontal and vertical. (3)	9	
	Negative covenants ☐ Negative covenants are agreements not to do something. (3) ☐ Negative covenants generally meet the touch and concern requirement. (3)	6	
App.:	☐ The covenant was within the deed so there was notice. (3) ☐ Because the covenant was in the deed for the property, it satisfies the Statute of Frauds. (3) ☐ The covenant was created as a part of a subdivision plan and so there was likely intent for it to continue. (3) ☐ The covenant references the character of the neighborhood, which makes it likely to have the intent to run. (3) ☐ This is an agreement not to do something, so it is a negative covenant, which will meet the touch and concern requirement. (3) ☐ The covenant was created within the sale of property, so horizontal privity exists. (3) ☐ We do not have information about vertical privity. (3)	21	
Concl.:		6	

Continued

Continued

Issue:	Is the negative easement for light enforceable?	6	
Rules:	☐ Negative easements must be express (written). (3) ☐ At common law negative easements were valid only for light, air, support, and stream water. Modern law has added conservation easements. (3) ☐ A negative easement must be appurtenant to be enforceable. (3)	9	
App.:	☐ The easement is within the deed, so it is express. (3) ☐ The easement is for light. (3) ☐ The easement is oddly written for a light easement, and may really be a restriction on aesthetics. (3) ☐ The easement was created to benefit neighboring properties and is appurtenant. (3)	12	
Concl.:		6	
		Total	

Mean Score for sample law student groups: 156

Designer with Inspiration Hypothetical

Time to read and write your answer: one hour.

Heading off on a trip from London (KY) to Paris (KY), eco-luxury designer Katy Bell notices a pink plaid cashmere sweater folded across one of the train station benches. The sweater is reasonably well made, but not by a top designer. Katy figures it is worth maybe $20 on the used clothing market at most, but it appeals to her designer's eye. Katy looks around for its owner, but does not spy any likely candidates. As she reaches for it a conductor passes by and says, "Oh, is that yours? I found it last week and folded it there. No one's touched it since then." The conductor, who thought himself to be acting quite carefully and conscientiously, works for a private company that owns and operates this new luxury train system that runs through the Midwest.

After a bit of debating with herself, Katy takes the sweater for her designer brand, "Lost Property of London." Back in her studio where she is preparing for London's Fashion Week (the other London this time), Katy discovers an interior pocket on the sweater. It contains a lovely and rather unique diamond ring, which Katy sets aside, thinking it would be perfect for her show. Katy cuts the sweater, reusing the cashmere to make a very chic clutch purse for the fashion show.

Katy's Eco-Luxury line is a hit at fashion week, where she has one of the models wear the diamond ring along with the clutch purse. After the show, Katy sells the clutch for $2,500, but no one can find the ring.

Unfortunately for Katy, the ring was recognized by the owner during the fashion show. The owner just happens to be (via Murphy's Law) Katy's neighbor and fellow designer, Arch Rivalry. Arch had originally owned not only his property, but also the property where Studio Eco, Katy's studio, is now located. When it was conveyed, the property was used by an accountant who never had client visitors at his office. (The accountant sold to Katy.) When Mr. Rivalry conveyed the property to the accountant, he included with the deed a right to cross his own property described as a "right to use the adjacent driveway to access the rear part of the conveyed property, but only for the limited use of a small homemaker-type business." The same notation was made on a deed for another property, Shady Acres Windmills, also formerly owned by Mr. Rivalry. Katy's business uses only the small studio on the property, where it employs four people and accepts regular deliveries of fabric and regularly loads new designs onto courier vans for delivery to celebrity clients.

In the meantime, the owner of Shady Acres Windmills is renovating his property. He is claiming a right to cross Katy's property because he cannot maneuver a cement truck close enough to his property to pour the new foundation without driving the truck across Katy's parking lot. If the truck is not permitted to cross the lot, then the cement must be moved to the new foundation via wheelbarrows, which would be nearly impossible during the winter.

Scoring Rubric for Designer with Inspiration Hypothetical

Section			
Issue:	Who is the "finder" of the ring/sweater?	6	
Rules:	***Traditional common law rules regarding the place of finding***		
	☐ The finder of lost property in a public place acquires rights against all others except the rightful owner. (3)	12	
	☐ On private property, the presumption is that the real property owner constructively possesses everything on the property, so long as the owner is in actual possession of the real property. (3)		
	☐ If private property is open to the public, a finder gets possession unless the item is within the actual control of the real property owner or the owner's agent. (3)		
	☐ Right of possession is not ownership; ownership remains with the true owner, if that person can be located. (3)		
	Characterizations of the object		
	Some jurisdictions use the nature of the object to determine who should have legal possession:		
	☐ Lost—finder gets possession (3)	30	
	☐ Mislaid—premises owner gets possession (3)		
	☐ Treasure trove—finder gets possession (3)		
	☐ The treasure trove rule usually does not apply to cash, but a minority of jurisdictions apply the rule to cash as well as coins. (3)		
	☐ Abandoned—title, not possession, goes to the first finder. (3)		
	☐ Abandonment is based on the circumstances of finding and the location, but not necessarily the passage of time. (3)		
	☐ Embedded—goes to the owner of the land where found (3)		
	☐ Embedded is defined as being within the earth or buried. (3)		

Rules:	☐ Statutes provide for eventual termination of the true owner's rights if the property remains unclaimed. Possessors then become title owners. (3) ☐ Stolen property has a void title. (3)		
App.:	***First finder*** ☐ The conductor discovered the sweater. (3) ☐ The conductor did not see the ring. (3) ☐ The conductor had no reason to believe anything other than a sweater was there. (3) ☐ A ring is unlikely content for a sweater. (3) ☐ Katy first held the ring. (3) ☐ Katy first saw the ring. (3) ☐ If Katy stole the sweater, this makes her possession of the sweater and any contents a void title. (3)	21	
	Ownership ☐ The true owner is known. (3) ☐ Because the true owner known, others can only get possession, not title. (3)	6	
	Property type for location of finding ☐ The sweater was found on private property because the train is a private enterprise. (3)	3	
	Category of found property ☐ With a sweater, it is likely to be intentionally placed and then forgotten, and therefore it would be a mislaid item. (3) ☐ It is also common to lose an item of clothing while traveling. (3) ☐ Abandonment of the sweater is possible, but unlikely for the ring, given its value. (3) ☐ It is possible that the sweater was abandoned, without understanding that the ring was in the pocket, so the intent would be to abandon the sweater, but not the ring. (3) ☐ No significant time has passed. (3) ☐ Katy took what she knew was not hers—so the sweater is stolen property. (3)	18	
Concl.:		6	

Continued

Continued

Issue:	Is Katy responsible for conversion of the sweater and ring?	6	
Rules:	☐ Conversion is the wrongful exercise of dominion over another's property. (3) ☐ There are multiple causes of action/remedies: Trover for value, replevin for item, etc. (3)	6	
App.:	☐ As non-owner Katy had rights only if she was the first finder. (3) ☐ The conductor was the first finder, at least of the sweater, so Katy had no rights to it. (3) ☐ Both the original item value and the new value are possible as measures of damages. (3)	9	
Concl.:		6	
Issue:	Can Katy claim mistaken improvement (title by accession)?	6	
Rules:	☐ One whose property has been appropriated without authority generally has the right to recover the property, even if it has increased in value by the addition of labor or money. (3) ☐ There is an exception to this rule where there has been a destruction of substantial identity of the original property. (3) ☐ Destruction of identity might be measured by the value difference. (3) ☐ Destruction of identity can be measured by a change in the nature of the item. (3) ☐ Jurisdictional split: some states find that bad faith may prevent the defense entirely, despite a substantial change in character. Other states are interested in the change to the item, not the mindset of the person who changed the item. (3)	15	
App.:	**Good/bad faith** ☐ Katy does not seem to have acted in good faith, because she knew that the sweater was not hers and someone else on the train might claim it. (3)	3	

App.:	**Destruction of substantial identity**	18	
	☐ The change in value is significant (100X greater). (3)		
	☐ The object is now a purse, not a sweater, so it is a different category of item now. (3)		
	☐ The object is still cashmere fabric. (3)		
	☐ The object is still within the clothing/accessories category of goods. (3)		
	☐ Labor has changed the form of the item. (3)		
	☐ The item has been cut and has changed shape. (3)		
Concl.:		6	
Issue:	Is there a bailment with Katy of the sweater and ring (for the benefit of the true owner of the items)?	6	
Rules:	☐ An effective bailment requires: a transfer of personalty with mutual assent or constructive assent. (3)	15	
	☐ Mutual assent requires acceptance in the context of a delivery. (3)		
	☐ Jurisdictional split: There is a traditional three-tiered set of different duties of care based on the type of bailment. The modern rule says the duty is always ordinary care. (3)		
	☐ In an involuntary bailment, if the party exercises dominion, the duty is ordinary care. (3)		
	☐ If the item is not returned, then the courts presume negligence. (3)		
App.:	**Benefit and duty**	6	
	☐ This would be a constructive bailment, created by taking dominion over a lost/mislaid item. (3)		
	☐ The benefit in a constructive bailment is usually to the true owner, but here Katy took advantage of the bailment to use the item for her own benefit. (3)		
	Divisibility	6	
	☐ Katy did not know of the contents when she took the sweater. (3)		
	☐ But when Katy discovered the ring and did not try to return it, she created an additional bailment of the ring, even if the ring would not have been previously included with the sweater. (3)		

Continued

Continued

App.:	**Breach** ☐ Katy used the ring for her own purposes in a show. (3) ☐ Katy lost the ring. (3) ☐ Katy has destroyed the sweater. It may be more valuable now, but it is not a sweater, which is what the true owner had (and presumably wanted). (3)	9	
Concl.:		6	
Issue:	Was there a bailment with the conductor/station?	6	
Rules:	☐ As above		
App.:	**Creation** ☐ The conductor picked up the lost/mislaid sweater, so this is a constructive bailment. (3) ☐ Where the finder is an agent of a business, there is a benefit to both parties, because there is an indirect benefit to a commercial establishment for customer good will. (3) ☐ The conductor is an agent of the train company. (3) ☐ The duty of care for a mutual benefit bailment is ordinary care. (3) **Breach** ☐ The conductor allowed Katy, who he knew was not the owner, to take the sweater, which suggests negligence. (3)	12 3	
Concl.:		6	
Issue:	Is the conductor or train company liable for the ring or only the sweater if there was a bailment?	6	
Rules:	**Liability for contents in bailment** ☐ Bailments may be divisible, with contents being separate from a container. (3) ☐ Bailments generally cover ordinarily expected contents, but not valuable or extraneous ones without specific knowledge of the contents. The question is what is a foreseeable item within the container. (3)	6	

App.:	☐ The value of the ring far outweighs the value of the sweater. (3)	12	
	☐ The value of the ring is high for it to be stored in a pocket without a box or anything else to secure it. (3)		
	☐ The pocket was hidden so there was no reason the conductor would expect any contents within the sweater. (3)		
	☐ Because jewelry is often carried in a purse, putting a ring in a pocket may not be that strange. (3)		
Concl.:		6	
Issue:	What type of easement, if any, is held by Katy and the windmill business?	6	
Rules:	**Categorize traits of an easement**		
	☐ An easement is affirmative if it is a right to make a physical entry; it is negative if the easement restricts someone from doing something. (3)	21	
	☐ An easement is referred to as express or non-express, depending on whether there is a writing. (3)		
	☐ An easement can be exclusive or nonexclusive, meaning you can use it alone or share it with other neighbors. (3)		
	☐ An easement is appurtenant if it is of value to the dominant tenement. (3)		
	☐ An easement is appurtenant if there is an intent for it to run with the land. (3)		
	☐ An easement is a right to enter, but does not give an ownership right in the property. (3)		
	☐ Easements only run with the land (go to next owner) if there was an intent for the easement to continue. (3)		
	Implied easement test		
	☐ There must be a single owner of multiple or later subdivided tracts. (3)	12	
	☐ The easement must provide to the other property a benefit or advantage, which is not minor, and must approach necessity. (3)		
	☐ An implied easement must be apparent, continuous, and appear permanent. (3)		
	☐ An implied easement is not written into a later conveyance. (3)		

Continued

Continued

App.:	**Traits**		
	☐ There is a writing, so this is an express easement. (3)	12	
	☐ This is a right to cross the property, so it is an affirmative easement. (3)		
	☐ This easement is nonexclusive because it is shared with a neighbor. (3)		
	☐ This easement is appurtenant because it has value to the user of the easement. (3)		
	Running		
	☐ There is value to the business, so this suggests the easement would be created to run with the land. (3)	3	
	Implied		
	☐ There was a single owner of the properties. (3)	18	
	☐ It is unclear if this easement was written into any later conveyance, but there is no proof that it was. (3)		
	☐ The easement provides a significant value. It is beneficial for deliveries and provides better access to the property. (3)		
	☐ Better access does not make the easement necessary, only convenient. (3)		
	☐ Given the current use, the easement appears necessary to operation of the business. (3)		
	☐ There are not a lot of facts on this point, but the use appears to be continuous. (3)		
Concl.:		6	
Issue:	Have Katy and the windmill business burdened the easement, or improperly extended the scope of the easement?	6	
Rules:	☐ An attempt by the dominant property owner to significantly change the use of the easement will not be permitted, because it is an invasion of the rights of the servient tenant. (3)	9	
	☐ The right of the easement holder is unlimited reasonable use. (3)		
	☐ Use may increase by volume through time, but the type or kind of use should be consistent. (3)		

App.:	☐ The homemaker suggests the easement meant to accommodate some type of small home business. (3)	33	
	☐ But homemaker is also a word used for someone who does not have a job outside of the upkeep and management of a household, so it is unclear. (3)		
	☐ Katy does not have a studio open to clients, so her use is less of a burden than that would be. (3)		
	☐ Most small businesses do delivery and shipping, so this is a reasonable use and probably existed before. (3)		
	☐ Katy has celebrity clients, which suggests this is not a small business. (3)		
	☐ Katy's business is very different from being an accountant in terms of shipping and deliveries. (3)		
	☐ Both an accountant and a designer might have no client visits at home. (3)		
	☐ There are only four employees. (3)		
	☐ Four employees are a lot for a home business. (3)		
	☐ The type of traffic has remained the same over time. (3)		
	☐ Volume has increased over time. (3)		
Concl.:		6	
Issue:	Does the windmill business have an easement by necessity across Katy's property?	6	
Rules:	**Necessity**		
	☐ Easements by necessity are generally created by being landlocked. (3)	12	
	☐ Landlocked means a property lacks an accessible route to the public highways. (3)		
	☐ There is a high standard for necessity. (3)		
	☐ Necessity is something much more than convenience (3)		
App.:	☐ The windmill business is not landlocked, so there is no true necessity. (3)	12	
	☐ The problem is access for new work, not getting to the existing structure, so again this does not suggest necessity. (3)		

Continued

Continued

App.:	☐ The need is limited and seasonal. (3) ☐ It is possible to work around the need to access in this way (i.e., using a wheelbarrow). (3)		
Concl.:		6	
		Total	

Mean Score for sample law student groups: 161

Egyptologists in Love Hypothetical

Time to read and write your answer: one hour.

Alexandria tried not to think. It was not working. The brain has a tendency to be constantly in motion, pushing forward and prodding the paths of least resistance, ideas, memories, and old wounds. Actually, though, she was not trying not to think in general. She was trying not to think about Luca.

They'd met at dinner on the first night at the practice dig in Virginia where they would set the staging for later international travel. That was four weeks ago. Since then, they had spent hours working together, chatting about their lives — hers in Atlanta and his in Rome. For hours, they roamed the island, exploring every cove and corner, sharing their love of history and archeology. One particular nest in the old dovecote became their mailbox for small love letters. It was silly, quaint, a gesture to the past, but it fit the two of them. Still, with lives and families and careers on two continents, they made no promises to each other.

A few days before the end of the program, their professor interrupted breakfast with an announcement. "I'm sorry to say that Luca has left the program early due to his mother's sudden illness." Alexandria looked up sharply in surprise. He hadn't even said goodbye.

She put her hand into the pocket of her cardigan and felt the ring she carried there. It was an antique; her grandfather had bought it in Rome in 1910. He had given it to Alexandria years before, suggesting that she someday give it to the man who held her heart. She might never see Luca after that summer, but she had meant to give it to him anyway.

In the days that followed, Alexandria walked numbly through her tasks. She finished her group's notes and tried to stuff an island summer's worth of souvenirs into her suitcases. Finally, when it wouldn't all fit, she dropped off some of her older clothes at the local charity shop. The pink sweater that she wore on the day Luca left was too painful a reminder. It had to go.

Rue ran her hands along the old worn stones of the walls, the sleeve of her cardigan catching on the edges of the stones. "Where did you get that sweater?" Elise asked.

Rue answered, still busying her hands with exploring the dovecote. "I bought it at the secondhand store, the charity shop in town that has old clothes and jewelry and stuff like that. I went to find something for the '80s dance at school next term, but this seemed cute and it has been chilly in the mornings here so far."

"Hmmm." Elise responded, trying not to roll her eyes at her sister's wardrobe choices.

"Anyway," Rue said, "Did I show you what I found? After I bought the sweater, I was going to put it in the wash, and I felt something down in the bottom of the pockets. It's a ring." Rue reached into her pocket and withdrew the ring to show her sister. "I think it's old and pretty neat. Someone's added an engraving to it — it says "For Luca" inside. And I got it for the price of a second-hand sweater. To be specific, $2.50."

"It's probably silver-plated, not worth anything," Elise dismissed the ring.

"I bought it whether I meant to or not, I like it, and I am keeping it." Rue ignored her sister, put the ring back in her pocket, and continued her exploration of the dovecote. Curious to feel what was inside, Rue slipped her hand into one of the nests, reaching far back into the wall. She frowned suddenly as she felt something. Something just out of reach.

"Hey, Elise, there is something in here. Do you think you can reach it? I can't quite get my hand in far enough."

"Eww. Yuck. Birds. I do not want to stick my hand in there," Elise replied. But as she said it, she walked toward Rue and rolled up her sleeve. "Go on, get out of the way." Elise reached far back into the corner of the nest, pulling free a small metal box.

Rue reached for the box immediately, taking it from Elise's hands. "I wonder what is in there?"

"Whatever." Elise ignored her sister and went back to wandering the dovecote.

Rue released the catch and lifted the lid of the box. The first thing she saw was an ornate gold, jeweled cross fitted with rubies. "Wow." It was all she could say. Beneath the cross she found a brittle piece of paper that she unfolded.

Dearest Alexandria,

I have a flight to Rome in an hour. There is no time. But I know you'll look in our mailbox one last time. This cross has been in my family for two hundred years. I have worn it always until this night. I am leaving it here, because I know you will not leave me without it. If I leave it with you, you will come to Rome. You would return it to me. But what I hope is that you will return with it, and then, if I have your heart, you will stay with me and keep the cross to wear as your own.

All my love, Luca

Rue never got around to figuring out who Luca and Alexandria were.

Scoring Rubric for Egyptologists in Love Hypothetical

Section			
Issue:	Did Luca make a valid, conditional inter-vivos gift of the cross to Alexandria?	6	
Rules:	*Intent* ☐ Gifts generally require an intent to transfer a present interest permanently. (3) ☐ Conditions violate the common law rule because the condition means there is no present intent. (3) ☐ Modern jurisdictional split: ☐ It is a valid gift with a valid condition. (3) ☐ It is a valid gift, ignore the condition. (3) ☐ It is a failed gift, which makes a bailment. (3)	15	
	Delivery and acceptance ☐ Delivery of the object to the new owner is required. (3) ☐ Delivery may be actual or constructive. (3) ☐ Acceptance by the new owner is required. (3) ☐ Acceptance is presumed for things of value to the recipient. (3)	12	

App.:	*Intent*		
	☐ Luca left the cross in their secret mailbox, which indicates he meant for her to have it. (3)	6	
	☐ Luca left a letter for her with it, explaining the circumstances and asking her to bring it to Italy, suggesting a conditional intent. (3)		
	Present interest		
	☐ The letter says she will return the cross to Rome, but not necessarily to him. (3)	6	
	☐ Luca seems to want her to keep it only if she stays with him, so the intent seems conditional. (3)		
	Delivery		
	☐ Luca put it in their agreed-upon mailbox. (3)	9	
	☐ He "knew she would check," and so delivered to it to the checkpoint, which is a constructive delivery. (3)		
	☐ She never checked the mailbox to actually get it, so there was no actual delivery. (3)		
	Acceptance		
	☐ The cross has jewels and so is valuable and acceptance can be presumed. (3)	3	
Concl.:		6	
Issue:	Who is the first possessor (finder) of the cross?	6	
Rules:	☐ Finder's law attempts to identify the "first possessor" and reward that person. (3)	12	
	☐ The question is when the item is found in the legal sense, meaning that someone has dominion and control. (3)		
	☐ Finding may include discovery of contents of a container or removal from the area. (3)		
	☐ Possession can be divisible if the contents are enclosed and unknown. (3)		
App.:	☐ Rue was the first to touch the box, so she was the first to control, but she did not maintain it. (3)	24	
	☐ She would have gotten the box herself, but needed help to reach, so she had the intent to possess when she asked for help. (3)		

Continued

Continued

App.:	☐ Elise did not want to help, so she was acting as agent for Rue. (3)		
	☐ Elise was the first to hold the box, so she had first actual possession, at least of the container. (3)		
	☐ Rue immediately took the box from Elise without Elise's objection, which indicates the agent relationship. (3)		
	☐ Elise says "whatever" and does not seem to care about opening the box, so she capitulates to the agent relationship. (3)		
	☐ Rue is the first to open the box, so she is the first to have knowledge of the contents. (3)		
	☐ Rue is first to hold the cross, so she is the first to have full dominion. (3)		
Concl.:		6	
Issue:	How would finder's law assign rights to the cross?	6	
Rules:	**Traditional common law rules regarding the place of finding**		
	☐ The finder of lost property in a public place acquires rights against all others except the rightful owner. (3)	12	
	☐ On private property, the presumption is that the real property owner constructively possesses everything on the property, so long as the owner is in actual possession of the real property. (3)		
	☐ If private property is open to the public, a finder gets possession unless the item is within the actual control of the real property owner or the owner's agent. (3)		
	☐ Right of possession is not ownership; ownership remains with the true owner, if that person can be located. (3)		
	Characterizations of the object		
	☐ Some jurisdictions use the nature of the object to determine who should have legal possession:	30	
	☐ Lost—finder gets possession (3)		
	☐ Mislaid—premises owner gets possession (3)		
	☐ Treasure trove—finder gets possession (3)		
	☐ The treasure trove rule usually does not apply to cash, but a minority of jurisdictions apply the rule to cash as well as coins. (3)		

Rules:	☐ Abandoned—title, not possession, goes to the first finder. (3)		
	☐ Abandonment is based on the circumstances of finding and the location, but not necessarily the passage of time. (3)		
	☐ Embedded—goes to the owner of the land where found (3)		
	☐ Embedded is defined as being within the earth or buried. (3)		
	☐ Statutes provide for eventual termination of the true owner's rights if the property remains unclaimed. Possessors then become title owners. (3)		
	☐ Stolen property has a void title. (3)		
App.:	**Abandoned**		
	☐ There is no evidence that the Luca has definitively relinquished the cross. (3)	12	
	☐ Luca knows where it was and never came back, which may indicate an intent to give up the claim. (3)		
	☐ It is a long way to come back from Rome, so not coming may not indicate intent to abandon. (3)		
	☐ Luca seems to assume Alexandria has it, so maybe he does not know where it is. (3)		
	Lost		
	☐ Luca knew exactly where it was. (3)	9	
	☐ A long amount of time has passed with no one returning for it, so it may have been forgotten. (3)		
	☐ Alexandria does not know the cross was there. (3)		
	Mislaid		
	☐ The cross was placed deliberately. (3)	9	
	☐ Luca did not intend to come back. (3)		
	☐ Luca did intend for someone else to pick it up. This is not the normal situation for mislaid property. (3)		
	Treasure trove		
	☐ Treasure trove normally includes coins, gold and jewels, and the cross includes jewels. (3)	6	
	☐ This is not, however, an ancient treasure, but a modern item. (3)		
Concl.:		6	

Continued

Continued

Issue:	☐ Is Rue a buyer in the ordinary course of business (BIOCB) of the ring?	6	
Rules:	☐ An item acquired by fraud has a voidable title and an item acquired by theft has a void title. (3) ☐ When a seller has a voidable title, a buyer can get a good title if they meet the BIOCB test. (3) ☐ A buyer is a BIOCB when there is entrustment to a merchant of goods of the kind, a sale transaction, and good faith of the buyer with no knowledge that the sale violates the rights of another. (3) ☐ Entrustment means voluntarily giving the item. (3) ☐ Goods of the kind means goods that match the one involved in the problematic sale. (3) ☐ The parties must follow customary business practices in the transaction. (3)	18	
App.:	**Entrustment** ☐ Alexandria gave the ring to a charity shop that has vintage jewelry. (3) ☐ Alexandria did not mean to give the ring, only the sweater. (3) ☐ Alexandria appears to have left the ring in the pocket accidentally. (3) ☐ The charity shop may not have accepted the entrustment as they did not notice the ring either, but they did accept the sweater, which contained the ring. (3)	12	
	Good faith ☐ Rue had no bad faith. (3) ☐ Rue had no knowledge of the ring. (3) ☐ Rue had no intent to violate another's rights. (3)	9	
	Transaction ☐ This was an ordinary purchase at the store. (3) ☐ This was a sale, not a gift. (3)	6	
Concl.:		2	

Issue:	Does Rue owe bailment duties to Alexandria?	6	
Rules:	☐ An effective bailment requires a transfer of personalty with mutual assent or constructive assent. (3) ☐ Mutual assent requires acceptance in the context of a delivery. (3) ☐ Jurisdictional split: There is a traditional three-tiered set of different duties of care based on the type of bailment. The modern rule says the duty is always ordinary care. (3) ☐ In an involuntary or constructive bailment, if the party exercises dominion, the duty is ordinary care. (3) ☐ If the item is not returned, then the courts presume negligence. (3)	15	
App.:	**Mutual assent** ☐ There is no delivery with mutual assent of the parties, so this is not an ordinary bailment. (3) ☐ This is a lost/mislaid item, and Rue has possession of it now, which creates a constructive bailment. (3) ☐ Rue has taken control of the ring, so she has exercised dominion, which is all that is necessary for a constructive bailment to create a duty of ordinary care. (3)	9	
Concl.:		6	
		Total	

NINETEEN

Supersize Hypos with Estates Issues

The Aspiring Actress and the Gun Runner Hypothetical

Time to read and write your answer: one hour.

In the late evening Ms. Amber Glass, an aspiring soap opera star, stops by O'Sullivan's Pub in Lexington, Virginia, for a drink. Having just failed her tenth audition, Ms. Glass is not in the best of spirits. She takes a seat near Tobias Finn, a notorious border gun runner who has just been listed on the FBI's most wanted list under the name "Lucky Striker."

Mr. Finn is also not in the best of moods. He has just learned of his newly promoted status on the FBI's list. And his divorce from Ms. Pamela Rhodes was just finalized.

After many, many margaritas and an escalating flirtation, the bartender teasingly says, "You two are really hitting it off. I think you should keep this one, Mr. Finn." In their inebriated state, Ms. Glass and Mr. Finn think this is a just fabulous idea. Mr. Finn's driver takes them to Gatlinburg, Tennessee, which happens to be the Las Vegas of the east coast for quickie weddings. By morning they are, rather accidentally, but quite legally, married.

The next morning is, well, rather interesting. The chapel attendant recognizes Mr. Finn's photo on CNN's morning broadcast about the updated most wanted list; he immediately reports Mr. Finn's whereabouts. In the meantime, Mr. Finn has awoken and is feeling both guilty (because his car and driver made the Tennessee escapade possible) and regretful (because he really does like Ms. Glass and wishes he could make a life with her). While she is still sleeping, he arranges for the delivery of an extraordinary 14-carat diamond ring. Mr. Finn leaves, placing the ring box and a note beside her on the bed. He has scribbled, "I wish things were different."

As he leaves the hotel, the FBI surrounds Mr. Finn. Mr. Finn, unarmed, wants to surrender and become an informant, but the agents assume he is armed and shoot too quickly, killing him instantly.

Mr. Finn had never revised his will after Ms. Rhodes filed for divorce. The will reads as follows:

I leave Vibrant Vines, my Virginia Winery, to my wife, so long as she does not re-marry after my death, but if she does then to my brother, Trent. I leave Vista, my mountain estate, to my wife for life, and then to my surviving nieces, but if there are none, then to my brother, Trent. I leave my condominium in D.C., 345 Avenue K, to my wife for life, then to my nephews who have issue to carry on the family name, so long as the nephews graduate from college. The residual bulk of my estate shall go to my heirs at law.

Scoring Rubric for the Aspiring Actress and the Gun Runner Hypothetical

Section			
Issue:	Is there an effective inter-vivos gift of the ring?	6	
Rules:	☐ Valid gifts require intent, delivery, and acceptance. (3) ☐ Intent should be present and permanent. (3) ☐ Delivery may be constructive or actual and fitted to the circumstances or nature of the item. (3) ☐ Acceptance may be presumed for things of value. (3) ☐ The burden of proof falls on the recipient of the gift. (3)	15	
App.:	**Intent to create a present interest** ☐ The ring was purchased for her. (3) ☐ He left not intending to return (intending to surrender) so the intent seems permanent. (3) ☐ The note suggests finality. (3) ☐ But if this is an engagement ring, then those may be viewed as conditional gifts. (3)	15	

App.:	☐ But an engagement ring is an odd way to think of the ring, given that they are already married. Also, if there was a condition, then it has already been met by the marriage. (3)		
	Delivery		
	☐ He left the ring with her in the locked hotel room. (3)	9	
	☐ He left the ring with a note for her, making delivery clearer. (3)		
	☐ She was sleeping, so she was unaware of the delivery, making it somewhat incomplete. (3)		
	Acceptance		
	☐ The ring has value, so acceptance is presumed. (3)	3	
Concl.:		6	
Issue:	Is the ring a gift causa mortis?	6	
Rules:	☐ The donor must intend to make a gift. (3)	21	
	☐ The intent should be conditional on death. (3)		
	☐ The donor must apprehend death. (3)		
	☐ Apprehension may be inferred from the circumstances. (3)		
	☐ The gift must be delivered. (3)		
	☐ Constructive delivery is acceptable. (3)		
	☐ Death must occur to make the gift irrevocable. (3)		
App.:	*Intent*		
	☐ The ring was purchased for her, but it is not clear that the motivation is connected to the possibility of death. (3)	9	
	☐ He left the ring not intending to return (intending to surrender), so his intent seems permanent. (3)		
	☐ The note suggests finality, and he is aware of the risk of facing the police, but there is no reason he would want her to have the ring only if he died. (3)		
	Delivery		
	☐ He left the ring with her in the locked hotel room. (3)	9	
	☐ He left the ring with a note for her, making delivery clearer. (3)		

Continued

Continued

App.:	☐ She was sleeping, so she was unaware of the delivery, making it somewhat incomplete. (3)		
	Apprehension		
	☐ He did not know that he was surrounded at the time of the gift, which reduces the immediacy of any apprehension. (3)	21	
	☐ He did know he was on the most wanted list, which creates some risk of death at any time. (3)		
	☐ Police generally are not supposed to kill, but sometimes do, sadly. (3)		
	☐ He operates a very high-risk business. (3)		
	☐ His business is weapons, which is how he died, so that seems expected. (3)		
	☐ He leaves planning to surrender, so as far as he knows, he should not die. (3)		
	☐ He is unarmed so a gunfight is not expected. (3)		
	Death		
	☐ He did, in fact, die. (3)	3	
Concl.:			
Issue:	How would a court interpret the devise to his "wife," in light of the date of the will, the divorce, and remarriage?	6	
Rules:	☐ Jurisdictional split: some jurisdictions invalidate gifts to spouses when the will is dated before the divorce, some jurisdictions allow the will to stand as written, especially if it is a recent divorce. (6)	6	
App.:	☐ There was a recent divorce. (3)	6	
	☐ Jurisdiction is not assigned in the hypothetical, so the outcome would depend on the state. (3)		
	Interpretation of "my wife"		
	☐ If "my wife" is interpreted as meaning prior wife (as of time written), then perhaps strike (as above). (3)	9	
	☐ If "my wife" is interpreted as a position/station, rather than a person, then the will refers to the new wife. (3)		

App.:	☐ If this provision is not interpreted to apply to the new wife, then the estate will need to meet any statutory minimum for spouses, which will partially defeat devises. (3)		
Concl.:		6	
Issue:	What are the property interests in Vibrant Vines?	6	
Rules:	**Common law versus modern and heirs language**		
	☐ At common law, the language "and heirs" was required to have more than a life estate in the property. (3)	6	
	☐ Under modern law "to X" is enough to create a fee estate. (3)		
	Life estates and remainders		
	☐ "For life" creates a life estate. (3)	36	
	☐ An interest that follows a life estate is a remainder. (3)		
	☐ If an estate cuts off another property interest by forfeiture, then it is an executory interest. (3)		
	☐ When there is a condition precedent on a bequest, the recipient must do something before taking the property. (3)		
	☐ Survivorship is generally a condition precedent. (3)		
	☐ If there is a condition subsequent on a gift, then the recipient can take then meet the condition. (3)		
	☐ The language "but if" suggests a condition subsequent. (3)		
	☐ A secondary clause after the granting words suggests a condition subsequent. (3)		
	☐ A suggestion of termination during ownership indicates a condition subsequent. (3)		
	☐ A condition precedent creates a conditional remainder (CR). (3)		
	☐ A condition subsequent creates a vested remainder subject to divestment (VSTD). (3)		

Continued

Continued

Rule:	☐ If more people can join the class to take, it is a vested remainder subject to open. This only works if no other conditions need to be met. If there are other conditions, then it must be a remainder vested subject to divestment (VSTD) or a contingent remainder (CR). (3)			
	Rule Against Perpetuities			
	☐ Rule Against Perpetuities (3)	6		
	☐ Contingent remainders, remainders vested subject to open, and executory interests are all subject to the Rule Against Perpetuities. (3)			
	Fee estates			
	☐ A fee that is divested to a third party on a condition is a fee simple subject to an executory limitation (FSSEL). (3)	3		
App.:	**Common law interpretation**			
	☐ "To my wife" creates a life estate only. (3)	15		
	☐ There would be a condition on the life estate, making it two separate interests: one ends by death, one by forfeiture (3)			
	☐ Trent takes on forfeiture, so this creates an executory interest of a life estate *pur autre vie* (measured by the life of the wife). (3)			
	☐ Trent would also have a remainder that would vest if the property were never forfeited, but only passed to him by the death of the wife. (3)			
	☐ The grantor holds a reversion. (3)			
	Modern law			
	"To my wife" creates a fee estate. (3)	12		
	☐ The estate is subject to a condition. (3)			
	☐ The condition divests to a third party, so the wife has a fee simple subject to an executory limitation (FSSEL). (3)			
	☐ Trent has an executory interest because he takes on forfeiture. (3)			
	Rule Against Perpetuities			
	☐ The executory interest is subject to the Rule Against Perpetuities (under common or modern law). (3)	9		
	☐ The measuring life is most sensibly the wife, who is the central taker of the property. (3)			
	☐ The condition will vest or fail within her lifetime, so there is no Rule Against Perpetuities problem. (3)			

Concl.:		6	
Issue:	What are the property interests in Vista?	6	
Rules:	☐ As above		
App.:	**Life estate and remainders** ☐ "For life" creates a life estate in the wife. (3) ☐ "Then to" after a life estate creates a remainder. (3) ☐ There is a requirement of surviving, so there is a condition precedent (as generally interpreted). (3) ☐ The nieces have contingent remainders because there is a condition precedent. (3)	12	
	Survivorship ☐ The will is unclear on when to measure survivorship. (3) ☐ In this situation it could be measured at the death of the grantor. (3) ☐ It could be measured at the death of the life estate holder. (3) ☐ If the condition is measured at the death of the grantor, then the contingent remainders vest immediately. (3) ☐ If it is measured at the death of the life tenant, then the interests can continue as contingent remainders, and holders are divested if they die before the life tenant. (3) ☐ Contingent remainders that did not divest earlier would vest at the life tenant's death. (3) ☐ Trent can only take if there are no surviving nieces when the condition is measured, so he must follow a life estate; his interest may be best understood as a remainder, not an executory interest. (3) ☐ Trent has an alternative contingent remainder. (3)	24	
	Rule Against Perpetuities ☐ Contingent remainders and executory interests are subject to the Rule Against Perpetuities. (3) ☐ The measuring life will likely be the life tenant because this is the central figure whose life determines outcomes. (3) ☐ The interests will vest or fail at end of the life estate at the latest, so there is no Rule Against Perpetuities problem. (3)	9	

Continued

Continued

Issue:	What are the property interests in the condominium?	6	
Rules:	As above		
App.:	**Life estate and remainders** ☐ "For life" creates a life estate in the wife. (3) ☐ "Then to" after a life estate creates a remainder in the nephews. (3) ☐ There are two conditions. (3) ☐ These conditions could be conditions precedent or subsequent, depending on the interpretation. (3)	12	
	Issue as a condition precedent or subsequent ☐ If "issue" is a condition precedent, then it creates contingent remainders. (3) ☐ The interest would continue as a contingent remainder until the holder has a child, then it would vest. (3) ☐ If the holder dies without offspring, then the interest fails. (3) ☐ If "issue" is interpreted as a condition subsequent, then the interest is a remainder vested subject to divestment. (3) ☐ This type of remainder again vests on having a child. (3) ☐ Holders are divested if they die without offspring. (3)	18	
	Ambiguity in family name ☐ There is an ambiguity because "family name" could mean that the parent must give the children that last name." Alternatively, the testator may have written about carrying on the family name only as an explanation for wanting there to be children. (3) ☐ If this language means the parent must give the last name to the child, then this suggests having issue is a condition precedent, not a condition subsequent, because it logically pushes for a precursor to taking the property. (3)	6	

App.:	**When to evaluate the condition of having issue**		
	☐ Issue can be evaluated at multiple points, and the deed is unclear as to when it should be evaluated. (3)	3	
	Evaluate at grantor's death		
	☐ The court can evaluate as of the grantor's death. (3)	6	
	☐ In this approach, it must be a condition precedent, so it creates contingent remainders, either failing immediately or vesting immediately. (3)		
	Evaluate at life tenant's death		
	☐ The court could evaluate the condition at the life tenant's death. (3)	12	
	☐ In this scenario, the condition could be a condition precedent or subsequent. (3)		
	☐ This means the interests could be either a contingent remainder or a remainder vested subject to divestment, depending on whether the court views the condition as subsequent or precedent. (3)		
	☐ The class would be open so long as there are potential parents alive. (3)		
	Evaluate at the interest holders' deaths		
	☐ This means the condition would be measured as within the lifetimes of the people who hold the property interest. (3)	18	
	☐ In this scenario, the condition may be a condition precedent or subsequent, and the court will choose because it is ambiguous. (3)		
	☐ If the interpretation is for a condition precedent, then it creates a contingent remainder that vests on having children, and the class is open. (3)		
	☐ If the interpretation is for a condition subsequent, then the property interest is a remainder vested subject to divestment. (3)		
	☐ If the holder has a child, then it vests, subject to open. (3)		
	☐ If the holder dies without a child, then that person is divested at death. (3)		

Continued

Continued

App.:	**Condition of graduation**		
	☐ There is a second condition of graduating from college. (3)	27	
	☐ This also could be a condition precedent or subsequent. (3)		
	☐ If there are two conditions, then it is likely that the first is a condition precedent, and the second a condition subsequent. (3)		
	☐ A second clause after the granting language here pushes in favor of a condition subsequent. (3)		
	☐ If the court finds that it is a condition precedent, then the holders have a contingent remainder until they go to college. (3)		
	☐ If both were conditions precedent, then holders of the interests must have a child and graduate for the interest to vest. (3)		
	☐ Like having issue, the question of whether someone has graduated from college could be measured at multiple points (repeat of above patterns). (6)		
	☐ Heirs at law will take any reversions. (3)		
	Rule Against Perpetuities		
	☐ Contingent remainders are subject to the rule. (3)	12	
	☐ The measuring life (life in being) is likely the life tenant. (3)		
	☐ It is more logical to use the same measuring point for conditions as for the measuring life for Rule Against Perpetuities purposes. (3)		
	☐ Applying the rule of convenience could save some interests here by closing the class at the life tenant's death. (3)		
	Evaluating conditions at grantor's death		
	☐ If the point of evaluation for conditions is the grantor's death, then there are no problems because all interests vest or fail at that time. (3)	6	
	☐ This does not change if the measuring life (life in being) is the life tenant or the interest holder. (3)		
	Evaluating conditions at the life tenant's death		
	☐ If the moment of evaluating conditions is the death of the life tenant and the measuring life (life in being) is the life tenant, then interests would vest or fail at end of the life estate at the latest, so there is no perpetuities problem. (3)	3	

Continued

App.:	*Evaluating conditions as of the interest holder's death*		
	☐ If you measure conditions as within their own lifetimes, then the remainders fail the rule if life estate is the measuring life because an interest holder could have a child 40 years after the life tenant's death. (3)	3	
Concl.:		6	
		Total	

Mean Score for sample law student groups: 167

Wannabe Spy Hypothetical

Time to read and write your answer: one hour.

Cecil Rolfe thoroughly enjoys his retirement in Lexington, Virginia, where he operates a small farm more as a hobby than as a commercial enterprise. Cecil, who regrettably never was accepted into the CIA, spends his time spying on his neighbors and creating elaborate escape routes through the alleyways in case the police think he has had one too many scotches at the Southern Inn.

When new neighbors, Mr. and Mrs. Smith, rent the house and farm beside Cecil's, Cecil is thrilled to have new potential targets for his mock espionage. Having become thoroughly bored with his spy efforts to date, Cecil begins repurposing his heavy farm equipment to dig listening tunnels underneath his neighbors.

Mr. and Mrs. Smith, who have rented a larger, more commercial farm that houses thousands of chickens, are not aware that Cecil's tunnels extend underneath the Smith farm. The Smiths are simply upset about the digging enterprise. The machines groan and creak and whirrr late into the night. Blowing dust covers the lovely white barns of the Smith farm.

When Cecil finishes his tunnels, he acquires the equipment to build some excellent listening gear. (You could once find all you needed at Radio Shack, in case you wondered.) To Cecil's surprise, he quickly learns that Mr. and Mrs. Smith are indeed spies employed by a former European royal family that has plans to invade Spain with the help of some disgruntled Americans. (Lexington is the perfect place when you need to not be found.)

Of course, the Smiths have noticed Cecil's rather clumsy spying, even if they have not realized the location of the tunnels. Cecil overhears the Smiths discussing the potential need to create a "little farming accident for Mr. Rolfe if he continues to be such a pest."

Cecil has no proof of the identity of the Smiths and plans to continue to use his tunnels to obtain such proof. In the meantime, he arranges for the delivery of his collection of antique spy equipment to his niece, Jane. A hastily scribbled note from Cecil to Jane simply says, "I want to make sure you have this. Just in case. Serious operation under way at the farm. Danger high."

Cecil passes away in a small farming "accident" the next week. His will reads as follows:

> I leave my beach cottage to my niece Jane for life, and then to my surviving nieces and nephews and their heirs, so long as they have issue to carry on the family name.

Cecil's only sibling is Howard. Howard has three children — Jane, Carol, and Beth — who are all living at Cecil's death. (Cecil, therefore, has three nieces, and no nephews.) Carol has a daughter, Anna, who is born before Jane dies. Carol does not survive Jane. Jane dies without children. Beth has one son, Ben, who is born after Jane dies.

Scoring Rubric for Wannabe Spy Hypothetical

Section			
Issue:	Is there an inter-vivos gift of the antique spy equipment?	6	
Rules:	**Elements of inter-vivos gift** ☐ Valid gifts require intent, delivery, and acceptance. (3) ☐ Intent should be present and permanent. (3) ☐ Delivery may be constructive or actual and fitted to the circumstances or nature of the item. (3) ☐ Acceptance may be presumed for things of value. (3) ☐ The burden of proof falls on the recipient of the gift. (3)	15	
App.:	**Intent** ☐ "Make sure you have this" sounds like it includes all circumstances. (3) ☐ "Just in case" suggests there is a condition on death. (3) **Delivery** ☐ "Arranges for" does not necessarily mean completed. (3) ☐ "Arranges for" may be constructive, like giving a gift to an agent or intermediary to complete the delivery. (3) **Acceptance** ☐ Antique suggests the gift has value. (3)	6 6 3	
Concl.:		6	
Issue:	Is there a gift causa mortis of the antique spy equipment?	6	
Rules:	☐ The donor must intend to make a gift. (3) ☐ The intent should be conditional on death. (3) ☐ The donor must apprehend death. (3) ☐ Apprehension may be inferred from the circumstances. (3) ☐ The gift must be delivered. (3)	21	

Continued

Continued

Rules:	☐ Constructive delivery is acceptable. (3)		
	☐ Death must occur to make the gift irrevocable. (3)		
App.:	**Intent**		
	☐ "Just in case" suggests the intent is conditional on death. (3)	6	
	☐ "Want to make sure" suggests the intent is for the recipient to have the gift on his death. (3)		
	Delivery		
	☐ "Arranges for" does not necessarily mean completed. (3)	6	
	☐ "Arranges for" may be constructive, like giving the gift to an agent or intermediary. (3)		
	Apprehension		
	☐ He is trespassing with spies and knows it. (3)	18	
	☐ He says there is a "high danger," indicating apprehension. (3)		
	☐ He says this is a "serious operation," indicating a known danger. (3)		
	☐ He has overheard a specific threat against him. (3)		
	☐ All of this danger is or may be avoidable danger if he would alert the authorities. (3)		
	☐ He is making an intentional entry into a dangerous situation, which means this is unlike the traditional apprehension of an unavoidable death such as one by illness. (3)		
	Death		
	☐ He died of an accident. (3)	3	
Concl.:		6	
Issue:	Trespass for Rolfe and for dust?	6	
Rules:	**Elements of trespass**		
	☐ There must be an entry across the boundary. (3)	9	
	☐ The entry must be onto the property or possessory interest of the plaintiff. (3)		
	☐ The intent can be intentional or unintentional, but only intentional trespasses create the possibility of punitive damages. (3)		

App.:	**Entry**	
	☐ Cecil made entry made within his neighbor's property boundaries via the tunnel. (3)	6
	☐ Dust created by Cecil also crosses the boundary. (3)	
	Private property of another	
	☐ Cecil is title holder of the other property as well. (3)	6
	☐ But a lease prevents his unauthorized entry except for specific actions such as repairs. (3)	
	Intentional or unintentional	
	☐ Cecil made an intentional entry. (3)	9
	☐ Intentional entry creates the potential for punitive damages. (3)	
	☐ The entry of the dust was not done intentionally; the dust blew onto the property inadvertently. (3)	
	Visibility/tangibility	
	☐ Dust is tangible, visible. (3)	6
	☐ Dust is only tangible or visible with accumulation, so it is tangible in a limited fashion. (3)	
Concl.:		6
Issue:	Do the neighbors have a nuisance claim against Cecil for the dust and noise?	6
Rules:	**Procedural**	
	☐ There is a short statute of limitations (two to three years). (3)	6
	☐ Continuous behavior resets the clock, but there is a jurisdictional split as to what remedies are available (i.e., only equitable remedies or both equitable remedies and damages). (3)	
	Basic test	
	☐ A nuisance requires an invasion of another person's use and enjoyment of property. (3)	15
	☐ The plaintiff must show significant harm. (3)	
	☐ In Restatement jurisdictions, actions should be either "intentional and unreasonable" or "abnormally dangerous." (3)	

Continued

Continued

Rules:	☐ Unreasonableness is measured by the social and geographical context of the activity. (3) ☐ Compensation is automatic if a case is proven, but an injunction is discretionary. (3)		
App.:	***Unreasonable interference with use and enjoyment*** ☐ Dust is dirty and unwelcome. (3) ☐ Dust is particularly visible and problematic on a home exterior, especially if it is a lighter color. (3) ☐ Heavy equipment is intentional and creates noises and vibrations that are disturbing. (3) ☐ The use of equipment at night is disruptive for sleep. (3) ☐ Groan, creak, and whirr do not sound pleasant. (3) ☐ This was Cecil's farm equipment, so it was likely used in the neighborhood, anyway. (3) ☐ Thousands of chickens suggest an industrial context, so noises are normal here. (3) ***Significant harm*** ☐ Noises will disturb rest at night and disrupt proper sleep habits. (3) ☐ Dirt makes home exteriors unattractive. (3)	21 6	
Concl.:		6	
Issue:	What are the property interests in the beach cottage?	6	
Rules:	***Life estates and remainders*** ☐ "For life" creates a life estate. (3) ☐ An interest that follows a life estate is a remainder. (3) ☐ If an estate cuts off another property interest by forfeiture, then it is an executory interest. (3) ☐ When there is a condition precedent on a bequest, the recipient must do something before taking the property. (3) ☐ Survivorship is generally a condition precedent. (3) ☐ If there is a condition subsequent on a gift, then the recipient can take then meet the condition. (3) ☐ The language "but if" suggests a condition subsequent. (3)	36	

Rules:	☐ A secondary clause after the granting words suggests a condition subsequent. (3) ☐ A suggestion of termination during ownership indicates a condition subsequent. (3) ☐ A condition precedent creates a conditional remainder (CR). (3) ☐ A condition subsequent creates a vested remainder subject to divestment (VSTD). (3) ☐ If more people can join the class to take, it is a vested remainder subject to open. This only works if no other conditions need to be met. If there are other conditions, then it must be a remainder vested subject to divestment (VSTD) or a contingent remainder (CR). (3) **Rule Against Perpetuities** ☐ Rule Against Perpetuities (3) ☐ Contingent remainders, remainders vested subject to open and executory interests are all subject to the Rule Against Perpetuities. (3)	 6	
App.:	**Life estate** ☐ To Jane "for life" creates a life estate in Jane. (3) ☐ "Then to" following a life estate creates remainders in the nieces. (3) **Condition of survivorship** ☐ There are multiple interpretations of when to evaluate survivorship, so the will is ambiguous. (3) ☐ The court could measure at two places: survive the grantor or survive the life tenant. (3) *Evaluating the condition as surviving grantor* ☐ If the court evaluates the condition at the death of grantor, then the interests are contingent remainders that would vest immediately. (3) ☐ If the court evaluates the condition as of the grantor's death, then all three nieces meet this condition. (3) *Evaluating the condition as surviving the life tenant* ☐ If the court evaluates the condition at the death of the life tenant, then the interests can continue as contingent remainders; the holders will be divested if they die before the life tenant, and their interests vest at the life tenant's death. (3)	6 6 6 9	

Continued

Continued

| App.: | ☐ Evaluating the condition at the death of the life tenant does not make as much sense in this context because Jane is both the life tenant and also has the potential to take in the remainder, which would make surviving her odd wording. (3)

☐ If the condition is evaluated as within the life tenancy, then Jane is dead, Carol is dead, and only Beth can take. (3)

Condition of having issue

☐ The conditions could be conditions precedent or subsequent because the deed is unclear in wording and structure. (3)

☐ If "issue" is a condition precedent, then it creates a contingent remainder. (3)

☐ This interest would continue as a contingent remainder until the holder has a child, and then it would vest. (3)

☐ However, Beth's interest would not have vested as of Jane's death, because she did not have a child before Jane died. (3)

☐ If "issue" is a condition subsequent, then the remainder is vested subject to divestment, vesting on having a child. (3)

☐ Holders would be divested if they die without offspring. (3)

☐ Carol's becomes a vested remainder on Anna's birth. (3)

☐ Applying the rule of convenience and closing the class at the life tenant's death could prevent Beth from taking. (3)

Ambiguity of family name

☐ There is an ambiguity because "family name" could mean that the parent must give the children that last name." Alternatively, the testator may have written about carrying on the family name only as an explanation for wanting there to be children. (3)

☐ If this is a requirement to give the child that last name, then it creates an additional condition besides having a child. (3) | 24

6 | |

App.:	**When to evaluate condition of having issue and interest created**		
	☐ The condition can be measured at multiple points: the grantor's death, the life tenant's death, or the interest holder's death. (3)	9	
	☐ If the court measures the condition at the grantor's death, it would be a condition precedent, creating a contingent remainder (which would fail immediately) or a vested remainder (if the grantee has a child). (6)		
	Rule Against Perpetuities		
	☐ Application of the rule depends on who is the measuring life, which may be logically different depending on when you choose to measure "having issue" and "survivorship," so consider for each interpretation of when, so long as it is a contingent remainder and therefore subject to the rule. (6)	6	
	Evaluating conditions at the grantor's death		
	☐ If all the conditions are evaluated at the grantor's death, then any contingent remainder vests or fails at the grantor's death, which means there is no problem no matter who is the measuring life (life in being) for purposes of the Rule Against Perpetuities. (3)	6	
	☐ No one takes the property under this scenario. (3)		
	Evaluating conditions at the life tenant's death		
	☐ If all the conditions are evaluated at the life tenant's death, the Rule Against Perpetuities applies only to the contingent remainders. (3)	6	
	☐ The interests will pass scrutiny under the rule if the class closes at the life tenant's death, no matter if the tenant or an interest holder is the measuring life. (3)		
	Measuring conditions in the interest holder's lifetime		
	☐ If either condition is evaluated at an interest holder's death, then those that are contingent remainders are subject to the rule. (3)	12	
	☐ This interpretation will be okay under the Rule Against Perpetuities if you use the interest holder as the measuring life. (3)		

Continued

Continued

App.:	☐ If the life tenant is the measuring life, then there is a problem. There could be a new child 22 years after the life tenant's death, so this interpretation would violate the Rule Against Perpetuities. (3) ☐ The interests could be saved by using the rule of convenience to close the class at the death of the life tenant. (3)		
Concl.:		6	
Issue:	Was there a breach of the lease due to failure to deliver exclusive possession?	6	
Rules:	☐ The landlord has a duty under a lease to deliver full, actual — not just legal — possession of a premises. (3) ☐ Even partial nondelivery is a breach of this duty. (3) ☐ The tenant has a right of full, exclusive possession. (3)	9	
App.:	☐ Entry below ground and the creation of the below-ground tunnel for spying purposes suggests nondelivery of full possession. (3) ☐ There is no reason, however, to suspect that the tenants needed or wanted access to the deep ground beneath the house, so the tunnel may not indicate nondelivery of full possession. (3)	6	
Concl.:		6	
	Total		

Mean Score for sample law student groups: 166

Dovecote Hypothetical

Time to read and write your answer: one hour.

Dovecote—noun, a historical type of building, usually of stone with thick walls and tiny niches, creating individual nesting spaces for doves.

Sean Doughoregan, standing beside his bedroom window, watched apprehensively as 20 graduate students from around the world poured out of three oversized vans. Suitcases, duffle bags, and backpacks tumbled to the brown pea gravel of the courtyard. Sean eyed their progress with suspicion. For the next six weeks, these students of archeology would excavate the area surrounding the now only partially standing eighteenth-century dovecote. The manor stretched across 25 coastal acres, seven of them protected marshlands. The fields and barns stretched across another 10 acres. The rest of the lands contained the main manor house, two enormous servants' quarters adjacent to it, and nearly an acre of formal gardens. All of it dated back to an eighteenth-century grant.

He already half regretted inviting the students. He had plenty of room for them — they could even have individual rooms in the renovated servants' quarters. And partnering with the prestigious U.N.C. program that brought students from around the world would make quick work of the excavation. He would know a little more of his family, of the slow building of the manor, maybe even of the farming techniques his ancestors had brought with them from Ireland. And he was happy to have people 50 years his junior on the estate with all their positivity and easy happiness.

The problem, as always, was family politics. Ten years ago, and just before he died, Sean's father, Patrick, had split the southernmost portion of the estate from the main parcel, deeding the ancient row of eighteenth-century manor cottages to his half-sister, Yvonne. And Yvonne was, well, difficult to manage. Sean sighed just thinking of it. If he had to put words to it, Yvonne was resentful and jealous, always thinking of her lesser share. On top of that, she was the most scatterbrained and forgetful person he'd ever known. If you worked out a peaceful agreement with her about anything, she probably did not remember it 10 minutes later.

Sean winced and rubbed his forehead just thinking about it. He had spoken to Yvonne about the graduate students. The students would be shown the property line — they would not cross over onto Yvonne's property. The only problem was the dovecote path. The dovecote path dated back centuries. The wide, sandy path always had been the way that cottage renters accessed the beach, crossing the Manor property. The path was entirely on Sean's property, as was the dovecote.

Originally, the path had been the primary path of access to the dovecote, from which the cottagers had a right to take doves for their dinners. The path did not go all the way to the beach, only as far as the dovecote, but the beach was only another 200 feet or so past the dovecote. Of course, the dovecote itself had half fallen down during Hurricane Maude in 1934 and had not been used to hold doves since then. Only half of the old walls remained. But because the dovecote was so close to the sea, the path made a good trail to the waters and the cottagers had always used it that way, both when they rented from Sean and now when they rented from Yvonne. Of course, Yvonne herself never used the path. She rarely set foot on the island. He could only hope that Yvonne did not kick up a fuss about having the place crawling with graduate students. Sure, the students would be in the way, their equipment and pits blocking the paths. It wouldn't matter except there really weren't other ways to the beach from those cottages. And normally Sean did not care, in fact, after the old dovecote walls fell, he'd told the cottagers it was fine to keep using the path. Now, the only problem was Yvonne kicking up a fuss. Ah, well, when they spoke on the phone, Yvonne agreed.

Sean Doughoregan watched his two granddaughters, Rue and Elise, from the window. Both would be spending the summer holidays with him, taking a break from college life. He was thrilled to see them both. Why were grandchildren always so much less trouble than their parents? Their mother, Grace, exhausted him. Sean had spent nearly his entire life trying to manage Grace's alcoholism. And to protect his granddaughters from it.

Now, though, Sean was content. He had signed a new will. This will would keep everyone on track when he was not there to watch them:

> I devise the Manor estate to my wife, Anna, for life, and then, for life, to my daughter Grace, provided that she remains sober, and then to my grandchildren who have issue, and provided that my grandchildren graduate from college, but if they do not, then to my half-sister, Yvonne. The residual of my estate shall go to my grandchildren.

Sean sighed as he watched his granddaughters wander into the old dovecote. Everything would be fine. That evening Sean and his wife Anna died together in an accident.

Scoring Rubric for the Dovecote Hypothetical

Section			
Issue:	Is there a servitude when Sean owns all of the property and rents to cottagers (but Yvonne owns nothing yet)?	6	
Rules:	☐ You cannot create an easement benefiting the property that is also being burdened. (3)	3	
App.:	☐ It is the same piece of property—all one estate. (3) ☐ It is possible to view the property as severed now because it is separated into the main part and the rented part. (3)	6	
Concl.:		6	
Issue:	Was there a profit?	6	
Rules:	☐ A profit is a right of entry, like an easement, but accompanied by a right to take something from the property. (3)	3	
App.:	☐ There was a right to enter to take doves. (3) ☐ This included a right of access, but the primary point was to take the doves. (3) ☐ Logically, the profit rights would stop at the dovecote, and would not create access rights to the beach. (3)	9	
Concl.:		6	
Issue:	Did the profit end when the residents stopped using the dovecote for raising doves?	6	
Rules:	**Rules for terminating a profit or easement** ☐ It is proper to terminate a profit like you terminate an easement. (3) ☐ A profit can end by expiration, when the underlying purpose no longer exists. (3) ☐ A profit can end by abandonment, but only with a clear demonstration of the intent to abandon. (3) ☐ A profit can end by destruction, if the access or relevant property becomes nonexistent due to a natural disaster. (3)	12	

Continued

Continued

App.:	**Expiration**		
	☐ In modern life, very few people eat doves or keep them to eat. (3)	9	
	☐ The building no longer serves the purpose of keeping doves. (3)		
	☐ Cottagers use the route to access the beach, not the dovecote itself. (3)		
	Abandonment		
	☐ The lack of use of the dovecote for housing doves suggests it has been abandoned. (3)	9	
	☐ Such a lack of use is, however, not affirmative evidence of abandonment. (3)		
	☐ The dovecote is still used, just for a different purpose. (3)		
	Destruction		
	☐ A hurricane destroyed the building years before. (3)	9	
	☐ The access path still exists. (3)		
	☐ But the hurricane destroyed the reason for using the path. (3)		
Concl.:		6	
Issue:	Is there some type of non-express easement?	6	
Rules:	☐ An easement is a right to enter or do something in particular, and does not give an ownership right in the property, only a right of access. (3)	6	
	☐ There are multiple types of non-express easements: implied from prior use, prescriptive, and easements by necessity. (3)		
	Implied easement from prior use test		
	☐ There must be a single owner of multiple or later subdivided tracts. (3)	12	
	☐ The easement must provide to the other property a benefit or advantage, which is not minor, and must approach necessity. (3)		
	☐ An implied easement must be apparent, continuous, and appear permanent. (3)		
	☐ An implied easement is not written into a later conveyance. (3)		

Rules:	**Prescriptive easement**		
	☐ A prescriptive easement looks like adverse posses-sion. (3)	27	
	☐ But a prescriptive easement does not require exclu-sivity. (3)		
	☐ A prescriptive easement requires possession that is actual and open. (3)		
	☐ Possession must be continuous. (3)		
	☐ The possession must be adverse or hostile. (3)		
	☐ The claimant must use the easement for the dura-tion of the statute of limitations. (3)		
	☐ There is a presumption in favor of an easement being created if the plaintiff proves uninterrupted, adverse possession. (3)		
	☐ The presumption can be rebutted by permission. (3)		
	☐ The general public cannot create an easement for a private holder. (3)		
	Necessity		
	☐ Easements by necessity are generally created by be-ing landlocked. (3)	12	
	☐ Landlocked means a property lacks an accessible route to the public highways. (3)		
	☐ There is a high standard for necessity. (3)		
	☐ Necessity is something much more than conve-nience (3)		
App.:	☐ There is no express easement because there is no writing. (3)	3	
	Implied from prior use		
	Single owner		
	☐ This was not true until the land was split to give Yvonne a share, but seems to be true after that. (3)	3	
	Benefit must approach necessity		
	☐ The benefit might have approached necessity when access to the doves was necessary for food, but that is no longer the purpose. (3)	6	
	☐ Today the easement is only access to the beach for cottagers, so it is not needed now. (3)		
	Apparent, continuous		
	☐ There has been a tradition of long-standing access. (3)	3	

Continued

Continued

App.:	Not written		
	☐ There is no evidence of a written easement. (3)	3	
	Prescriptive easement		
	Open/notorious/visible		
	☐ Sean is aware of the use; Yvonne is aware of the cottagers' use as well. (3)	9	
	☐ The cottagers' use is a long-standing practice. (3)		
	☐ The use is significant enough to keep the path worn. (3)		
	Continuous		
	☐ There is no evidence of interruption. (3)	3	
	Adverse/hostile		
	☐ This element can be presumed if the claimant meets the other requirements. (3)	3	
	Time period		
	☐ There is long-standing use, so this should meet most requirements, which are 7–15 years. (3)	3	
	Permission		
	☐ Access appears to be with Sean's consent. (3)	3	
	Necessity		
	☐ Here, there is no evidence that any part of the property is landlocked from the highway, so there is no necessity. (3)	3	
Concl.:		6	
Issue:	What is the proper ownership of the manor based on the will?	6	
Rules:	**Life estates and remainders**		
	☐ "For life" creates a life estate. (3)	36	
	☐ An interest that follows a life estate is a remainder. (3)		
	☐ If an estate cuts off another property interest by forfeiture, then it is an executory interest. (3)		
	☐ When there is a condition precedent on a bequest, the recipient must do something before taking the property. (3)		
	☐ Survivorship is generally a condition precedent. (3)		

| Rules: | ☐ If there is a condition subsequent on a gift, then the recipient can take then meet the condition. (3)
☐ The language "but if" suggests a condition subsequent. (3)
☐ A secondary clause after the granting words suggests a condition subsequent. (3)
☐ A suggestion of termination during ownership indicates a condition subsequent. (3)
☐ A condition precedent creates a conditional remainder (CR). (3)
☐ A condition subsequent creates a vested remainder subject to divestment (VSTD). (3)
☐ If more people can join the class to take, it is a vested remainder subject to open. This only works if no other conditions need to be met. If there are other conditions, then it must be a remainder vested subject to divestment (VSTD) or a contingent remainder (CR). (3)
Rule Against Perpetuities
☐ Rule Against Perpetuities (3)
☐ Contingent remainders, remainders vested subject to open, and executory interests are all subject to the Rule Against Perpetuities. (3) | 6 | |
| App.: | **Present estates**
☐ "For life" gives a life estate to Anna. (3)
☐ "For life" gives a life estate to Grace. (3)
☐ Anna can't take the life estate because she is dead. (3)
☐ Grace's life estate has a condition, so it is a conditional life estate. (3)
☐ Grace can be divested at death or on breach of the condition. (3)
Future interests
☐ Rue and Elise can take on the forfeiture of the life estate, so they have executory interests. (3)
☐ Rue and Elise can also take at the end of the life estate, so they also have some kind of remainder. (3)
☐ Rue and Elise must meet conditions, so it is not a vested remainder. (3) | 15

18 | |

Continued

Continued

App.:	□ There are two conditions on their remainders, so the court must interpret whether these are conditions precedent or subsequent. (3) □ Rue and Elise must graduate college. This condition follows after the granting language, so it looks like a condition subsequent. (3) □ Rue and Elise must have issue, which can be a condition precedent or subsequent. (3) *When to evaluate the condition of having issue* □ Having issue can be evaluated at three points, so there is an ambiguity here. (3) □ The court can evaluate the condition as within the grantor's life, but this does not make sense as much for a will creating a life estate. (3) □ The court can interpret the provision as requiring compliance before a life estate ends, but with two life estates, this interpretation is confusing. (3) □ The court can evaluate the condition as within the lifetimes of the beneficiaries. (3) *Meeting the conditions* □ Rue and Elise are on college break, so they have not met the graduation condition yet. (3) □ Rue and Elise have no issue, so they have not met the issue condition yet. (3) □ If having issue is a condition precedent, then Rue and Elise have contingent remainders. (3) □ If having issue is a condition subsequent, then Rue and Elise have remainders that are vested subject to divestment. (3) □ Yvonne takes if Rue and Elise do not meet the condition. (3) □ If Rue and Elise have contingent remainders, then Yvonne has an alternative contingent remainder. (3) □ If Rue and Elise have a remainder that is vested subject to divestment, then Yvonne has an executory interest, because she would take on a forfeiture. (3) □ The class is open if more members can be created and Grace is still alive. (3) □ If the interests are all contingent remainders or alternative contingent remainders, then the grantor's estate has a reversion. (3)	12 27	

App.:	**Rule Against Perpetuities**		
	☐ The rule is applicable to any contingent remainders or executory interests here. (3)	6	
	☐ Having issue can be measured at three points, to apply the rule to each option as a potential interpretation. (3)		
	Conditions evaluated at the grantor's death		
	☐ No matter who is the measuring life, all interests should pass because the measurements close then. (3)	3	
	Conditions evaluated at a life tenant's death		
	☐ The life in being (measuring life) is usually a life estate holder, but there are two, so it could be either. (6)	12	
	☐ It would be awkward to evaluate a condition at one tenant's death and use the other tenant as a measuring life for the Rule Against Perpetuities, so this is an unlikely interpretation. (3)		
	☐ If the court uses the second life tenant as a measuring life for the rule and also evaluates conditions as of that point, all interests should pass. (3)		
	Conditions evaluated at the interest holder's death		
	☐ If the conditions are measured within the interest holder's life, but the court uses either of the life tenants as the measuring life, then there is a problem because an interest holder could complete the condition 22 years after the life tenant's death. (3)	9	
	☐ But this scenario passes the rule if an interest holder is the measuring life instead of the life estate holder. (3)		
	☐ It is awkward to use an interest holder as a measuring life if it is a class of beneficiaries, such as nieces, so this is a less likely interpretation. (3)		
Concl.:		6	
		Total	

Mean Score for sample law student groups: 173

PART THREE

DIAGNOSING AND FIXING
PROBLEMS WITH
TECHNIQUE

TWENTY

Diagnosing Problems with Hypothetical Answers

Thematic or Comprehensive Errors

What is a thematic or comprehensive error? It is not an error of law; it is a — usually pervasive — error of analysis or technique. A thematic error can't be corrected by learning more law. For example, not knowing the elements of adverse possession is a legal error — a problem of either knowledge or memorization. On the other hand, if you know the elements, but when you try to answer a hypothetical, you skip the application of the elements to the facts and just write a conclusion, then you have a thematic error: being conclusory or skipping applications.

Thematic errors are more problematic for multiple reasons. First, thematic errors cannot be corrected by simple memorization, rereading your class notes, or re-listening to lectures from class.

Second, errors of law are generally obvious to you once you see the scoring rubric. Thematic errors take more effort to see and it can be a challenge to see your own. Note: the remainder of this chapter explains how to spot these errors, but it is always harder in your own work. Therefore, this is one of those moments when it is a great idea to use this book with a partner or small group and exchange your work for grading purposes.

Professors regularly mirror the techniques of proper analysis, but frequently do not stop to alert you to the fact that they are doing exactly that. When you are a 1L, it can be hard to see. This is especially true as 1Ls tend to generalize far more than is advisable in law school. In other words, you may think "Professor Fraley is talking about the *Popov* case," but your professor thinks, "I am applying the rules of actual possession to a skirmish in the stands over a valuable baseball."

Neither do professors usually provide much explicit instruction on how to do these things properly or how to correct the errors. Most of the learning is based on mimicry and not all students learn well that way.

When you get feedback on exams, professors often point out thematic errors, but rarely provide specific techniques for correcting them. In your defense, it is not helpful for a professor to say only, "You were conclusory and did not really apply the rules to the facts." This is especially true when what you want to say back is, "I thought I did!" And/or "How the heck do I do that?"

Finally, thematic errors are a big deal because you are likely to make them pervasively, not just when responding to one issue. That means thematic issues can seriously ruin your final exam score if not corrected.

Here is the good news:

1. There are only a few thematic errors.

2. You can, with relatively little effort, use a scoring rubric in this book to identify the thematic errors you make. And if you struggle with this, a study partner can help.

3. This book provided you with a primer in the first chapters, designed to help you avoid these common thematic errors. You can reread the relevant sections and practice more.

4. The remainder of this chapter provides you with additional techniques specific to some of the more common errors.

The Most Common Thematic Errors

If professors created a list of the most frequent problems with exam answers and those most detrimental in terms of scores, here it is:

Most common thematic errors that reduce exam scores:

1. Failure to spot issues
2. Many conclusions, little to no application
3. Factual errors or speculation about nonexistent facts
4. The answer is too short when compared with other students' work

Any one of these errors, if prevalent, is enough to drop a score to a B+, or worse. With that said, many lower-scoring exams have more than one of these problems. Ideally, a professor gives you feedback and identifies these problems in your exam. Then the professor gives you strategies for overcoming these problems. Regrettably, in law school the first of these only happens sometimes and the second happens rarely.

Using the Rubric to Diagnose Thematic Errors Generally

In many ways, the rubric itself is the solution to one, and sometimes both, of these problems. Once filled in, the rubric provides specific feedback about what is missing from an answer. It tells you what you did include, but also what you should have included. But this is only a part of the rubric's function.

Most importantly, the rubric can help you very quickly diagnose not only the specific things you could have said, but it can also help you diagnose the broader problems that prevent you from achieving a higher score.

The section divisions of the rubric provide the crucial information: The rubric is divided into sections that help you to identify these broader problems in the list above.

Using a Scoring Rubric to Diagnose Common Thematic Errors	
Rubric Feature	*Likely Problem*
Entire IRAC groups are blank—zero points	Issue spotting
Within IRAC groups, there are 0–12 points within the Application section at a bare minimum. Application section points often hit only one or two of a longer list of elements	Conclusory, or lacking application
Answer is long, but there are few points on the rubric	Factual errors or speculation
Within application sections, there are points in only or mostly the yes section or the no section, not both	Picking sides or one-sided applications
Overall score is at or below a suggested mean for a rubric and there are few points or no points in the Rules sections	Lack of knowledge of the rules (prevents rule points as well as proper application)
Overall score is at or below a suggested mean for a rubric, but does not contain other features mentioned above. Also likely: you spotted issues when reading the hypothetical and writing the answer, but did not have time to address them	Lack of speed (comparatively)

Diagnosing Problems: Issue Spotting

Provided that you have a scoring rubric to pair with a hypothetical prompt, this one is easy to diagnose. When you read the rubric, you see issues listed that you just did not recognize when reading the fact pattern. The riskiest thing about this problem is that students rarely see scoring rubrics for hypotheticals. Most professors do not make them available. You can compare answers with a study partner, but then there is the possibility that one of you invented issues that aren't actually there. (Students do that all the time.) You need to practice hypotheticals then score yourself on a scoring rubric to see if you have this problem or not.

STRATEGIES FOR SUCCESS

Getting Better at Issue Spotting

Issue spotting requires a sufficient knowledge of the rules to read a fact pattern and notice the types of facts that usually generate an issue. This book labels those facts "triggering facts" because they should trigger the IRAC analysis for an issue. Additionally, issue spotting requires ready knowledge of what the issues and sub-issues are likely to be. The best strategies are responsive to these two requirements.

Strategy 1: know the possibilities

Most students make an outline, which in some ways contains the issues, but the list is not quickly available and sub-issues are sometimes hidden in the depths. Make a quick reference list that is literally just a list of the issues and sub-issues covered in class. Part of a list for your property class might look something like this:

Inter-vivos Gifts

Gifts Causa Mortis

Adverse Possession

    Tacking

    Permission

    Laches

Mistaken Improvers

Note that elements are not sub-issues. That is because elements should always be covered if there is a potential cause of action. Sub-issues are sometimes relevant and sometimes not. In other words, every analysis of adverse possession should talk about whether or not there is open and notorious possession, but only sometimes is there a question of tacking.

Strategy 2: getting to know those triggering facts

It is very helpful to create a list for yourself of what key facts generally create an issue. You can do this by briefly looking back to the facts of the cases you read that included each issue. Once you have glanced at the facts, generalize those into a basic scenario or two. Do this for each issue. You can create a quick chart. It might look something like this:

Issue	Probable Triggering Facts
Nuisance	Someone uses their property in an annoying way, creating noise/dust/germs/smells/injury/etc.
Adverse Possession	Adjacent property owner wants to take land without purchase *or* Mistakes in construction where one owner's stuff (fence/garage/sidewalk/house etc.) is accidentally built across the property line

Continued

Continued

> If there is only one case in your textbook for an issue, or you are having trouble seeing the commonalities, try running a search in a legal database for cases on that issue. Skim the beginning paragraphs of a few cases to begin to look for similarities.

Diagnosing Problems: Student Prefers Conclusions over Applications

This is the most common problem for students and it generally takes some amount of practice to resolve. If students try to label their own hypothetical answers with I, R, A, and C, they frequently label as an application, something that is actually a conclusion. Consider these sentences from an exam:

Kara trespassed because she entered the property.

This is a legal conclusion. It posits one of the required elements (entry) and draws the conclusion (trespassed) without reference to the facts at all. Not a good plan, but it is probably not clear to you that it is a conclusion.

How about this one? Is it any better?

Kara trespassed because her car entered Jules' property.

Here is the structure of the sentence above:

[Defendant] [legal conclusion] [connecting word] [legal sub-conclusion].

You might say, "But wait! Her car entering the property is a fact." No, actually it isn't. Within the context of trespass, entry is a term of art and, more specifically, an element of the cause of action. To be able to analyze the facts, and to conclude whether there was or was not an entry, you need to know how courts or statutes have defined entry.

As you can imagine, the statutes provide details. All sorts of qualifying words might limit what constitutes an entry. Examples include: direct, indirect, intentional, unintentional.

How could you state just the fact? Kara's car traveled onto Jules' driveway. What indicates that this sentence contains only the facts and not a sub-conclusion? Any person who knows where the boundary falls can say whether or not Kara's car traveled onto the driveway of another property by just looking at it. It takes an attorney (or successful law student) to know whether the car "entered" the property.

While overall conclusions may be obvious, students often neglect to write proper applications because they have assumed a particular sub-conclusion. How do you know if a particular term generates a legal conclusion? Elements of any cause of action will each have sub-conclusions. Examples include: intentionally, willfully, grievous bodily harm.

Additionally, watch for definitions of terms. These can come from either courts or statutes. For example, in the context of a DUI or DWI, most jurisdictions define "motor vehicle." As a result, the charge might or might not succeed against someone who is driving a snowmobile, depending on whether the statutory definition of "motor vehicle" included "wheels."

One study technique is to color-code all of the words that would require you to make a legal conclusion. Then, as you reread your notes and outline, you will be programming yourself to remember that you should not just toss around these words. You must remember to use the facts to prove them.

Whether it is the stress of exams or the time pressure, students often skip portions of the analysis by grasping quickly onto a sub-conclusion. It is not the end of the world, but it does mean that you are losing points for that particular part of the application. Repeating that same mistake frequently could significantly reduce your final score.

Finally, remember that many of the tips and techniques in the primer section of this book are geared specifically to making sure that you write a thorough application. If you are still struggling with that, then reread the relevant primer sections, and make sure to get extensive practice with hypotheticals before an exam. There are a few other strategies that can be useful if you continue to have problems.

STRATEGIES FOR SUCCESS
Writing Applications, not Conclusions

Strategy 1: use the successful hypothetical factors checklist

Print a copy of the factors list and place it beside you as you work through the hypothetical. Check off items as you complete them. Some may be more difficult than others to tell that you have completed them. Make your best guess and use all of your time allotted.

Strategy 2: create a personal checklist of things you often forget

Create a short list of key items to remember, such as: make sure to cover all the elements, do not forget both sides for each element. Use the checklist as you write the next hypothetical answer.

Strategy 3: create a bubbles checklist for facts

As you read the hypothetical prompt, draw a small circle by each fact. Place a checkmark in the circle each time you use the fact as you write your answer. By the end of the application, you should have at least one checkmark in each circle; many circles should have two.

Strategy 4: pause after each fact

While writing a hypothetical answer, each time you use a fact, pause for a few seconds to make sure that you have connected the fact to the rule. Explain why the fact is important in light of the existing rules.

Diagnosing Problems:
Factual Errors or Speculation

Often student answers either analyze the wrong fact (by misremembering the fact) or speculate about things that are out of the bounds of the hypothetical prompt. Either one of these can be extremely detrimental to your score.

The problem with factual errors is that they often lead to incorrect issue spotting. First, students sometimes just miss an issue due to a factual error. The professor only knows for sure that this is what is happening because the answer will say something like, "There can't possibly be a nuisance claim here, because none of the dust ever entered the neighboring property." The problem is that the facts said the dust did enter. But the student has already chosen to skip that issue.

Even worse, students occasionally misremember the facts of the hypothetical prompt in a way that creates an issue that is not there. For example, the student begins analyzing trespass and notes that John entered the neighbor's property. In the prompt, the hypothetical clearly stated that he never crossed the boundary. In the rush and anxiety of an exam, the student has forgotten the facts. It happens more often than you might think. The problem here is that the student will spend 10 or 20 minutes analyzing an issue that does not exist. That is time lost for the issues that were there. The student will either not finish the exam or write too little about the real issues.

Finally, some students like to write their own exam. In other words, they start imagining facts that are not in the prompt. The problem with speculation is that you are writing in the air on an imaginary rubric. There are no points for this analysis. To determine whether you are speculating, try running a word search in your hypothetical answer. The one to look for, of course, is "if." But sometimes it also helps to search "might" and "could."

It is important to note that there is a difference between a lack of facts and speculation. It is not usually worth pointing out a lack of facts in a hypothetical. (The professor knows very well those facts are not there. She wrote it.) But sometimes a lack of facts in a story is in itself an important thing. Then you may want to briefly discuss the omission. For example, a lack of injury or a lack of safety actions might be a fact worth discussing briefly.

STRATEGIES FOR SUCCESS
Fixing Factual Errors or Speculation

Strategy 1: read the hypothetical question twice

To prevent critical mistakes of fact, read the fact pattern twice before you proceed to the analysis. This may feel difficult to do in the time constraints, but it is time well spent if it helps with issue spotting and avoiding mistakes of fact.

Strategy 2: create a bubbles checklist for facts

As you read the hypothetical, draw a circle by each fact. Place a checkmark in the circle each time you use the fact. If you look for a fact to check off and do not find it, skim to be sure it really existed in the prompt.

Diagnosing Problems:
Arguing One Side Only or Mostly

You may be able to reread your answer and tell immediately that you have written for only one side of an issue (or more than one). Most students can't do it, though. It is hard to reread your own analysis and see it. One option is to ask a study partner to do it for you. They may see it more easily. But with a little more effort, you can do it yourself. Here are a few different methods that can help you see if this a problem for you.

Multiple options for diagnosing:

1. For hypotheticals in this book, rubrics often divide the yes/no sides. After you have graded your answer and totaled your points, go back to the rubric beginning and reread. See whether your checkmarks are evenly distributed between the two on all issues.

2. If you use a strict format of issue, rule, application, and conclusion, and then break the application into yes/no paragraphs for each element, you can just scan your answer. If paragraphs in the application are of very unequal length or you are missing one, you are likely arguing only or mostly one side.

3. If you are using old exams, etc. or perhaps do not have a rubric to go with a hypothetical, reread your answer with a pen in hand. In the margins beside each sentence, write an element or rule block and Y or N for yes or no. Example: The hypothetical contains a potential inter-vivos gift. If your answer says, "James intended for the ring to be a gift, because he presented it wrapped for her birthday." In the margins, you would write, "Intent-Y" because this sentence argues on the element of intent and argues that yes, there is intent. Do this beside every sentence. At the end, look at the sentences for each issue/element and count. Are there five Intent-Y, but only one Intent-N? This is unbalanced.

STRATEGIES FOR SUCCESS
Avoiding Arguing Only One Side

Strategy 1: do not be too sympathetic

Identify emotive prompts and do not fall for them. If a hypothetical's facts are particularly sympathetic for one party, flag this for yourself and make a particular effort to argue the other side. The best way to do this is for that issue, try a temporary heading as a reminder. Something like: Misfortune Wins!

Strategy 2: label it

Use a strict format structure (as taught in the primer), so you can see a lack of balance as you are working. Use labels to help you do this. Save a blank document with labels and use it to answer hypotheticals. Make the yes/no labels BIG.

Strategy 3: get iffy

Begin each problem with an iffy statement of the issue to get in the right frame of mind. You can delete it later. But start by clarifying for yourself that the answer is unclear.

Strategy 4: get a client

Sometimes students who write for one side do not see the facts that support the other side on a first reading. Write an initial answer to the hypothetical, allowing yourself to be one-sided, but leaving headings for the other side. Now assume that your client is the other side. Then reread the hypothetical prompt, looking for facts to help you. And finally, fill in the other side under the headings that you created. Note that this is going to be slow initially. It is something you must practice through multiple hypotheticals.

Diagnosing Lack of Knowledge of the Rules

This one may be easy. In other words, you may know that you do not know them. However, this is not always true. The quickest check is to look at a scoring rubric you have filled in and focus on the Rules sections. Are there no checkmarks or only a few? Did you know the rule and just forget to write it down or skip that step? If not, then you need to work on learning the rules more thoroughly.

In particular, learn by using spaced repetition. This is how the scientists understand that the brain likes to get its information: bite-sized and regularly spaced pieces. There are apps for your phone and computer that create perfect, scientifically accurate, spaced repetition. You can also go with old-fashioned flashcards. They work. But to get the best results, it is important to not do them by bingeing, but rather at intervals.

Additionally, you can use what scientists know about habits to create a learning habit. New habits, science says, are hard to form. The best way to do it is to find a way to make the new habit tag along with one you already have. Do you sit at the same spot every morning to eat your yogurt? Put your stack of index cards in that spot. When you eat the yogurt, go through the cards once or twice. This will help to both create the new habit of studying the index cards and also encourage intervals rather than bingeing.

Diagnosing Lack of Speed

A lack of speed is often easy to diagnose. You worked for an hour or an hour and a half on answering a hypothetical, but there was more you wanted to write. You saw issues and just did not have time to deal with them.

Lack of speed is a frequent complaint from students. There is a reason for this. Recall that one of the big differences between undergraduate study and law school is that nearly all of law school grading is comparative. That means the question is not how much the professor expects you to get done in the time allotted. The question is how many people are being more efficient than you are in generating points. If you type slowly and/or prefer to think slowly, these may not be problems as a practicing attorney (depending on the type of work you do and the type of billing). But they are problems for exam writing in law school and for the bar.

STRATEGIES FOR SUCCESS

Tackling Speed and Time Management Issues

Speed and time management problems are really a group of problems rather than a single problem. There are different potential solutions, depending on the source of the problem.

Problem: Good analysis, just too slow

Strategy 1: keep going

Answering hypotheticals is most likely a new skill. It is not reasonable to expect to be great at it immediately. All students get faster with practice. Keep doing hypotheticals and set a timer to monitor yourself and check the word count in your document. Keep track of your pace, just like you would if you were trying to build your skills as a runner: words per minute instead of miles per hour. Keeping track can help you see your progress and gain confidence.

Strategy 2: pre-study

Take time to get in the right frame of mind first. Do not begin reading and answering a hypothetical until you have spent at least 10 minutes studying your recent notes/outlines or, for this book, reading the rules and outlines in the chapters. You will move through the problem faster if "property thinking" is already your operating mode.

Strategy 3: bump up rule knowledge

Make certain that you know the rules very thoroughly. If you are stopping to remember details or work out confusion, then you are wasting time.

Strategy 4: sink into structure

Use a format to create a strong structure in your answer. This is basically to prevent any staring at the blank page or not knowing where to go or what to do next. Additionally, make sure you make the list of issues as you read the hypothetical, for just the same reason. It works as a task list.

Strategy 5: figure out when you stop

Figure out what you are doing when you are wasting time and correct accordingly: This requires a study partner who is willing to watch you work. This person monitors your work, noticing when you stop typing for more than a few seconds to think. The person then prompts you, "What are you doing right now?" This person makes a list of your responses. Later you can look over that list and determine whether it is a lack of knowledge of the rules, confusion of the rules, lack of understanding of the facts of the hypothetical, or not knowing where to go next that is causing the problem. Once you know the precise cause of time wasted, you can correct accordingly using other strategies in this book.

Problem: Over-writing one issue, neglecting others

Strategy 6: periodic alarms

If you tend to get caught up on one issue and not move on to others, try setting a periodic alarm on your computer or watch that will alert you every 15 or 20 minutes. This can help remind you that it is time to move on. Remember for the exam that you will need this alarm to be silent, therefore a pop-up on your computer is probably best.

Dealing with Anxiety

Anxiety is a common problem for law students for many reasons. High-stakes exams are a part of the problem, of course. If anxiety during exams is a problem for you, here are a few suggestions.

1. Be careful where you study. Anxiety seems to be contagious. Do not catch more of it from your classmates.

2. Know what you are facing. Get a copy of old exams for your classes if at all possible. Do not wait until the very last second to do them. (Students often save them until the last minute.) If you are anxious, knowing what the exam looks like is calming.

3. Do your hypothetical practice. The more comfortable you are with the process of writing hypothetical answers, the more it will feel like an everyday thing when you are in the exam.

4. Make that list of issues and sub-issues for each class. It helps to see that there actually are not that many of them. You covered less than you think in some ways.

5. Make sure you are doing only the work that matters. Not all time spent studying counts equally. Learn rules, practice hypotheticals. Ask your professor what time spent on studying and preparing for class should look like. Remember that the best preparation for class is not actually exactly the same as the best preparation for exams. For example, for cold-calling in class, it helps to know facts well. This is rarely useful on exams.

Extra Practice for Issue Spotting

Instructions:

Read each hypothetical. Use the blanks below to list the issues you recognize. N.B.: The number of blanks is no indicator of the number of issues present. You may find that you have too many or too few blanks.

Note that there may not be facts to support every element of an issue or two sides to every element or issue. That is not the question. The question is whether there are there enough facts to suggest that the issue might be there, and therefore should be addressed. Remember you should never draw conclusions (i.e., there is not a trespass) without going through the analysis if there are facts that provide at least some of the elements.

You will find answers at the end of all the questions.

ONE

When Brief & Pleasant Law School admitted Deliah, she was busy — really busy. So, she set up her living accommodations online via a local Facebook group. Toby advertised an apartment on Facebook, noting that it was a structure fully attached to his own home, but inaccessible from inside his home. Toby described the apartment as "in an 1840s farmhouse on a quiet, large farm in small-town Virginia." When Deliah arrived, she found that the apartment was essentially the original unattached summer kitchen. The large wood-burning fireplace in the kitchen is the only way to heat the apartment. The summer kitchen is now attached to the house via a bathroom. The bathroom has one door going into the main house and a second door going into the apartment. There are no locks on either door. When Deliah arrives, she finds that she can only access half of the shower because the other half is filled with stacks of metal crates. Toby says, "Oh, I'm sure I'll find a use for those and move them in a few months."

Toby did not mention that he is a metal artist. He makes giant mixed-metal sculptures (things like skeletons on bicycles) that also contain speakers for broadcasting heavy metal music. Toby's artistic process involves hours of loudly banging on metal, testing speakers, and drilling through metal. When Deliah can't effectively study due to the noise, she yells at Toby, but when he is nonresponsive to her plight, she finally moves into the apartment owned by the family next door (because she does not have a car to move her stuff any further). Even next door, Deliah can often hear terribly loud noises from the metalwork.

TWO

Exhausted after a long day at her laboratory, Erika comes home and collapses on her bed. It would have been comfortable except that there was paper stuffed into her pillow. Erika opened the pillow cover and pulled out a set of papers. On the top was a letter.

> *Dear Erika,*
>
> *I think I've figured out this time travel thing finally. I'm going to try to go to tomorrow to get the lottery numbers! Of course, if this does not work, it is quite likely to kill me. The machine is temperamental and only a beta test version. It is already killed two monkeys this month. Anyway, I'm almost certain I've worked out the kinks now! In the meantime, you can have my gold S. Hawking necklace. It should be a collector's item someday!*
>
> *Your loving roommate,*
>
> *Margery*

Erika shuffled to the second page and found a handwritten will. The will left Margery's vacation home in Williamsburg, Virginia "to my sister Amelia, but she needs to stay on her meds, but she can keep the house so long as she stays on the meds, or until she goes off them, and then the house reverts to me, or if I'm not around then to my heirs, whoever they are."

_____

_____

_____

_____

_____

_____

_____

_____

_____

_____

THREE

Hollon and Hildreth share ownership of a farm left to them by their grand-mother, Ailish, when she died seven years ago. Both Ailish and her next-door neighbor, Amaranth, collaborated on a remarkable project for domestic and national security. Ailish and Amaranth raised a rare species of bioluminescent arctic jellyfish. The jellyfish have unique cells that are remarkably impenetra-ble. These evolved to protect the creatures from sharp shards of ice. Until her sudden death, Ailish and Amaranth had been genetically modifying the jel-lyfish skin cells to create a type of body armor. Amaranth, the one with more engineering skills, had built an extensive outdoor tank system to hold the jel-lyfish. The tank, which sat on Ailish's land, unfortunately leaked some of the genetically modified cells onto the ground. The cells have been multiplying and moving onto neighborhood lands. It creates a constant, soft glow at night, and the neighbors have some concerns about the safety of the genetically modified animal cells, particularly given that they seem to be now naturally reproducing in the non-marine environment.

Ailish and Amaranth had been good friends and never put any of their business or property ownership arrangements on paper. They shared a lab on Amaranth's property and housed the jellyfish on Ailish's property. Most of the business records resided on Ailish's property. Ailish left her property to "Hollon and Hildreth, my dear granddaughters, jointly and severally and to the last one."

Hildreth, a clothing designer, has not visited the property in the last seven years of ownership. Hollon, a biologist, has taken over working with Amaranth. To secure the paperwork and their inventions, Hollon changed all the locks two years ago. Hollon would prefer to just pay Hildreth for her share and give her the part of the property that does not have the jellyfish tanks. Hildreth does not want the property, but would rather have some money out of it. Hildreth says the tanks are a big part of the value of the property and she wants her share of that.

_____

_____

_____

_____

_____

_____

_____

FOUR

Eleanor owns an older house in Lexington, Virginia. Eleanor's house and her neighbor's house were both a part of a larger lot that contained three houses owned by three sisters. When Eleanor bought the property 20 years ago, her neighbor Allison told her that the driveway on Eleanor's property was shared between the two and always had been. Eleanor did not object and therefore Allison has been sharing the driveway. This is particularly convenient for Allison, because without the driveway she cannot use the alleyway to access her garage. (She can access the other end of the garage — one bay only — from the main street.)

Recently, the city of Lexington has suffered extraordinary snow loads. The snow has been so deep that the city has been unable to push it back from the roads enough to allow cars to pass through. In response to this situation, the Virginia legislature passed a law allowing local cities to forbid homeowners from using access routes to roads other than the main streets. In other words, the city could forbid the use of the driveways that accessed the alleys so that the city could use the alleys for dumping snow. Eleanor is not sure if her property owns any part of the alley itself, but it might. Eleanor definitely owns a driveway that accesses the alleyway — the one that she shares with Allison.

To comply with the new law, Eleanor wants to block off her driveway to prevent access. Allison objects, insisting that Eleanor must make a new driveway (open to both of them) that would access the main road. When Eleanor starts digging a ditch to block off the alleyway, Allison runs out of her house to object. Allison is standing on the driveway when Eleanor shovels up a small brown box. Eleanor is reaching for the box when Allison grabs it first and opens it, revealing a gold ring with a huge ruby.

_____

_____

_____

_____

_____

_____

_____

_____

Answers

ONE

Rescind lease due to misrepresentation of quiet farm
Rescind lease due to misrepresentation of private access
Constructive eviction of tenant
Violation of the covenant of quiet enjoyment due to failure to provide full possession
Violation of the warranty of habitability due to improper provision of heating
Nuisance

TWO

Gift causa mortis
Inter-vivos gift
Identifying present estate and future interest
Void for vagueness problem
Rule Against Perpetuities

THREE

Type of co-tenancy created
Ouster accomplished
Partition
Personalty versus realty
Nuisance
Aesthetic nuisance for the glow
Trespass
Adverse possession
Easement — Prescriptive for Amaranth

FOUR

Easement implied by prior use
Easement implied by necessity
Prescriptive easement
Changing of an easement's bounds
Interference with an easement by title holder
Scope of the easement holder's rights

Termination of an easement
Takings
Regulatory takings
Finder: characterize item
Finder: first possessor
Finder: public/private (i.e., rights of easement holder)

Conclusion

The purpose of this book is to make real practice with meaningful feedback possible so that law students can use their study time wisely to level up their abilities. Accessible hypotheticals with scoring rubrics fundamentally change the world for law students.

Answering hypotheticals gives students a chance to bring together and practice all of their knowledge and their skills. This is what attorneys do daily: combine high-level skills with solid knowledge. This is what the student needs to do to score well on an exam. The scoring rubrics allow the student to self-grade and to generate meaningful feedback that can be put to use in the next round of practice. The rubrics also guide students in diagnosing more holistic or thematic problems, such as failure to spot all of the issues or a tendency toward making conclusions rather than applying the rules.

This kind of practice is critical for most students to perform well, but it is hard to find in law schools, which rarely provide much in the way of sample hypotheticals or scoring rubrics. This book contains 18 hypotheticals with scoring rubrics for each one. There are also sample answers, annotated answers, and more tools to help students succeed. Together these resources form a solid base for building the skills every law student needs to do well on exams.

Index